Weimar Germany

The Republic of the reasonable

Paul Bookbinder

Manchester University Press
Manchester and New York
Distributed exclusively in the USA by St. Martin's Press

Published by Manchester University Press
Oxford Road, Manchester M13 9NR, UK
and Room 400, 175 Fifth Avenue, New York, NY 10010, USA

Distributed exclusively in the USA by
St. Martin's Press, Inc., 175 Fifth Avenue, New York,
NY 10010, USA

British Library Cataloguing-in-Publication Data
A catalogue record for this book is available from the British Library

Library of Congress Cataloging-in-Publication Data
Bookbinder, Paul.
Weimar Germany : the republic of the reasonable / Paul Bookbinder.
p. cm.
ISBN 0–7190–4286–0.—ISBN 0–7190–4287–9 (pbk.)
1. Germany—Politics and government—1918–1933. 2. Germany—Intellectual life—20th century. 3. Germany—Social conditions—1918–1933. 4. Germany—Ethnic relations. 5. Germany—Civilization—Jewish influences. I. Title.
DD240.B63 1996
320.943—dc20
95–47914
CIP

ISBN 0 7190 4286 0 *hardback*
0 7190 4287 9 *paperback*

First published 1996

00 99 98 97 96 10 9 8 7 6 5 4 3 2 1

Typeset in Great Britain
by Northern Phototypesetting Co. Ltd, Bolton
Printed in Great Britain
by Bell & Bain Ltd, Glasgow

Contents

Abbreviations

AEG	Allgemeine Electrizitatsgesellsch
BBB	Bauernbund or Peasants' League
BDF	League of German Women's Associations
BVP	Bavarian People's Party
DDP	German Democratic Party
DHV	Deutschnationale Handlesgehilfen Verband (Germany's largest white collar union)
DNVP	German Nationalist People's Party
DVP	German People's Party
JFB	Judischer Frauenverband (Jewish Women's Association)
KPD	Communist Party
MSPD	Majority Socialist Party
SPD	Social Democratic Party
SA	Sturmabteilung
SS	Schutzsbaffel
USPD	Independent Social Democratic Party
USPD	Independent Socialists
WSDAP	National Socialist German Workers' Party
Zentrum	Catholic Center Party

To Judy whose book this is in every way

Introduction

The Weimar Republic was born in defeat, lived through long periods of crisis and ultimately was succeeded by the genocidal dictatorship of Adolf Hitler and the Nazis. Like the proverbial cat, in many ways, it had nine lives. It seemed to some to die on the streets of Berlin and Munich in the Winter and Spring of 1919; to others it ended as the Erhardt Brigade entered Berlin in 1920. Some saw its death in the Ruhr, in a Munich Beer Hall or in Saxony and Thuringia in 1923. Still others saw it suffer an electoral death as early as the elections of 1920, others in the presidential election of 1925, many more in the elections of 1932. Many talked of its economic death in the inflation of the early twenties or the depression of the early thirties. And yet it lived.

It lived burdened by the legacy of Bismarckian and Wilhelmine Germany and by "The Great War." This legacy was determined by the *Sonderweg*, the "special way" in which Germany developed. Germans defined community in a different and more exclusive way than did other western Europeans and Americans during this period. Concentration on the "other", mainly the Jew but also the Pole and even the Catholic, was important to self-definition and political development in Germany and had serious future implications. Germany's different way of industrializing and the unique characteristics of class relationships played an important role in influencing developments as well. The aristocracy which retained great power and influence beyond the period of industrialization and urbanization contributed to Germany's particular conditions. A women's movement which had not concentrated on political suffrage or equal rights as had the Anglo-Saxon movements led to differences. The lack of a democratic tradition or a critical electorate and the situation of political parties which only knew opposition and never had power or responsibility all affected the Weimar Republic.

The Weimar Republic, born from monarchy and followed by dictatorship, is too often viewed only in terms of its origin and what rose from its collapse. However, its life was entwined with the major developments of the twentieth century, and, in its own terms, it speaks to us today of changes and problems that we face. It was a noble experiment and provided many lessons in both its failures and its successes. It was a Republic of those who were willing to be reasonable, to put aside short-term self-interest and work for the longer-term interests of the broader community.

However, not enough people enthusiastically supported this reasonable Republic, the first truly democratic state in German history. Even while its leaders missed opportunities for positive changes and sometimes lacked vision and courage, they accomplished much under difficult circumstances. Yet, the public often denied them the support the Republic deserved. Women and young men who were enfranchised by it found it wanting and rejected it. Clergymen and educators did not recognize the freedom of thought and action the Republic offered and did not preach and teach the values and skills needed to sustain it. Industrialists and land owners often refused to sacrifice any of their profits to preserve the new state that had protected them from radical revolution that had threatened their property and their opportunities to make those profits. Labor union leaders did not moderate their demands or show any willingness to make concessions for the Republic that had allowed them to make unprecedented gains for their working-class constituents. Political party leaders and elected officials might have spoken about representing all of the people, but few acted as if they did. Many intellectuals who had greater scope to create than ever before concentrated on the flaws of the Republic and offered it little support. Conservatives often demonstrated a greater desire to destroy than to conserve, and liberals seldom confronted the haters within the new German society. The pulpit and the classroom were often sources of anti-Semitism and divisiveness rather than acceptance and a broad sense of community.

The Weimar Republic had to deal with defeat in a long and costly world war, a weakening and demanding peace treaty, inflation, revolution, political violence and depression. Clearly these factors placed limits on the freedom of action and the ability to control events for the new Republic's leaders. As the historian Donald Kagan says in writing about a far different topic, the outbreak of the Peloponnesian War, "Leaving aside the metaphysical question of free will versus determinism, we may still raise legitimate questions as to the extent of man's freedom to make political decisions. There can be no doubt that some apparent choices in the realm of human affairs are in fact precluded by previous events while others are made more likely. But men can make decisions that alter the course of events." One of the most important questions facing historians dealing with the Weimar years is, as Kagan says, to "distinguish between relatively open choices and those that were only apparent."[1]

How much room for maneuver did the reasonable men and women have who wanted to make the Weimar Republic a success and how well did they make those open choices? There were successes within the overall failure that characterized the Weimar Republic. The Prussian police demonstrated that it was possible to reverse an authoritarian tradition in at least one institution and create a police force committed to Republican government and democratic values. The artists who built the Bauhaus struggled to make art serve the society and created a body of theory and work of significant beauty and value which influenced subsequent developments in architecture, painting and design shaping the modern environment. A Jewish women's group battled against the twin handicaps of anti-Semitism and anti-feminism to work for expanded economic and educational opportunities for women and for general sexual enlightenment providing a model for later efforts.

In general, the Weimar years left a legacy on which the Federal Republic of Germany and the current reunited Germany could build. It also exposed pitfalls that the post-war Republic has worked to avoid. Its fourteen-year history, replete with revolution, political terrorism, gender conflicts and economic crisis, stands as a unique case study in the attempt to create a representative Republic which would protect all its citizens and give them enhanced opportunities during a time of change and great danger. Our mandate is to appreciate its problems, rejoice in its accomplishments and learn from its failures.

Notes

1 Donald Kagan, *The Outbreak of the Peloponnesian War*, Ithaca, New York, 1978, p. 4.

1

Wilhelmine Germany on the eve of the First World War

The Weimar Republic was born out of the chaos which followed Germany's defeat in World War I. While it is true, as H. Stuart Hughes has claimed, that the war changed everything, it is also true that what Germany became at the end of the war was intimately related to what Germany was before the great struggle.[1]

Germany was a relatively new nation in 1914 unifying, after centuries of conflict, only in 1871 around the core of Bismarck's Prussia. The new nation was a strange constitutional structure, a federal monarchy, created by an association of former kingdoms still led by their royal families: "His Majesty, the King of Prussia ..., His Majesty, the King of Bavaria, His Majesty the King of Württemberg ..."[2] While the conservative Bismarck, as Chancellor of the Empire, chose to experiment with a lower legislative house elected by manhood suffrage (all men twenty-five years in age or over could vote), he loaded the constitution with provisions which severely limited the power of this Reichstag. Considerable power was left in the hands of the state (*Land*) governments, the largest of which by far, Prussia, retained its old three-class voting system based on taxes. Each of three strata of society could vote for representatives according to their own class. Each group of representatives voted separately in the Landtag, and the vote of any two groups carried the day. Thus two groups of deputies representing the wealthiest and best educated segments of society could outvote the representatives of the far more populous lower classes.

The federal constitution also provided for an upper legislative house, a Bundesrat, whose consent was needed for constitutional change and whose members were chosen by the state governments. Prussia's block of seventeen delegates was sufficient on its own to prevent constitutional changes. The constitution also put great power in the hands of the chief executive, the Emperor or Kaiser, who was also the King of Prussia. The chief administrative officer of the state, the Chancellor, and his cabinet were responsible to the Kaiser but not to the legislature.

The personality of the Kaiser, Wilhelm II, who was Germany's ruler in 1914 at the beginning of World War I, and the nature of his inner circle of confidants were important factors in the evolution of this society. The Kaiser began his rule in 1888 as a young man who proclaimed concern for the working people of Germany and who did not appear to be a rigid conservative. His parents had embodied the liberals' hope for the future of Germany. His father, Friedrich and his mother, who was the eldest daughter of Queen Victoria of England, were intent on moving Germany towards a true constitutional monarchy where class, ethnic and religious differences would be of less importance. Wilhelm's father was critically ill with cancer when he inherited the throne from his brother Wilhelm I and died within three months. His son was in many ways closer in outlook to his uncle than to his father or mother. He rebelled against their generally more liberal orientation and veered sharply away from any early promise of moderation.

By the turn of the twentieth century, Wilhelm II had surrounded himself with those who encouraged his limited and most reactionary instincts. As Isabell Hull describes Wilhelm's circle of intimates, "Their milieu fostered the narrowest and most conservative aspects of Wilhelm's eclectic *Weltanschauung*." He spent most of his adult life trying to be something he was not. "Wilhelm lived out his life in an elaborate masquerade. He paraded as the consummate soldier-warlord, always fierce, hard, decisive, steady, an amalgam of the 'masculine' virtues." Wilhelm, in fact, could not have been further removed from his ideal. He was "slightly feminine in appearance, with delicate health, hypersensitive, squeamish, nervous as a caged animal, and steady as an aspen leaf."[3]

The Empress, who cared greatly for her husband, but seemed to have a disastrous effect on him, embodied in her world-view characteristics typical of the dominant class in Wilhelmine Germany. She personified the class prejudices of much of the aristocracy and represented those who were hostile to all that was not Protestant Christian and long-established German. Her influence contributed to Wilhelm's increasingly narrow definition of the community of true Germans and to his fear of the "other." This perspective led, as John Röhl has recently described, to the Kaiser's development into a fierce hater of Jews and a believer in a type of racism not far different from that of the Nazis.[4]

Yet assessments of the Wilhelmine state are not unanimous. Karl Marx described the German Empire as, "A parliamentarily be-figleafed, feudally-reinforced, bureaucratically-contracted, police-tended military despotism."[5] Geoff Eley has challenged this judgement:

> My own view, ... is that the strictly reactionary elements were considerably more isolated and less powerful in the political system, that the constitution was considerably more flexible, and that modernizing forces had achieved considerably less penetration – indeed that the traditional elements were considerably less 'traditional' than most historians have tended to believe.[6]

Contrary to Geoff Eley's assertion, it seems less important whether the industrialists (the "modernizing forces") were more feudal or the land owners (the "traditional elements") were more modern than that both groups were willing to co-operate to limit the power of the middle and lower classes. This combination of heavy industry, which was a significant part of the industrial camp, and agriculture led to a program known as *Sammlungspolitik,* designed to keep power in the hands of the upper classes. Both the old agricultural elite and its new industrial counterpart were inflexible in not wanting to share power with the middle or working classes.

Geoff Eley and David Blackbourn are right to point out that Germany's development during the Bismarckian and Wilhelmine periods did not make the failure of the Weimar Republic inevitable. It is also true that many of the individual features of Imperial Germany from its family structure to its educational system were shared by other western industrial nations. However it was the unique combination of these factors that made the German experience a different one. Germany was, indeed, never the totally homogeneous society that most Germans imagined it was, as a significant number of foreign workers from eastern and even southern Europe were present during the Imperial period. However, an overwhelming number of Germans believed in their unique homogeneity thus making perception more important than the reality.

The domination of upper-class interests led to a risk-taking program which, through its colonial expansion and naval construction, antagonized the British.[7] The industrialists and land owners supporting this program hoped to use naval construction, which also had strong middle-class support, and an assertive foreign policy to shift the focus away from domestic discontent and reduce challenges to their position of political power. However, since the British based their security on naval superiority and they and the French worried about challenges to their colonial supremacy, German moves in these directions made the possibility of war more likely. Fritz Fischer ignited an historical controversy by being the first major German scholar to suggest that German risk-taking foreign policy was indeed the major factor leading to the outbreak of the First World War.[8]

Like Fischer, Hans-Ulrich Wehler sees the style of politics of Wilhelmine Germany as being distinct from that of France, England or the United States.[9] Wehler cites Bismarck's strategy, which he calls negative integration, of creating cohesiveness by carefully delineating the insiders from the outsiders in the Empire and thereby unifying the insiders against their enemies, the outsiders. Hostility to minorities, particularly Jews, was a key factor in the policy of negative integration.

The constitutional structure of the German Empire and the inflexible attitude of the German aristocracy created a situation where the forces who represented electoral interests other than those of the conservative Protestant land-holding and business elements of the population were viewed as the enemy by those who ran Wilhelmine Germany. "Thus political Catholicism, parliamentary liberalism, Social Democracy and liberal Judaism were built up as the true enemies of the Empire."[10]

It is important to note that these minorities collectively represented the great majority of the German electorate. However, the structure of the German Constitution and strong class antagonism between the bourgeoisie and the working class made it difficult for the true majority to assert itself. The Jew as the "progressive enemy of the Empire" became a target of particularly heavy criticism. The stress on division within the society and the polarization of people into friends and enemies was intense in connection with ethnic minorities as it was with political minorities. The clearest targets of these feelings were Poles and Jews. Pre-World War I Germany had about one million Poles within its borders and about 570,000 Jews. The Jews were particularly vulnerable to being labelled as enemies because they were perceived both as dangerously progressive or liberal and as an alien ethnic group. The growing popularity of racial biology gave a new meaning to the divisions among people. For Jews, racial differences were now added to religious and political ones as a basis for their alienation from true Germans.

The emphasis on the Empire's enemies had major effects on the development of German political culture. These enemies were discriminated against as second-class citizens by means of formal legal distinctions aimed at the Social Democrats and national minorities or through informal mechanisms which affected Jews and Catholics. This practice was implemented in federally controlled areas such as the army and civil service and in other areas as well. The targeted groups were excluded from spheres where merit criteria should have been applied irrespective of person. As people became accustomed to this situation of inequality, the level of tolerance of such illiberal tendencies gradually increased. The belief that one had some neighbors who were inferior became part and parcel of everyday life during the fifty years of the Empire's existence and helped foster a mentality which polarized citizens. Although many Germans referred to minorities as a "problem", their own prejudices were the real problem. "For that matter, even the so-called Jewish problem was really a German problem- or rather, the effect of Germany's isolation from the rest of the world. The average German, unlike the British or French, had no experience of foreigners or foreign ideas."[11]

The Wilhelmine state followed a policy of "Germanizing" in which those people who lived within the Empire who were not German speakers were pressured to give up their own culture and language. While the immediate effect of laws against non-German speakers was discrimination, there were also longer-range consequences:

> The laws which operated to the detriment of those citizens of the state who spoke a different language had a double-edge to them. They helped prepare the way for dismantling the 'state based on the rule of law' and its constitutional principles by the use of legal methods sanctioned by the state itself. They also encouraged a situation in which discrimination against minorities came to be accepted. Expulsion and expropriation, social ostracism and a 'germanizing' repression, all played a part in the Wilhelmine Empire. Had it not been for the acceptance of such public injustices the path towards the violent events of a latter period could never have been made so smooth so soon.[12]

Germans in the pre-World War I period were socialized in families, educated in schools and preached to in churches which often fostered values that were fundamentally undemocratic. While each of these factors taken separately could not determine a general climate, taken together they exerted a multiplier effect on each other. The result was a German citizen characterized by Heinrich Mann as *Der Untertan*. In a letter to his brother Thomas, he described those "subjects" as representative Germans: "They despise parliamentary government before it is even reached, public opinion before it is heard."[13] While he was writing his novel, a searing critique on Germans in the first decade of the twentieth century, Heinrich described his evaluations to Thomas:

> I am making notes. How an unimportant member of the mass is treated when he or she buys a slice of bread. How at almost every opportunity each acts as the superior and the enemy of the other: openly and brutally as nowhere else in the world. On the station platforms, in the sweaty cafes. I sometimes have the feeling: if suddenly a police troop were to burst in and cut down ten or twenty of those present with their swords, the others would neither miss their train nor let their pudding get cold.[14]

The alienated attitude of *Der Untertan* began in the family. The German family was paternalistic, rigid and repressive. German fathers had a reputation for austerity, dominance and brutality. However the pattern of the German family was not, as Wehler explains, an uncommon one:

> The New England Puritan, the Victorian Englishman and the Republican Frenchman were scarcely outdone in terms of the severity by the Wilhelmine father-figure. An authoritarian family

> structure would thus appear to be quite compatible with very different kinds of 'political' culture. On its own it could hardly establish political authoritarianism for the society as a whole. If, on the other hand, it is embedded in a society which uses authoritarian models and codes of conduct in general, it may well act as a kind of multiplier.[15]

Wehler's multiplier effect correctly characterizes the inter-relationship among such factors as the family, the schools, the churches and the political culture. With regard to German schools, Wehler stresses that the environment and administration were cold, and the faculty was impersonal and authoritarian. Most teachers were conservative nationalists who shared the narrow political perspective of their fellows among the educated elite whom Fritz Ringer has called the "German Mandarins".[16] They were anti-democratic, anti-socialist and anti-Semitic. The textbooks that they used reflected their values and presented history in a stark black and white fashion. Most Germans of the pre-war period who have written memoirs had overwhelmingly negative things to say about their school experiences.[17]

German schools were strongly involved with political education of an anti-revolutionary, anti-individualist variety. They "obeyed the various directives on imparting attitudes and translated them into a code of virtues such as diligence, fear of God, obedience and loyalty."[18] Independent thinking, critical observation and participatory practices were not goals of the education process. The values which came from the pulpit were similar to those which emerged in the classroom. Critics of the churches such as Carl Amery have argued that churches stressed secondary virtues such as diligence, loyalty and obedience, while the primary religious virtues of charity, mercy and brotherhood of all people received very little attention.[19]

Germany's ruling classes, bred in pre-war schools, homes and families, developed a narrow class identity and the inclination to conflate their interests with those of the nation. This tendency extended to other groups as well such as the middle class, the industrialists and the workers. It would outlast the war and become a feature of the Weimar Republic. However, it clearly manifested itself in the pre-war foreign and domestic policy of the ruling elite.

Aristocrats such as Bernhard von Bülow who were primarily motivated by their own domestic agenda convinced the Kaiser to support a policy of maximum risk which was only very questionably in the national interest.[20] They sought to use an aggressive foreign policy and military building program to break the growing power of the Social Democrats and the unions. Aristocrats and industrialists viewed the Social Democrats as unpatriotic and disloyal trouble-makers who were leading the workers astray. They were willing to engage in risky foreign adventures which might lead to war in their hope to weaken the Social Democrats and the unions and win the loyalty of the workers to the national "cause". However there was a clear danger that these "sabre rattling" policies in areas such as colonial Africa might push the British and French towards war and destroy the domestic peace they were designed to promote.[21]

While Germany's aristocrats valued the power that industry and commerce had brought to their nation they were philosophically opposed to what they called modernism. Their attitude was shared by elements of the middle class, especially the old middle class – craftsmen, independent artisans, and retailers with small stores – and by members of Germany's academic and cultural elite. Modernism was identified with the city, big business and finance, changes in the position of women, and cultural movements of change and experimentation. Many also identified modernism with the Jews who were seen as the prime agent for the breakdown of traditional values and the traditional society.

This resistance to modernism had gathered around the *völkisch* movement which had developed at the beginning of the nineteenth century. It was an effort to find a basis of political unity for a divided Germany where people were often more attached to their provincial identities than to their national identity. This movement, which stressed a linguistic, cultural and historical basis for unity among all Germans, aided the German states in their battles against the occupying French troops of Napoleon and in their quest for a national state. During the course of the nineteenth century the movement helped propel Germans towards the unity which finally resulted in the founding of the German Empire in the year 1871 under the leadership of Bismarck and Wilhelm I of Prussia.

During the course of the nineteenth century, the *völkisch* movement underwent two important modifications. It became a focus for resistance among the most traditional elements within German society opposed to the changes brought about by the rapid industrialization and urbanization of Germany. It also became a center for the new racial biological school of thought which defined groups of people according to the tenets of the new "racial sciences" which were becoming popular and academically respectable in the nineteenth century. These *völkisch* thinkers identified a German racially as well as by language, culture and history. They contributed, to a significant degree, to fostering the attitude of hostility toward minority groups that the Kaiser and his circle encouraged. *Völkisch* study of the roots of culture was complemented and legitimized by the development of the "cultural sciences" which included diverse disciplines such as ethnology, anthropology, *Völkerpsycholgie*, and cultural history.[22]

Although leaders of the electrical and chemical industries who were modern in their outlook saw no possible accommodation with the *völkisch* agenda, some of the leaders of German heavy industry such as the coal, iron and steel magnates looked for a *modus vivendi* through which they could find common purpose with *völkisch* groups. Viewing their own position in a semi-feudal way, they hoped to find common ground against those forces of modernism that they opposed: worker emancipation, socialism and unionism. While nineteenth- and early twentieth-century French, English and American industrialists were overwhelmingly oriented toward profits, fought unionization, and in general showed little concern for the working and living conditions of their employees, German industrialists, particularly those in heavy industry, seemed to demonstrate these characteristics in the most extreme form. This predisposition stemmed, at least in part, from the fact that they expected paternalism to come from the aristocratically dominated state which was more involved in industrialization than were the English, French or American governments. The German state, had been the leader in creating social legislation such as unemployment and accident insurance to offer workers some form of security and protection. However the actual payments to workers were quite low and the intransigence of the industrialists contributed to the rapid growth of unions and the Social Democratic Party.

The Social Democratic Party had been formed in 1875 by a

merger of the two major socialist groups active in Germany resulting in a strange amalgam of Marxist rhetoric and a rather moderate policy of reform. Its language was created by Karl Marx and Frederick Engels, but its policies were those of Eduard Bernstein. Bernstein had taught that socialism could come to German society through parliamentary reform and that class revolution was neither necessary nor desirable. The leaders of the Social Democratic Party such as Friedrich Ebert and Philipp Scheidemann embodied this philosophy. They had careers as skilled workers, joined and participated actively in labor unions, and worked their way up through the party structure. By the time they reached the higher ranks, they had achieved middle-class status and lived like comfortable middle-class citizens. Most of these men had never been very radical . While it is true that there were more extreme elements in the party, generally in the small intellectual party circle, it was, as Carl Schorske has demonstrated, leaders like Ebert who represented the heart of the party and were most in touch with the rank and file.[23] The irony in all this is that the aristocratic ruling circle around the Kaiser advocated a confrontational policy in foreign affairs, which contributed to the outbreak of World War I, because they feared the radicalism of the working masses under the leadership of the Social Democratic Party. This fear was highly exaggerated. While the economic, social and political advances of the workers and electoral and parliamentary reform were indeed a threat to aspects of the imperial system, the SPD did not fundamentally threaten property or the basic nature of that society. David Blackbourn's conclusion regarding the hostile reaction of the leadership of the Catholic Center Party to the SPD sheds much light on this question. Blackbourn argues that it was "the negative tactics and the bitterly critical tone" of the SPD that were particularly disliked by Center Party leaders who were eager to demonstrate their commitment to the national cause and the status quo in late Imperial Germany.[24] Many of the dominant elements of imperial Germany would recognize, in the post-war period, that the SPD and union leaders were their best hope for changing society in a way that would leave their basic interests intact.

However, economic and social changes that had taken place in Germany at the end of the nineteenth and at the beginning of the twentieth century had created a society in which domination by an agrarian aristocracy was an anachronism. Only the peculiarities of the German national constitution, particularly its Prussian counter-part, and the inability of the middle- and working-class parties to form an effective alliance had allowed the aristocrats to maintain their preponderant power and influence. To push the irony of aristocratic policy further, it was the war, toward which their risk policy contributed, that finally broke their power.

Certainly the attitudes and policies of the aristocratically dominated military exacerbated the internal intolerance of German society and its incautious and abrasive foreign policy. The German military was a collection of state forces dominated by the Prussian army, where aristocrats controlled the officer corps and minorities had no place. The survey of 1911 showed that there was not one regular Jewish officer in the Prussian army. This situation existed at a time when in Italy with a much smaller Jewish population there were fifty Jewish generals. The arrogance of the military leadership was evident in the policies carried out by the army in Alsace. This former French province had become German territory after France's defeat at the hands of Prussia in 1870. Alsace's status was unusual because it was treated in some ways as a part of Germany and in other ways as occupied territory and thus had both German civilian and military officials in positions of authority. The often considerable tension between the German military and the local population burst into open conflict in 1913 fueled by the alienated attitude of the military. As critically analyzed by David Schoenbaum, "It was inevitable that Prussian officers would feel uneasy about a population so Catholic, so liberal, so bourgeois, so egalitarian, in any case so different from themselves ..."[25]

The pre-war Germany characterized by intolerance towards minorities, archaic domination by the aristocracy and a provocative foreign policy was also a country of rising real wages and standards of living and of considerable economic stability. While this relatively new nation had faced numerous years of economic depression from the 1870s through the mid-1890s, the period from 1896 to 1913 had been one of the most substantial growth periods in modern western history. Life expectancy had risen and the working week had been reduced. While German wages were still not on a par with Britain, France and the United States, the rise had been quite impressive and Germans had more social welfare benefits, modest though they may have been, than workers in the other major industrialized nations. German bonds were among the most secure in the world, and the unemployment rate was about one per cent. Germany was regarded as a great power and a center of culture and education.

German women began to change their economic, social and political role in German life during this period. They founded many types of women's organizations to address their points of view and their needs. One of the most significant of these groups was the German Women's Association (BDF) founded in 1894 and dominated particularly by middle-class women. These organizations grew and agitated for greater freedom and more opportunities for women planting the seeds for developments during the Weimar years.

World War I changed everything for Germans as it did for all Europeans and for many of the rest of the world's people. The outbreak of hostilities was greeted with enthusiasm by large numbers of Germans as it was by large numbers of Europeans in general. However those most enthusiastic tended to be male rather than female and middle or upper class rather than members of the working class. The famous scene in the Odeonplatz in the center of Munich with the young Adolf Hitler throwing his hat in the air as an anonymous member of a cheering throng was a representative scene for the time. For many in the middle class, the war promised adventure, excitement, a respite from routine jobs and family responsibilities. It gave these young men a chance to put the nationalism of their teachers, their leaders and their families into operation and to actualize reserve commissions that they had worked hard to earn. For many of the aristocrats, it was a call to follow the Kaiser and to do what their class had been bred to do. The war that most expected was to be a short struggle which would allow scope for individual heroism and would end in glorious victory. Even many avant-garde artists welcomed the war as a cleansing force which would burn away the crust of materialism, phoniness and alienation that characterized pre-World War I Germany and produce a new society and a new German person.

The initial reactions to the outbreak of the war seemed to substantiate the hope of the conservatives that a foreign adventure would create unity and heal the class divisions without the ruling classes having to make any significant concessions to the lower classes. In a move which startled and delighted the circle around the Kaiser, the Social Democratic Party voted to support the war effort by voting for war credits for its financing. This vote was a rejection of the Marxist view of wars as instruments of policy by the financiers and industrialists to boost their profits and an assault on the solidarity of the working men of the European nations. The leaders of the Social Democratic Party justified their actions by choosing to see the war as a defensive action against a ring of hostile powers who surrounded Germany and threatened her existence. They stressed the particular danger from Russia which they depicted as an aggressive, barbaric power which threatened German culture, civilization and values with its hordes of uncultured and brutal Cossack warriors. This rhetoric was only a smokescreen for the basic patriotism and nationalism which many of the Social Democratic leaders shared with aristocrats and members of the middle class. They carried the overwhelming number of their Reichstag deputies with them and only faced opposition from a small hard core of radical intellectuals within their own ranks led by Rosa Luxemburg.

This early almost complete unanimity among the leaders of the Social Democratic Party would slowly dissolve as would the initial solidarity among all the political parties which existed in the early stages of the war. This solidarity known as the *Burgfrieden* was not only represented by close to unanimous Reichstag votes but also by a reduction of expressions of class hostility and a commensurate decrease in verbal attacks on minority groups, particularly the Jews.

The differences between the expectations of what the war would be like and the actual nature of the combat soon became evident. When the initial German offensive in the west failed and France did not fall, the war became bogged down and turned into a struggle for yards, trenches, barbed wire, with staggering casualties and little scope for individual heroism. The expectations of a short struggle with much opportunity for glory turned out to be an illusion.

Germany's hope of a speedy victory was based on a plan developed in the 1890s by the head of the General Staff, Count Alfred von Schlieffen, which called for a mass invasion in the west while fighting a holding action in the east. Schlieffen hoped that a great encircling action taking German troops through Belgium and the

Netherlands and isolating Paris would lead to a speedy exit of France from the war and a quick German victory. The plan itself was illusory as it called for more troops than Germany ever had, underestimated Russian power and the speed of their mobilization, and discounted the possibility that this action would force Britain into the war in time to make a difference.

Many who welcomed the outbreak of the war soon became disaffected. The artists who had been so enthusiastic were among the first to become depressed about the war itself and hostile to those who had led Germany into it. Writing in May of 1915, the later prominent expressionist painter Max Beckmann described the horror of life at the front:

> The trenches wound in meandering lines and white faces peered from dark dug-outs. A lot of men were still preparing the positions, and everywhere among them there were graves. Where they sat, beside their dugouts, even between the sandbags, crosses stuck out, corpses jammed in among them. It sounds like fiction – one man was frying potatoes on a grave next to his dug-out. The existence of life here really became a paradoxical joke.[26]

During the approximate fifteen hundred days of this struggle, an average of six thousand men were killed each day. In some of the larger battles, the carnage was incredible. On the first day of the Battle of the Somme River in August of 1916, for example, the British alone lost forty thousand men. In total, Germany lost two million young men in the war, and another four million Germans were wounded. Two million seven hundred thousand of these wounded soldiers were permanently disabled by their wounds.[27] Five-hundred and thirty-three thousand women became widows, and several million more lost the prospect of obtaining husbands. One million, one hundred and ninety-two thousand children became fatherless, and those whose mothers did not remarry grew up without fathers. While about forty per cent of the war widows remarried between 1919 and 1924, remarriage was much more likely for widows without children.

One of the main reasons for the high casualty counts and stalemates that developed was that weapons of defense far outstripped weapons of offense in the first years of the war. The machine gun and barbed wire, typical defensive weapons, carried the day until the tank, the airplane and the flamethrower shifted the balance towards the offense in the last stages of the war. The reactions of soldiers like Max Beckmann and Erich Maria Remarque, whose anti-war book *All Quiet on the Western Front* was a run away bestseller in the second half of the 1920s, were the dominant ones among the millions of German soldiers who fought in the war.[28] However there were also those like Ernst Jünger and Adolf Hitler who loved their war experiences and continued to fight a successful battle for the minds and hearts of Germany's young in the 1920s in opposition to the critics of the war.

The upheaval of the war brought significant political, economic and social changes to the home front. Morals and values changed as well. The class situation in Germany underwent strain and change. In many ways it was the middle class or *Mittelstand* that was most dramatically affected. The *Mittelstand* constituted a more rigidly stratified element of the society than did the middle class in the United States or the rest of Europe. It included the old middle class of artisans and shopkeepers and a second rapidly growing component of office workers and lower level government officials. This latter group operated on an annual salary rather than on hourly wages and prided itself on the white collars which its members conventionally wore. As Jürgen Kocka has observed, "From 1911 a series of Reich laws, at first concerned with social insurance, but soon with other areas as well, separated white collar from manual workers by awarding privileges to the former and, unlike England and the USA, by cementing a socio-economic differentiation ..."[29] As the war continued the two elements of the middle class diverged further and further from each other. The war hit the newer middle class, particularly the lower civil service and clerical part, harder than any other class in society in terms of their loss of relative position. Their fixed salaries were not raised while storekeepers and artisans were able to sell their products and services at higher prices. Kocka argues, "These lower-middle-class groups not only suffered badly from the almost intolerable economic situation, but also from the corresponding challenge to their status. War and its concomitant deprivations resulted in much more profound psychic shocks to their group than to the workers."[30]

All classes in Germany were expected to make sacrifices during the war. However the extremely unequal nature of the sacrifices created bitterness and tension within the society. In Kocka's words, "The entrepreneurs increased their wealth, on the average, relative to the working class; in many, though not all, respects the war was advantageous to them. Certainly the rich had to accept only very few reductions in their living standards up to the end of the War."[31] Everything was still available in any amount but at a high price. About a third of the commodities bought and sold during the war were bought and sold on the black market thus seriously damaging the efforts of government agencies to guarantee some degree of fairness in the distribution of goods and services during this period of hard times. For those who did not have access to the black market, by 1918 the official food ration covered only 57% to 70% of calories needed for light work and only 47% to 54% of the calories needed for heavy work. "In the face of increasing shortages of foodstuffs, clothes, coal and housing, this standard often fell below the subsistence level."[32] These conditions sometimes led to starvation, more frequently to malnutrition, and made the population extremely vulnerable to the fierce influenza epidemic of 1918 which killed millions worldwide.

Women were working in ever greater numbers during the war and not only at "women's professions" such as social work, nursing or teaching. They were working increasingly in offices and factories operating machines and engaging in skilled labor. Because labor restrictions were lifted to increase output, women were also working longer shifts and at night. Thus while opportunities were greater, the dangers of industrial disease and injury increased many times over during the war years. In factories such as those belonging to Daimler-Benz the automobile and airplane engine manufacturer, the increase in women in the work force was quite dramatic. However, the new women workers and those who were now doing work which required considerable skill and training were earning about fifty per cent of what male workers doing the same job were receiving. This increase in the number and skill of female workers led to a rapid rise in profit for the owners and managers of Daimler-Benz rather than a decline in prices of anything that they produced, even though most of what they produced was bought by a financially strapped government for the war effort.[33] While it is true that the substitution of women and very young men for experienced skilled men in some areas of production led to some "de-skilling" and, therefore, lower quality production, in many areas, the women in particular proved able relatively quickly to develop the skills necessary to do the job. Thus while there were losses in production during the transition phase, for companies such as Daimler-Benz, the production gap closed quickly and the extra profits which resulted from the lower wages for females were substantial. The Daimler-Benz experience was representative of many corporations.

When the war began it was not clear what the effects on German government might be. During most war situations, power consolidates dramatically towards the center, and the executive gains at the expense of the national legislature and state governments. However in Germany the Kaiser proved psychologically unable to assert himself and concentrate power in his own hands. Bernhard von Bülow, who was Chancellor of Germany from 1903–1909, indicated in his memoirs that he would have conducted a more aggressive, risk-taking foreign policy than he did but for the fact that he feared for the stability of the Kaiser:

> He was no fool, but he often lived in a 'fools' paradise'. I often feared for his mental balance, and one of the chief reasons, though not the most important of all, for my steady maintenance of a policy of peace [a questionable interpretation of his policies] for Germany was the conviction that unlike his father and grandfather, and still far more unlike the Great Frederick, William II was not mentally equipped to stand the heavy vicissitudes and ordeals of a great war.[34]

Since the Kaiser was unable to lead, the war situation offered a substantial opportunity for the Reichstag to assert itself. While it is true that the Reichstag did slowly increase its power, it did not do so sufficiently to lead Germany during the war. In addition to the difficulty of any legislature being able to assert clear and dynamic leadership, the German legislature had particular problems. Its political parties had no experience in actually governing, and the divisions between the parties were so severe that effective co-operation proved difficult to achieve. Since 1871, the Reichstag had functioned not by sharing power but by being in confrontation with those who held the reigns of power. The Kaiser and his inner circle, the Chancellor and the cabinet responsible to the Kaiser had ruled in the peaceful pre-war period; the Reichstag had debated.

The failures of the Kaiser and the Reichstag to act decisively created a power vacuum. The government had acted to organize the war economy and enlarge the armed forces. However, as the war progressed, the executive and legislature proved less and less able to make policy decisions as the Kaiser and Reichstag leaders provided little leadership. Thus power passed increasingly to the only unified national institution focused on the war – the army, in particular to the leaders of the Third Supreme Military Command, (Oberste Heersleitung-OHL) Generals Hindenburg and Ludendorff. These men, who were the heroes of the campaign against Russia, became the *de facto* decision makers and rulers of Germany, although they had no constitutional basis for the authority they assumed. Under the pressure of the war and with lack of other leadership, Hindenburg and Ludendorff moved increasingly towards military dictatorship.

While the experiences of the war radicalized much of German society, the working classes were the most likely group to be affected. They were part of a tradition that had an ideology of revolution even though it had been truly accepted by only some intellectuals and the most radical workers. German workers were among the most organized segment of the German population. The trade unions and the Social Democratic Party had large memberships and played a major role in the lives of many working-class families. By 1912, the overwhelming number of workers and one out of every three adult males voted Social Democratic. Protestant workers were much more strongly represented in the Social Democratic Party and socialist-oriented labor unions than were Catholic workers who often belonged to Catholic labor unions and voted for the Catholic Center Party, *Zentrum*.

Resistance to the war appeared first in the ranks of the Social Democratic Party and then spread to parts of some of the centrist middle-class political parties. Initially many Germans, including those who would later become prominent participants and supporters of the Weimar Republic such as Walther Rathenau and Gustav Stresemann, were in favor of a military policy which would lead to substantial territorial and financial gains for Germany at the expense particularly of Russia but also of Belgium and France. However, by 1917 a majority of Reichstag deputies supported a "Peace Without Annexations Resolution" introduced by Matthias Erzberger, the leader of the liberal wing of the

Catholic Center Party. By the end of the war the Social Democratic Party had split into several factions. The growing radical leadership was based in a splinter party called the Independent Social Democratic Party. A still more radical group called the Spartacist League was led by Rosa Luxemburg and Karl Liebknecht.

The prolongation of the war had led to a breakdown of the *Burgfrieden*, the early co-operation between the workers and the owners of the major industries particularly the heavy industries of coal, iron and steel. By 1916, even some conservatives were urging reforms to reduce these developing labor conflicts in order to keep the war industries and consumer products manufacturing working as well as possible under the trying conditions. Jürgen Kocka explains that:

> Under a continuing war situation within a class society which is perceived as unjust, and whose injustices become more acute if no conscious counter-measures are taken, there remains only the possibility of internal reforms; these are designed to establish mechanisms of the regulation of conflict and to fulfill at least some of the demands of the underprivileged, in order to retain their loyalty and to secure a minimum of social cohesion.[35]

While Stephen Shuker concluded that all European industrialists were profit-driven and greedy, German industrialists were the least willing to make concessions to their workers and the most confrontational in their attitudes.[36] Magnates like Alfred Hugenberg who represented the coal and steel interests in the Ruhr had to be forced to make concessions to workers. During the period of the war when army leaders Hindenburg and Ludendorff were making the major policy decisions, representatives of the army often intervened to force Hugenberg and other industrialists to make accommodations to labor in order to keep the domestic peace and prevent disruptions in war production.[37]

The advent of the Bolshevik Revolution in Russia and the growing unrest within Germany by the end of 1917 finally convinced many of even the most inflexible German industrialists that they had to deal with the essentially moderate unions and the majority elements of the Social Democratic Party if they did not want to face radical social revolution, Bolshevik style, in which they could lose everything that they owned. Thus at the end of the war a new although less inclusive *Burgfrieden* was established and one in which the interests as well as the patriotism of the leaders and members of the working class were represented. This agreement did not include the most hard-line industrialists or their representatives such as Hugenberg or the radical socialists such as Rosa Luxemburg.

The circumstances which led to the weakening of the *Burgfrieden* were also manifested in the growing overt hostility to the bellweather minority in Germany, the Jews. "Moreover, there arose an ever-more virulent anti-Semitism, especially after the end of 1915. Once the effect of the *Burgfrieden* had worn off, the Jews were accused, quite openly but completely unfairly of shirking military service as well as of usury and war profiteering."[38] The most extreme version of anti-Semitism was promulgated by the Fatherland Party founded in 1917 by Admiral von Tirpitz, Alfred Hugenberg, and the civil servant Wolfgang Kapp. Tirpitz had been the architect of Germany's aggressive policy of naval construction and risk-taking. Since Germany's fleet, with the exception of its U Boats and a few pocket battleships, had been reduced to the role of observer after initial battles, Tirpitz should have been thoroughly discredited. However, the mysterious reverence for high military officers, regardless of their effectiveness, was so pervasive in Germany that he remained a man of power and influence. The Fatherland Party was fiercely anti-Semitic in addition to being imperialistically expansionist at the time when growing dissatisfaction with the war led to the Reichstag's peace resolution. By July 1918, party membership numbered 1.25 million people, and corporate members included major businesses such as Siemens, Borsig, Duisberg and Krupp as well as middle-class and peasants groups. The Fatherland Party revived many of the doctrines of the much smaller but prophetic United Association of Anti-Semitic Parties which had in 1899 envisaged a "final solution" for the Jewish problem. "Since the Jewish problem will reach world proportions in the course of the twentieth century," the Fatherland Party explained, "it would have to be solved in the end by the complete exclusion and ... finally annihilation of the Jewish people."[39] At the end of the war, the Germany that emerged was, as Walther Rathenau put it in a memorable formula, "a state in which for centuries no one has ruled who was not a member or convert to military feudalism, the feudalized bureaucracy, or the feudalized, militarized and bureaucratized plutocracy."[40]

Notes

1 H. Stuart Hughes, *Consciousness and Society: The Reconstruction of European Social Thought, 1890–1930*, New York, 1954.

2 Louise W. Holborn, Gwendolen M. Carter, John H. Herz, (eds) *German Constitutional Documents Since 1871*, 1970, p. 19.

3 Isabell Hull, *The Entourage of Kaiser Wilhelm II 1888–1918*, Cambridgeshire, 1982, p. 17.

4 John C. G. Röhl, "Wilhelm II, Das Beste waere Gas," *Die Zeit*, 2, December 1994, pp. 6–8.

5 Karl Marx, *The Eighteenth Brumaire of Louis Bonapart*, with explanatory notes, New York, 1964, p. 34.

6 Geoff Eley, *From Unification to Nazism: Reinterpreting the German Past*, Boston, 1986, p. 102.

7 *Deutschland im ersten Weltkrieg*, Berlin, 1969, p. 83.

8 Fritz Fischer, *Griff nach der Weltmacht: Der Kriegszeitpolitik des kaiserlichen Deutschland 1914–1918*, Düsseldorf, 1961.

9 Hans-Ulrich Wehler, *The German Empire 1871–1918*, trans. Kim Traynor, Providence, Rhode Island, 1985.

10 *Ibid.*, p. 91.

11 *Ibid.*, p. 29.

12 *Ibid.*, p. 113.

13 Quoted in Nigel Hamilton, *The Brothers Mann: the Lives of Heinrich and Thomas, 1871–1950, 1875–1955*, London, 1978, p. 95.

14 *Ibid.*, p. 128.

15 Wehler, *German Empire*, p. 119.

16 Fritz Ringer, *The Decline of the German Mandarins: The German Academic Community 1890–1933*, Cambridge, Mass., 1969.

17 See as examples, Arnold Brecht, *The Political Education of Arnold Brecht: An Autobiography: 1884–1970*, Princeton, 1970; Franz Schoenberner, *Confessions of a European Intellectual*, New York, 1946.

18 Wehler, *German Empire*, p. 121.

19 Carl Amery, *Capitulation: The Lesson of German Catholicism*, trans. Edward Quinn, New York, 1967.

20 Gordon Craig, *Germany 1866–1945*, New York, 1978, p. 275.

21 Jürgen Kocka, *Facing Total War: German Society 1914–1918*, trans. Barbara Weinberger, Cambridge, Mass., 1985, p. 154.

22 Woodruff D. Smith, *Politics and the Sciences of Culture in Germany, 1840–1920*, New York, 1991.

23 Carl Schorske, *German Social Democracy 1905–1917*, Cambridge, Mass., 1955.

24 David Blackbourn, *Class, Religion and Local Politics in Wilhelmine Germany*, New Haven, 1980, p. 233.

25 David Schoenbaum, *Zabern 1913: Consensus Politics in Imperial*

Germany, London, 1982, p. 77.

26 Quoted in Richard Friedenthal, *Letters of Great Artists: From Blake to Pollock*, New York, 1963, p. 213.

27 Robert Weldon, *Bitter Wounds: German Victims of the Great War*, Ithaca, New York, 1984, p. 95.

28 Erich Maria Remarque, *All Quiet on the Western Front*, trans. A. W. When, New York, 1929.

29 Kocka, *Facing Total War*, p. 79–80.

30 *Ibid.*, p. 35.

31 *Ibid.*, pp. 39–40.

32 *Ibid.*, pp. 25–6.

33 Bernard Bellon, *Mercedes in Peace and War: German Automobile Workers, 1903–1945*, New York, 1990, pp. 96–100.

34 Bernhard von Bülow, *Memoirs of Prince Von Bülow*, trans. F. A. Voigt, Vol. II, Boston, 1931, p. 66.

35 Kocka, *Facing Total War*, p. 145.

36 Stephen Shuker, *The End of French Predominance in Europe: the Financial Crisis of 1924 and the Adoption of the Dawes Plan*, Chapel Hill, North Carolina, 1976.

37 Gerald Feldman, *Army, Industry and Labor in Germany 1914–1918*, Princeton, New Jersey, 1966.

38 Kocka, *Facing Total War*, pp. 123–4.

39 Wehler, *The German Empire*, p. 107.

40 *Ibid.*, p .99.

2

The founding of the Weimar State

By the Autumn of 1918 the military fortunes of Germany had deteriorated precipitously. Generals Hindenburg and Ludendorff had come to the conclusion that Germany could not possibly win the war and might very well face total defeat. With the Kaiser and the generals distracted by military necessity, the Reichstag took additional power which made it possible for them to participate more actively in the governing process. In November 1918 in acknowledgment of the deteriorated military situation, a new Chancellor, Prince Max von Baden, had come to power. He combined aristocratic position with more flexible ideas on government. Friedrich Ebert, the leader of the Social Democratic Party, agreed to serve in Prince Max's government and declared that "It is the birth of democracy."[1]

It is possible that, given a less chaotic set of circumstances following these changes, the Weimar Republic or a liberal constitutional monarchy could have been born more tranquilly and with greater prospects for success. Yet it was only because of the crisis and looming disaster that the aristocratic power holders in Germany showed any disposition to relinquish any of their control. Even as the generals turned more power over to civilian leaders and recognized the hopeless nature of Germany's military predicament, commanders at the front were saying that their troops were "stabbed in the back" by left-wing elements at home. This rhetoric of betrayal had been well established months before there was any sign of left-wing revolution in Germany.

Left-wing agitation in the military and in the cities, particularly

Munich and Berlin, intensified by the Fall of 1918. When the admirals decided to send the German fleet, which had been in port since the early days of the Battle of Jutland, into a last glorious battle with no prospect of victory, the sailors based in Kiel rose in rebellion. The naval revolt at Kiel brought sympathetic crowds into the streets in Berlin and Munich and convinced Hindenburg and Ludendorff that the German military machine was in the early stages of unraveling.

Generals Hindenburg and Ludendorff pressured the leaders of the Reichstag, now dominated by Social Democrats and the Center Party, to negotiate an armistice on an emergency basis. Matthias Erzberger, the Catholic Center leader who had introduced the "Peace Without Annexation" resolution into the Reichstag in 1917, and the Social Democratic leaders Friedrich Ebert and Philipp Scheidemann urged the generals to hold out longer so they could gain favorable armistice terms. The generals argued that they had no time and that great speed was essential.

Ironically, while this pressure to sue for peace was coming from the generals, rumors circulated among the Supreme Command that the front was being "stabbed in the back" by left-wing elements at home. The very people responsible for the politicians' reluctant agreement to a speedy armistice in November 1918, Generals Hindenburg and Ludendorff, themselves became promoters of the stab-in-the-back story which they, more than anyone else, knew to be untrue. Thus General Hindenburg, who would become Germany's president in 1925 by campaigning as a man of honor above politics, had worked to save his personal reputation and his political power by contributing to the development of the "big lie". Hindenburg was also the main force in convincing the Kaiser to abdicate so Germany could avoid socialist revolution. The Kaiser's abdication was an act of such great symbolism that, more than anything else, it would send a message to all Germans that major change was under way. This strategy reduced revolutionary pressure. The role that Hindenburg played in the abdication added another element of irony to his later pose as a politician who symbolized the better days under the Kaiser.

Germany was declared a Republic twice on the same day in November 1918: once by Philipp Scheidemann representing the moderate socialists and once by Karl Liebknecht representing the radical socialists. Scheidemann's announcement, which was considered premature by Friedrich Ebert, was designed to forestall action by the more radical elements. Both groups were committed to making major changes in Germany's government and society in general, but the goals of the radicals were set far beyond those of the moderates. Friedrich Ebert would have preferred a constitutional monarchy on the English model rather than the total elimination of the monarch. The high-ranking and long-term civil servant Arnold Brecht who loyally supported the Republic argued at the time and later as well that a more gradual move to a constitutional monarchy would have brought the new government a larger pool of potential supporters and increased its chances for survival.[2] However the pressure of the streets and the Spartacists, in addition to the urgings of the American President, Woodrow Wilson, suggested to Scheidemann that the luxury of time to make a more gradual, staged move away from the Wilhelmine regime was an illusion. Ebert and Scheidemann, the reformers, thought in terms of a parliamentary democracy with improved social programs and better working conditions for Germany's working men and women. Liebknecht and Luxemburg, the revolutionaries, envisioned a government of workers', soldiers' and peasants' councils and revolutionary changes on the Russian Bolshevik model.

In the last days of 1918 and the early days of 1919, the conservative forces were dispirited and in disarray. The situation in Germany looked so bleak and polarized that they were willing to turn to the moderate socialists as the best hope to prevent the Bolshevization of Germany. The degree to which the Social Democrats could use this situation to their greatest possible advantage became a key factor in the development of the Weimar Republic. In this crisis period, councils formed by workers, soldiers and left-wing intellectuals competed with Reichstag political parties for power and influence. The party leaders including the Social Democrats were hostile to the concept of councils and any role they could play in Germany's future. Wehler argues that the councils could have played a positive role. While acknowledging that the councils were an unlikely source of permanent government, he declares, "Nevertheless, in a situation of radical upheaval like that of 1918–1919 the councils which emerged in Germany could have been used to restructure society, if the political leadership of the time had encouraged such a course with more determination than it showed."[3]

The political view of the Social Democratic leadership and their reluctance to embrace the councils extended into many areas of their program. The councils were weapons that could have been used against political centrists and industrialists to gain concessions on working conditions, taxation and the redistribution of wealth as well as the administration of justice and education. Although the Social Democrats made positive moves in these directions while their opponents were in disarray, their clear hostility to the radicals and the subsequent actions that the Social Democrats took against these radicals convinced the conservatives that they could limit any concessions that they might make.

Certainly the situation of the Social Democratic leaders was a difficult one. They hoped to create a state based on co-operation with moderate forces whom they did not want to alienate. They also worried that radical reform, which might look like Bolshevization to the English, French and Americans, might not be accepted and might lead to a renewal of the war. Their plight becomes clear against the background of the actions of the radical left from November 1918 to April 1919.

In Prussia and Bavaria, particularly in the cities of Berlin and Munich, revolution was in the air and in the streets. However, these uprisings lacked the organized quality of the Bolshevik Revolution in Russia and the disciplined cadre of Lenin and his avant-garde. In Munich, power was seized by a collection of idealistic intellectuals led by Kurt Eisner. Eisner and his associates were able to prevail for a few months because of the vacuum created by the end of the war, the abdication of the Kaiser, and the departure of the Bavarian King Ludwig III who fled with his four daughters and whatever treasure he could carry. Eisner was not disposed towards dictatorship as Lenin had been and sponsored elections in April 1919. He and his radical supporters lost the election to more moderate Social Democrats, and he was on his way to the legislative building to resign when he was assassinated by a young aristocratic army officer, Count Arco Valley.

The assassination of Eisner inspired his followers to try to retain power by force and to create a soviet-style government. Their rebellion was suppressed in a bloody fashion by units of the regular German army and the *Freikorps*. The *Freikorps* were units formed at the end of the war to defend German territory in the east against occupation by Polish and Baltic troops who expected that their nations would re-emerge after the defeat of Germany and her allies.[4] They believed that the more territory they could actually control militarily the more territory they would ultimately receive in a peace settlement. The Germans, believing the same thing, wanted to hold on to as much territory as they could. However, many regular army units had fallen apart as a result of casualties, disease and desertion. Therefore, special units were formed which drew on volunteers. Some came from units that had already dissolved while others had been too young to enlist or had been rejected for reasons of physical limitation, emotional problems, lack of intelligence or criminal records. Although led by regular army officers, these units lacked the discipline of standard army groups and were often extremely brutal and prone to atrocities. The strange phenomenon of a socialist government calling in army troops, often followed by *Freikorps* units, to put down a people's rebellion contributed to a major split on the left which was not healed for the duration of the history of the Weimar Republic. Bavaria thus began its transformation from a short-lived, left-wing stronghold to a bastion of conservatism and radical right activity.

Revolutionary activity in Berlin took on greater importance because the city was the seat of the national government. Berlin became the center of radical agitation, and street demonstrations were endemic at the end of 1918. In January 1919 a series of major disturbances, often called the Spartacist Revolution, broke out. The Spartacists, members of the extreme left-wing of the Social Democratic Party, had agitated against the war and for radical socialist revolution. However, the Spartacist leaders, Rosa Luxemburg and Karl Liebknecht, were not planning revolution in January because they did not believe that the time was yet ripe for the type of revolution they envisioned. Seemingly without leadership or a specific plan, serious riots broke out in Berlin, and the outlines of spontaneous revolution appeared. While some of the demonstrations had been called by a group of revolutionary shop stewards, the uprising was amorphous.[5] It had no clear goals and no effective leadership. This uprising presented a major dilemma for Rosa Luxemburg and Karl Liebknecht who were reluctantly drawn into its vortex.

Liebknecht was the son of the co-founder of the German Social Democratic Party and one of its best orators. Yet, as *The New York Times* editors recognized, Rosa Luxemburg was the dominant member of the leadership: "She was undoubtedly a much stronger character than Liebknecht. She was the real 'man' in the Spartacus Movement ... and sometimes one had the impression that Liebknecht was almost childishly subject to her."[6] Born in Poland to upper-middle-class Jewish parents, Rosa Luxemburg had come to Germany for university study. One of the few women with higher education, she had emerged as a leading theoretician of socialism in Germany and a world socialist leader, intellectually on a par with Lenin and Trotsky. Among the German Social Democrats, she was one of the few who had opposed the war from the beginning. She suggested cynically that the Communist Manifesto be amended to say, "... workers of all countries unite in peace time, but in war slit one another's throats."[7] She was a determined opponent of the revisionist ideas which dominated the Social Democratic Party, particularly those of Eduard Bernstein. She disputed the notion that a new government, even one dominated by Social Democrats, could truly change things as long as the capitalist system still existed. She argued that revolution was necessary, and her theory of revolution began with spontaneous demonstrations when the conditions were right to bring crowds of the discontented into the streets on a regular basis.

Berlin in 1919 looked much like the picture of revolution which Luxemburg had often described, and yet she did not believe that Germany was ready for far-reaching change. However, her people were in the streets, and she believed that, although this movement was premature, she had to give some direction and sense of purpose to the uprising. Liebknecht joined her, and their decision led to their murders at the hands of some of the troops charged with restoring order. Luxemburg's and Liebknecht's decision to join the revolution made most contemporary and some later observers believe that the Spartacists had indeed planned and organized the revolution. Their revolutionary rhetoric and even their organization's name contributed to the misunderstandings. A *New York Times* editorial reflected the general view that the Spartacists believed they would succeed. In this light, it questioned their choice of name: "in choosing the name

(Spartacists) the German leader (Liebknecht) forgot to take into consideration that similar as he thought the present situation to Roman times, the movement of the original Spartacus has attached to it besides the glory of the temporary victories of the oppressed, the stigma of ultimate defeat."[8] In fact, as Rose Leviné Meyer, the wife of Spartacist leader Eugene Leviné, attested, they had no plan and little optimism.[9] When Luxemburg and Liebknecht went into the streets they had few illusions about their chance of success. Thus, when *The New York Times* talked of Spartacist expectations, they saw the hope of victory. However, the Spartacists leaders may have been motivated by a hopeless need to fight which was closer to the sentiments of the Roman slave leader.

The irony of January 1919 was that the decision to call in troops to restore order was made by the Social Democratic leaders led by Friedrich Ebert. Ebert saw Germany's defeat as an opportunity for real political and economic reform, but he was opposed to radical transformation. He feared that the specter of socialist revolution might provoke the English and the French to abandon the cease fire and invade Germany. He also feared that radical change would preclude co-operation between socialists and members of moderate parties which he believed was the basis for a stable democracy.

Ebert called upon the military to restore order. His connections to General Hindenburg and other members of the army general staff had been established during the war. Ebert's emissary in the operation was Gustav Noske whose effective action in implementing Ebert's decision made him a pariah in leftist circles and earned him the epithet "bulldog of counter-revolution." General Groener, who was the representative of the general staff in this operation, later played a complex role in the history of the Weimar Republic. In this instance, a deal was struck between the generals and the Social Democratic leaders. The generals would dispatch troops to Berlin to deal with the revolutionaries. In return, the Social Democrats would promise to leave the general staff in tact during the life of the new government. One of the consequences of this deal was a largely unreformed army which many historians believe contributed to the ultimate failure of the Weimar Republic. Army troops came to Berlin in sufficient strength to put down the uprising. However, they were followed by the far less disciplined and more brutal *Freikorps* who were responsible for a number of atrocities, including the murders of Luxemburg and Liebknecht.

The struggle on the streets of Berlin led to a split between the Majority Social Democrats under the leadership of Ebert, Scheidemann and Otto Landsberg and the Independent Social Democrats led by Hugo Haase, Wilhelm Dittmann and Emil Barth which broke up the six-man council that had dominated the political scene since December. The Social Democrats quickly moved to broaden the government and set up the machinery for the election of a National Assembly. Strife was avoided when the major body of soldiers' and workers' councils decided to support the election of the Assembly rather than demand a government totally dominated by councils.

On January 19, 1919, Germany had the most significant election in its history to choose a National Assembly which would write a constitution for the new Republic. It was the most democratic election in German history since, for the first time, women and young men could vote. Under the old constitution, only males over twenty-five years in age had been eligible to vote. The rules for the election of the National Assembly, later incorporated into the new constitution, enfranchised all Germans, female as well as male, twenty years of age or older. This election was a great victory for the forces committed to republican government for Germany. The three parties which were later at the heart of Weimar coalitions did extremely well. Four hundred and twenty-one seats were at stake. The Social Democratic Party led all others with 11.5 million votes and 163 seats; the Catholic Center Party held second position and received close to 6 million votes and 89 seats; and the Democratic Party came in third with 5.5 million votes and 75 seats. Most gratifying was the vote of German women who supported the pro-republic Weimar parties in great numbers. Little did the republicans know that this election was to be their high point. Many men and women who supported these parties in 1919 sooner or later drifted away towards more conservative or radical parties often in opposition to the Republic itself.

On February 9, the assembly met and chose Friedrich Ebert as President and Philipp Scheidemann as Chancellor. Fear of radical socialist revolution created a basis for co-operation between conservatives and moderate socialists and between industrialists and labor leaders. An agreement between the long-time head of the Socialist trade unions, Carl Legien, and the major industrialist leader, Hugo Stinnes, represented this phase of co-operation. The Assembly, meeting for the first time between the bloody battles in the streets of Berlin and Munich, faced the unenviable challenge of being responsible for the negotiation of the treaty that signalled Germany's defeat in the war.

The Versailles Treaty has been called the initial strike against the Weimar Republic from which it could never entirely recover. While it is true that the Republic did appear to recover from the effects of the treaty by the mid-twenties, its irritant quality endured through the period of relative prosperity and harmony from 1925 to 1929 and remained an issue until the Republic was finally destroyed. Many nationalists, Adolf Hitler the one most quoted, called the treaty *Die Diktat*. The term referred to the German belief that the treaty was imposed upon them and that they had no voice in its creation. While it was true that the German delegation had little chance to modify the treaty, they were the defeated party in a long, deadly and costly war.

The treaty played such a large part in the history of the Weimar Republic, and its provisions need to be weighed against the almost unanimous German claim that the treaty was, to use the words of the English economist John Maynard Keynes, a "Carthiginian peace which aimed to reduce Germany to a second rate power and led to the impoverishment of the German people."[10] The treaty confiscated Germany's colonial empire, returned the provinces of Alsace and Lorraine to France from which they had been taken in 1871, internationalized the Saar for fifteen years and took eastern German territory to give Poland a path to the internationalized port of Danzig. The settlement did not attempt to create a separate Bavaria or break the Rhineland away from Germany, although it was to remain free of German military force. The somewhat truncated Germany was still a large and populous nation with its industrial power largely in tact.

While the reparations demands of the treaty were high and planned for an excessively long period of time, the economic crisis of the 1920s was not solely the result of the treaty. A recent study of the negotiations at Versailles by Alan Sharpe also indicates that the terms of the treaty represented a compromise between those who wanted Germany to pay all the costs of the war and those who wanted Germany to pay only the civilian damages.[11] This compromise also produced the notorious Article 231, the war guilt clause: "The Allied and Associated Governments affirm and Germany accepts the responsibility of Germany and her allies for causing all the damage to which the Allied and Associated Governments and their nationals have been subjected as a consequence of the war imposed upon them by the aggression of Germany and her allies." Article 232 followed and qualified 231 by recognizing "that the resources of Germany are not adequate ... to make complete reparation for all such loss and damage. The Allied and Associated Governments, however require, and Germany understands that she will make compensation for all damage done to the civilian population ... and to their property." Thus Sharpe concludes, "The intention then, was to differentiate between what they claimed was their moral entitlement and their actual demands."[12] Whatever the conciliatory aspects of the provisions, many German political leaders and right-wing publicists in particular turned this article into a act of national humiliation perpetuated by the Allies and agreed to by traitorous Republican politicians. They vilified it as a stain that had be removed at all cost.

The territorial settlement was a great irritant as well. Germany suffered substantial territorial losses as a result of the Treaty. In the west, she lost the valuable provinces of Alsace and Lorraine that she had gained as a result of the Franco-Prussian War. The coal-rich province of the Saar was also separated from Germany and put under League of Nations control for a minimum of ten years. Alan Sharpe has observed, "The uncertainty over the eventual fate of the Saar reinforced Germany's fears in the west, but it was the loss of territory to Poland and the forced abandonment of German minorities in eastern Europe which most distressed the Weimar Republic about the territorial settlement."[13] Attempts to modify or destroy the Treaty of Versailles and regain Germany's prestige and territory motivated many of the developments during the Weimar years.

The negotiations which led to the treaty revealed the complexities inherent in the situation. In his private notes and dispatches, David Lloyd George, the British Prime Minister, evidenced a clear awareness that a treaty perceived as overly harsh could lead to future conflict: "The maintenance of peace will depend upon there being no cause of exasperation constantly stirring up the spirit of patriotism, of justice or of fair play."[14] In writing about the decision to station troops of the victorious powers on German soil in the Rhineland he noted that "nothing was more likely to create a feeling of bitterness and exasperation than the presence of a foreign soldiery under conditions of martial law in a land inhabited by a proud people."[15] He was aware of the warning of the Austrian Foreign Minister, Prince Metternich, who played a major role in negotiating the peace at Vienna a century earlier after the defeat of Napoleon. Metternich had warned that when any party left the negotiating table totally bitter and distraught the resulting treaty would never last, unless, as the Italian Renaissance writer Machiavelli had urged, the defeated party was completely destroyed and lost all future power to strike back. Lloyd George also expressed concern over the effects of an extreme treaty on the fledgling German Republic which he wished success. Yet he was the leader of the British Liberal Party whose spokesmen had promised the voters in 1918 that Germany would be mercilessly squeezed to compensate for the enormous losses that Britain had suffered. Lloyd George, who had played such an important role at Versailles, was much more the political leader who had witnessed the collapse of British liberalism in the December elections, than Lloyd George, the far-seeing diplomat.

Woodrow Wilson, the President of the United States, who had come to Europe with a vision for a new peaceful world and whose "Fourteen Points" offered the promise of a just peace also reacted to popular political realities. Germans based their greatest hope for a moderate peace settlement on an unrealistic assessment of the actual possibilities of Wilson's program. Wilson also faced practical political problems. "The loss of control over Congress in the November elections of 1918, the fight over American partnership in a League of Nations, and the relative indifference of the American public to all the details of the German settlement narrowed Wilson's freedom of action."[16] When the negotiations were over, Wilson had become a hypocrite and liar in the eyes of many Germans. Future generations of Germans would fear American presidents who spoke in idealistic terms in the language of evangelical Protestantism. During the Weimar years, enemies of republican government like Arthur Moeller van den Bruck would often begin their assault on democratic statesmen by launching an attack on Woodrow Wilson.[17] Georges Clemenceau, the Premier of France, who at eighty-four believed he had the right to characterize his fellow leaders, commented on what he saw as Lloyd George's political opportunism and Wilson's moralizing righteousness by declaring that sitting between them was like sitting between Napoleon and Jesus Christ.

The Versailles Treaty may not have been grossly unfair given the damage that Germany had inflicted on its rivals and considering the precedent that Germany had established with the Treaty of Brest-Litovsk which she had imposed on a defeated Russia. It may not have been unfair, but it certainly was unwise. The short-sightedness of the diplomats was compounded by conflicts among the Allies concerning how severely to deal with failures to meet obligations and by conflicts within Germany as to how much of a good faith effort to make to comply with the terms of the treaty while working to modify it.

The republican leaders did not want to sign the treaty just as they had not wanted to sign the armistice, but military leaders made it clear that Germany was in no position to resume the war. As Hajo Holborn has written, "the Allied armies would have marched into Germany and have occupied northern Germany as far east as the Weser River, cut off southern Germany, and established contact with Czechoslovakia."[18] Philipp Scheidemann resigned as Chancellor rather than sign the treaty. Finally Hermann Müller, the Social Democratic Foreign Minister and later Chancellor, reluctantly signed it. The same generals who told Müller that he had to sign the treaty were later to consider him a traitor for so doing, and radical rightists plotted his murder.

In the transition to the new government, there were winners and losers. The losers were extremely bitter, and many retained their bitterness for the entire life of the Weimar Republic. The winners often felt that they had not gotten all that they had hoped for and criticized the Republic for what they saw as its shortfalls without keeping in mind all that they had gained. As Machiavelli wrote in *The Prince*, "The reformer has enemies in all those who profit by the old order, and only lukewarm defenders in all those who profit by the new order." Among those who saw themselves as losers were aristocrats, industrialists, Protestant clergy, some civil servants, judges, university professors, army officers and other veterans, elements of the lower middle class, and the leaders of the radical left. Ominously for the Republic, few groups considered themselves to be winners, although parties committed to the Republic did win overwhelming support in the elections to the National Assembly. Some of this support came from those who feared revolution, despaired of leadership closer to their view of the world, and voted for the lesser of evils. Certainly there were those in the working class, in the women's movement, among the liberal segments of the middle class, German Catholics and Jews who did recognize the positive changes taking place. However, the intensity of their support, even for those who retained it throughout the life of the Weimar Republic, never matched the vehemence of the opposition.

The enemies of the Republic attacked early and often particularly in the period from 1920 to 1923. Coup attempts, political murders and attempts at popular uprisings threatened the Republic during this first crisis period. The character of the period is sharply focused in the history of the two largest German states, Prussia and Bavaria, and in two of the major institutions of Weimar society, the police and the judiciary. The language of the discussion of these events is anchored in the grammar of the Constitution and the political party structure.

Notes

1 Quoted in, Cuno Horkenbach (ed.), *Das Deutsche Reich von 1918 bis Heute*, Vol. I., Berlin, 1930, p. 11.

2 Arnold Brecht, *The Political Education of Arnold Brecht: an Autobiography, 1884–1970*, Princeton, New Jersey, 1970, pp. 110–11.

3 Hans-Ulrich Wehler, *The German Empire 1871–1918*, trans. Kim Traynor, Providence, Rhode Island, 1985, p. 229.

4 Robert Waite, *Vanguard of Nazism: the Free Corps Movement in Germany, 1918–1923*, Cambridge, Mass., 1952.

5 Eric Waldman, *The Spartacist Uprising of 1919*, Milwaukee, Wisconsin, 1958.

6 *The New York Times*, January 18, 1919, p.3.

7 Quoted in Elzbieta Ettinger, *Rosa Luxemburg: A Life*, Boston, 1986, p. 106.

8 *The New York Times*, December 15, 1918, p. 3.

9 Rosa Leviné, *Leviné the Spartacist*, London, 1972, p. 6.

10 John Maynard Keynes, *Economic Consequences of the Peace*, New York, 1920, p. 78.

11 Alan Sharpe, *The Versailles Settlement: Peacemaking in Paris, 1919*, New York, 1991, p. 79.

12 *Ibid.*, p. 87.

13 *Ibid.*, p. 129.

14 David Lloyd George, *Command Paper 2169 Anglo-French Pact*, p. 77.

15 David Lloyd George, *The Truth About the Peace Treaties*, New York, 1970, Vol. I, p. 312.

16 Hajo Holborn, *Germany and Europe*, Garden City, New York, 1971, p. 170.

17 Arthur Moeller van den Bruck, *Das Dritte Reich*, Munich, 1923.

18 Holborn, *Germany and Europe*, p. 182.

3

Constitution and political spectrum

The end of World War I and the beginning of the Weimar Republic brought significant changes across the whole German political spectrum. The idea of a political spectrum developed in the French Assembly during the nineteenth century where various groups sat in fixed positions within the assembly hall and became identified with those positions. Thus the idea of a left, center and right developed and became associated with specific political concepts. In the Reichstag during the Weimar period, the spectrum extended from Nationalists and National Socialists on the right to Communists and Social Democrats on the left. Political debate and conflict were framed by the ideas and composition of the major Weimar parties. These factors determined not only the relative position of a party from left to right but also its point of view as conservative, liberal or radical with many shades of difference in between. The drama of the political struggle was played out against the backdrop of the new Weimar Constitution.

The Weimar Constitution, like everything else connected with the Weimar Republic, was a compromise. It was an attempt to combine the British and continental parliamentary system, the American presidential system, and to a much lesser degree a Soviet system of worker councils. However, in contrast to the constitution of the Wilhelmine Empire which was a contract among monarchs, the Republic and its Constitution were created by the people as its preamble clearly indicated: "The German people, united in their racial elements and impelled by the will to renew and strengthen their Reich in freedom and justice, to serve the ends of peace at home and abroad and to further social progress, have established this Constitution."[1]

The Constitution defined the new German nation as a republic since the official head of state, the president, was to be elected by the people. It was a federal republic because it retained a state system in which the states shared power with the central government although central power and national law took precedence. The expectation of the writers of the Constitution was that the chancellor, chosen by the president, would be the major leader of the German government and would direct domestic policy and foreign relations. The chancellor would be the parliamentary leader capable of commanding a legislative majority in the Reichstag, the legislative body elected at least every four years by the vote of males and females twenty years of age and older. Voting was secret and legislative seats were distributed according to a proportional representation system whereby each party that received votes above a certain threshold was granted seats in proportion to the percentage of the popular vote it received. This system contributed to the proliferation of political parties during the Weimar years. The chancellor chose the cabinet which in turn had to be ratified by the Reichstag. If the chancellor lost a vote of confidence on a major issue in the Reichstag, he could reshuffle his cabinet, or if this proved unsuccessful the president could call new elections.

The president, to be elected by the people every seven years, was given the power of nominating the chancellor, appointing public officials, and commanding the armed forces. He was also given major crisis powers which in times of emergency he could use to suspend civil liberties, assume temporary dictatorial power, direct the armed forces to deal with domestic insurrection, and seize state governments which proved unable to control disturbances or provide republican rule. In spite of their inclusion of the emergency powers provisions, the jurists who wrote the Constitution, led by Hugo Preuss, believed that the normative situation, rather than the crisis situation, would prevail and would determine the nature of government. They expected that the chancellor and the Reichstag would dominate. They should have listened more closely to the jurist Carl Schmitt, a critic of the Weimar Republic on the far right, who argued that the crisis situation determined government power. He wrote, "Whoever decides in the exceptional case is sovereign."[2] In Schmitt's opinion, the Constitution gave the primary power to the president.

The Weimar Constitution provided for a broad range of civil liberties, including the rights of free speech, press, assembly, and due process protections against unlawful search and seizure. Article 118 of the Constitution which provided for free expression was not as sweeping as the American First Amendment because it allowed for some limitations. "Censorship is forbidden, but in the case of moving pictures deviations from this rule may be established by law. Legal provisions are also permissible for combating pornography and obscene publications and for the protection of young persons at public plays and entertainments."[3] In spite of this constitutional latitude for restrictions, the Weimar government allowed far more latitude in expression than had the Wilhelmine monarchy and was constantly accused by its opponents on the right of contributing to a decadent and immoral societal environment. The Constitution specifically provided for equality for women which will be discussed later and for the protection of children. It also contained provisions designed to promote economic justice. This constitutional framework provided the structure within and against which the political spectrum functioned.

A significant part of the Weimar political spectrum evolved in the atmosphere of what has been described as the "Conservative Revolution".[4] The term may have been first used by the poet Hugo von Hofmannsthal or possibly the Nobel Prize-winning author and converted supporter of the Republic, Thomas Mann. The term "Conservative Revolution" was not seen as an oxymoron during the Weimar years. As Thomas Mann put it, the conservative revolutionary "gets in on the other side of a one-sidedly overloaded boat."[5] Thus he or she tries to restore the balance between opposites. In broader terms, Keith Bullivant defines these conservatives by arguing that, "Above all, they attacked a rationalism that tried to condemn 'all living things to be part of a logical mechanism'."[6] These conservatives stressed emotion and instinct as opposed to reason and intellect as guides to finding the truth and individual decision-making. They were rebelling against English parliamentarianism, French rationalism and Roman law, all of which they condemned as alien forces corrupting German life. Many claimed to be above political parties, but most were hostile to the Republic and helped to create a climate which contributed to its decline and to the success of the Nazi Party.

Weimar conservatism and its party affiliations have also been traced by Klaus Epstein as an outgrowth of German conservative reaction to the French Revolution.[7] Epstein identifies three types of German conservatism: reactionary conservatism, status quo conservatism and reform conservatism. The reactionary conservatives longed to return to a previous age which they idealized. The status quo conservatives wanted no change in the society as it was. The reform conservatives believed that changes needed to be made, but they had to be made slowly and carefully and in terms of the traditions and historical developments of the particular people of a particular society. Conservatives in Germany in the pre-World War I period had generally been of the status quo variety. They were loyal to the monarchy and committed to a triad which included the monarchy, the Protestant Church and the aristocratically-led army. In the Weimar period, most conservatives took a reactionary point of view while a small group was willing to accept the new status quo and an even smaller group wanted more careful reform than the initial stages of the Republic produced. Ironically, in order for the larger number of reactionary conservatives to achieve their goals, they had to adopt a revolutionary posture and work to undo the Republic itself. Most of the conservatives were concentrated in the German Nationalist People's Party (the successor to the Wilhelmine Conservative Party) and the German People's Party. The German Nationalist People's Party would ultimately be dominated by reactionary conservatives who would work as "conservative revolutionaries" to undo the Republic.

German Nationalist People's Party (DNVP)

This party was created by a merger of the two conservative parties of the pre-World War I era. Its new name, including the word "People's", was a concession to the realities of the universal suffrage of all Germans female and male twenty years of age or older which became the law under the Weimar Constitution. The supporters of the party were generally Protestant and represented a mix of landowners and industrialists with crafts people and civil servants. It also attracted the more conservative elements among the white collar workers who were concentrated in the DHV, an association and lobbying group of middle level managers and clerical workers. It was militaristic, resistant to republican government, opposed to attempts to fulfill the terms of the Versailles Treaty and anti-Semitic. Members of the DNVP had close connections to the extremist Fatherland Party created during the war by Admiral Tirpitz. The party's chief publicist, Richard Kunze, was known as Knüppel Kunze (Kunze with a club) for his virulent attacks on Jews. The most important leader to emerge from the Nationalist People's Party was Alfred Hugenberg, who moved from being Managing Director of Krupp Industries to become Director of a right-wing media empire including newspapers, book publishers, a news-wire service and a major film studio. The reactionary conservatives who supported Hugenberg and made him master of the Nationalist Party by 1928 overwhelmed the status quo conservatives and forced a number of them to create a small breakaway conservative party during the last years of the Republic.

German People's Party (DVP)

The German People's Party descended from the National Liberal Party of the Bismarckian and Wilhelmine period. Confusingly this party was often in alliance with the conservatives and resisted the democratization of Germany. Its major leader, Gustav Stresemann, who will be discussed in more detail later, emerged as one of Europe's great statesmen of the 1920s and as a significant supporter of the Weimar Republic. However, during World War I, he was a fierce annexationist and militarist. The party represented small and medium-sized business interests and white-collar workers, and its support was much stronger among Protestants than Catholics. It lacked the rural base of the Nationalists and was more moderate in its nationalism and anti-Semitism. It had a core group which was willing to support and participate in Weimar coalition government, and these reform conservatives kept Gustav Stresemann as party leader. At the same time other People's Party members were never reconciled to the new Republic.

Wilhelmine liberalism, from which the People's Party derived its orientation, differed from English or American liberalism. In the nineteenth century, German liberalism was a middle-class doctrine that advocated constitutional representative government and extensive civil liberties for citizens. Liberals stressed the importance of suffrage although many resisted universal manhood suffrage and favored suffrage based on *Besitz und Bildung*, property and education. Liberals usually supported industrial and commercial development and a government policy favorable to business. There was a strong anti-clerical strain among some liberals, and they emphasized a secular "progressive" society. Many German liberals were extremely class-conscious resulting in less co-operation between German liberals and representatives of the working class than in other western nations. This lack of co-operation in the period before World War I had contributed to the aristocrats maintaining more political power and influence than their declining economic position would have otherwise allowed.

After the war and once the danger of radical social revolution appeared to have passed, most German liberals overcame their class-consciousness and supported the Republic. Many of Weimar's leaders could be classified as liberals. The Democratic Party was the major liberal political party during the Weimar years, but the Catholic Center Party had a strong liberal component as well, of course without an anti-clerical bias. The People's Party, while liberal in the older economic sense, co-operated only with difficulty with more politically liberal parties such as the Democratic Party.

Catholic Center Party (*Zentrum*)

In terms of ideology and class, the Catholic Center Party was more diverse than any of its Weimar rivals. Its one area of uniformity was its commitment to protect the interests of Germany's Catholics. Thus it is not surprising that the largest number of Center Party supporters were Catholic, although Protestants also supported the party and were included in its Reichstag delegation. While it had a left-liberal trade union wing and a right-conservative nationalist wing, the weight of its support and the orientation of its leaders placed the party at the center of the political spectrum. The Center Party was vital to the stability of the Republic, and it was a part of every Weimar government. Its leaders served as chancellors for nine administrations and were included in each of the twenty-one cabinets which ruled during the fourteen years of the Republic. The Center Party was noteworthy for the consistency of its support, and for most of the history of the Weimar Republic about fifty per cent of German Catholic voters voted for the Center Party. It also strongly advocated the extension of the vote to women in the Weimar Constitution, and Catholic women voted for the *Zentrum* in high numbers. However, when Monsignor Kaas replaced the four-time Chancellor Wilhelm Marx as party leader in 1928, the party began a drift away from strong support of the Republic towards its more conservative Bavarian wing which had evolved into the Bavarian People's Party. Independent of the national Catholic Center Party, it often positioned itself in opposition to the Weimar government.

Bavarian People's Party (BVP)

The Bavarian People's Party was the most important of a number of regionally based political parties which functioned during the Weimar years. While the party at times acted in league with the larger and more national Catholic Center Party, the BVP, although a Catholic party, was more conservative than most elements of the Center Party and wholly committed to Bavarian regional interests. The BVP dominated Bavaria from 1923 to 1933 and was not supportive of the Weimar Republic in contrast to the Center Party. Its regionalism and conservatism led the BVP to support the Protestant Hindenburg rather than the candidate of the Center Party, the Catholic Wilhelm Marx, in the presidential election of 1925. This decision by the BVP may have cost Marx the election and had serious consequences for the Republic.

German Democratic Party (DDP)

The German Democratic Party had its roots in the pre-war Progressive Party. Its largely Protestant membership was drawn from the middle class often from professional groups of lawyers, doctors and liberal academics. Some of its leaders were converts to democracy and republicanism, but the party was firmly supportive of the Weimar Republic and resistant to militarism and anti-Semitism. While the party fits on the left side of the political spectrum, it stressed its moderation. One of its most used posters showed a figure walking down the center line of a highway with the caption, "We never stray from the middle of the road". Unfortunately for the Weimar Republic, this party received its greatest vote total in 1919 and saw its support erode for most of the period. Contributing to the decline of the Democratic Party were the untimely deaths of Max Weber and Friedrich Naumann, its most prominent leaders, shortly after the founding of the party. No leaders of equal stature arose to take their place. Yet, in spite of its declining support, the DDP played a significant role during the Weimar years and was an eager participant in coalition governments. In an effort to revive its fortunes in the final days of the Republic, the Democratic Party reconstituted itself as the "State Party".

To the left of the Catholic Center and German Democratic Parties, were those parties that developed from the German socialist movement. However, the socialist movement irrevocably split during the earliest years of the Republic. The intensity of the bitterness between factions of socialists who had once been members of a common party became so severe that no co-operation was possible. Communists considered the Social Democrats to be their arch enemies for most of the period. The Comintern, the international communist organization based in Moscow, had as early as 1922 labelled the Social Democrats as Social Fascists. In the later Weimar years, they concentrated as much fire on the Social Democrats as they did on the National Socialists.

The Social Democratic Party (SPD)

The Social Democratic Party was the one party to carry over its name from the pre-World War I period. It drew its support from blue collar trade union skilled workers and at times from the more progressive white collar workers. While the party had proportionally more Protestant than Catholic supporters it did attract Catholic workers. The unified Social Democratic Party, which had been the largest political party in Germany on the eve of World War I, emerged from the war split into three parts. The largest and most moderate part of the party was the Majority Socialist Party (MSPD). A more radical smaller but significant part was the Independent Social Democratic Party (USPD). The

Spartacists constituted the smallest and most radical faction. At the end of 1918, the Communist Party (KPD) was also created out of the radical faction. While originally a very small group, it inherited the remnants of the Spartacists after their failed revolution in early 1919 and a part of the Independent Social Democratic Party when it dissolved in 1922. It grew to a significant size although up to 1930 it remained considerably smaller than the Social Democratic Party which in 1922 began using that name again as the Majority Socialists and the moderate part of the Independent Social Democratic Party recombined.

The SPD was committed to further future reform of Weimar society and hoped eventually to make the institutions and economy of Weimar more egalitarian. In spite of its equivocal heritage on this issue, the SPD was the party most resistant to racism and anti-Semitism. There had been anti-Semitism among founders of the movement and among the rank and file, but by the Weimar period these tendencies had been largely overcome. The Social Democratic Party was in most ways the bulwark of the Weimar Republic.

The Communist Party (KPD)

The German Communist Party was founded at the end of December of 1918 in the midst of revolutionary chaos. Its earliest members came from the ranks of the radical Spartacist group. The deaths of Rosa Luxemburg, Karl Liebknecht, Gustav Landauer and Kurt Eisner deprived it of those who might have been its ablest leaders. Its early core was composed of surviving Spartacists and the left-wing of the Independent Social Democratic Party. It was inspired by the Bolshevik Revolution in Russia and kept in close contact with Zinoviev, leader of the Communist International, and with Lenin and Trotsky. Drawing on a membership of more radical workers and a small group of radical intellectuals, the party was fundamentally opposed to the existence of the Weimar Republic. A number of major internal crises racked the party during the twenties. One concerned the extent to which the party would be bound to the will of Moscow. Paul Levi struggled hard in the early twenties to retain the party's autonomy, but his vision of an independent agent for substantial change lost out to the pro-Moscow radicals. His more reasonable approach was also sabotaged by those who saw the possibility of successful violent insurrection in Germany between 1920 and 1923. Once again Levi's realism and relative moderation was overridden. As Werner Angress has said of Levi's attempts to drive out the revolutionary radicals, "His decision to do so was that of a reasonable man who hoped to introduce an element of sanity into the revolutionary movement. But reason and revolution rarely mix, and his good intentions were in the long run condemned to failure."[8] Thus the Communist Party remained unresigned to the Weimar Republic and worked constantly to undermine it. While the party had the strongest feminist agenda, the only prominent women party leaders and the most women candidates for office across the political spectrum, this position did not translate into substantial female voting support.

National Socialist German Workers Party (NSDAP)

This party, founded in 1920 as the German Workers Party, began its move towards prominence when Adolf Hitler emerged as its principal speaker and leader. In the early twenties, it was one of a number of radical *völkisch* groups active in Germany. General Ludendorff, the military hero and virtual co-ruler of Germany during the last days of the war, was an early influential party member. The National Socialists initially attracted young men who had been in the military and had not been able to reintegrate themselves into the civilian economy. The party also drew support from members of the lower middle class who had suffered during and as a result of the war. They were shopkeepers, artisans and some white collar workers and were mainly Protestant males unequivocally opposed to the Weimar Republic. In 1923 they tried unsuccessfully to seize the government by force. After this failed attempt, the party reverted to a strategy of gaining power through the electoral process without ever changing its fundamental opposition to democracy and republican government. During the later twenties, the base of National Socialist support for the party expanded considerably. The party and its leader will be considered in more detail later.

Germany's political culture

In addition to these large parties which were a factor for the entire history of the Weimar Republic, there were also numerous small regional, narrow or one-issue political parties which proliferated during the Weimar years. In the election of 1928 during the peaceful period in the life of the Republic, there were thirty-one parties on the ballot. With the aid of proportional representation, fourteen of them gained representation in the Reichstag. The large number of political parties made coalition governments a necessity and limited the possibilities of decisive action.

The highpoint of support for the pro-Weimar parties was the elections to the National Assembly in 1919. By the time of elections for the Reichstag in 1920, votes shifted away from the pro-Weimar Democratic and Social Democratic Parties towards the German Nationalists. The pro-republican civil servant Arnold Brecht spoke of the seriousness of these election results: "The Weimar democracy had been dealt its mortal wound, a wound which would not necessarily be fatal to absolute monarchies, to dictatorships, or aristocracies, but which affects a democracy's very core: 'loss of majority' in its support."[9] This view that the Republic was mortally wounded in 1920 is too extreme, but clearly its existence and effectiveness were compromised by its inability to develop and maintain consistent majority support.

In addition to the large number of political parties and the fact that a number of them opposed the very existence of the Republic, the nature of Germany's political culture also made life difficult for the new government. Many educated middle-class Germans looked down on politics and had a very low opinion of politicians. Brecht's observations of pre-World War I political perception could also be applied to the Weimar period:

> That many middle-class Germans wanted and were able to lead a non-political life was not due to their lack of political power and education alone. Intellectually eminent people, in particular the 'Goethe-Germans' lived under the exalted delusion that it was not becoming for them to meddle in politics, that the entire political tumult belonged to a lower level, that it was better to be concerned with what was 'essential.'[10]

Middle-class Germans had not been unpolitical during the Wilhelmine period when they had belonged to a proliferating number of special interest lobbying groups.[11] However, these groups attempted to influence opinion, and did not directly engage in politics. The negative attitude towards politics persisted into the Weimar years even when the middle class had the real possibility of power. Furthermore, their antipathy intensified when they were exposed to the corruption and other abuses of party politics that resulted when parties had real power and patronage. These abuses are resented in any society, but, in Germany where people had not built up tolerances for them, they seemed unbearable.

The need to put together coalitions was a fact of life for the entire history of the Republic. During those years, depending upon the number of seats in any given Reichstag (as determined by total vote), it was necessary to have from 250 to over 300 votes to command a majority. Since no party ever reached those numbers and only the National Socialists came close in 1932, coalition governments were a way of life. The problems of putting disparate parties with no history of co-operation together and getting them to make significant compromises for the common interest plagued Republican leaders unremittingly. The consequences of the need for these coalitions echoed throughout the period and shaped the development of states as different as Prussia and Bavaria.

Notes

1 Constitution in Frederick Watkins, *The Use of Emergency Powers under the Weimar Constitution*, Cambridge, Mass., 1938, p. 180.

2 Carl Schmitt, *Die Diktatur-von den Anfängen der modernen Souveränität bis zum proletarischen Klassenkampf*, Munich, 1916, p. 222.

3 Watkins, *Emergency Powers*, pp. 203–4.

4 Arnim Mohler, *Die Konservative Revolution in Deutschland*, Stuttgart, 1950.

5 Keith Bullivant, "The Conservative Revolution," in Anthony Phelan (ed.), *The Weimar Dilemma: Intellectuals in the Weimar Republic*, Manchester, 1985, p. 55.

6 *Ibid.*, pp. 56–7.

7 Klaus Epstein, *The Genesis of German Conservatism*, Princeton, 1966.

8 Werner T. Angress, *Stillborn Revolution: the Communist Bid for Power in Germany, 1921–1923*, Princeton, New Jersey, 1963, p. 43.

9 Arnold Brecht, *The Political Education of Arnold Brecht: an Autobiog-*

raphy, 1884–1970, Princeton, New Jersey, 1970, p. 184.

10 *Ibid.*, p. 40.

11 Roger Chickering, *We Men Who Feel Most German; a Cultural Study of the Pan-German League 1886–1914*, Boston, Mass., 1984.

4

Prussia: bulwark of the Republic

Prussia's transformation from the pre-war aristocratic-dominated heart of the Hohenzollern Empire to the bulwark of the Republic and its strongest supporter among the states was one of the most dramatic aspects of Weimar history. In contrast to the central government where a pro-republican coalition was always fragile and difficult to maintain and where minority governments often ruled, Prussia maintained strong republican coalitions during almost the entire history of the Weimar government. Members of the Social Democratic, the Catholic Center, the Democratic and, even for long blocks of time, the People's Party were able to work together in relative harmony. Social Democrats Otto Braun, Carl Severing, and Ernst Heilmann and Catholic Center labor leader Adam Stegerwald were major figures in Prussian state politics and among the nation's most able political leaders.

Prussia's political strength and stability reflected its balanced demographics as the largest of the Weimar states. Berlin, its capital was Germany's largest city and the capital of the German nation. Prussia was a largely Protestant state but with a significant Catholic minority concentrated in its Rhineland area. The Prussian state economy was a mixture of industry and agriculture with a significant segment of workers concentrated in its cities and agricultural workers concentrated on the landed estates in the east.

Prussia had been the core around which Germany had unified in 1871, and the Prussian state was the wealthiest and politically dominant part of Germany from 1871 to 1918. Prussia was a bulwark of conservatism dominated by the Conservative and conservatively-oriented National Liberal Parties. The depth of Prussian resistance to change is evidenced by the disjuncture between the state's voting system and the suffrage granted by the national government. While the Constitution of 1871 created a lower national legislative house, the Reichstag, which was elected by universal manhood suffrage of all German males at least twenty-five years of age, the Prussian elections remained based on a three-class voting system which enabled a small minority of the population to control two-thirds of the seats in the Prussian Landtag and restricted the more popular Social Democratic Party to a mere handful of seats in this state legislative body.

During World War I, when the pressure of Social Democratic workers and even some factions of the military leadership for meaningful reform reached great heights, the Conservative and National Liberal forces in Prussia continued to resist significant change. The reform package called for universal manhood suffrage and the paliamentarization of Prussia. This change would make the Prussian cabinet responsible to the legislature rather than to the King. The position of the National Liberal Party stands out as particularly intransigent since the party's own national leader Gustav Stresemann and state leader Robert Friedberg had endorsed a suffrage reform plan. As Dietrich Orlow has analyzed the situation: "Germany's largest state, the foundation of Bismarckian and Wilhelmine Reich, now personified not the glory of Germany, but the immovable obstacle to peace and progress. In southern Germany a widely held view stated, 'If Prussia is not destroyed, Germany will be destroyed by Prussia.' "[1]

In the first days of the Republic, Prussia was the center of political turbulence with outbreaks of socialist revolution from 1918 to 1919. Although the revolutionary forces were strong in the capital, the first acts of revolution in Prussian territory began in the northern provinces and fanned out to the west and the south. It was not until the very end of the chain of events that the disturbances spread to the capital.[2] Confronted with revolutionary upheaval, the Prussian leaders agreed to support the national government in their effort to restore order and move towards parliamentary rule. It was in Prussia that the Spartacist Revolution was crushed.

Yet in spite of the turmoil of these early Weimar years, Prussia was building towards a strong republican entity which rested on a structure of coalitions aimed at reconciling radical extremes. While the Prussian Socialists were clearly divided between Majority Socialists and Independent Socialists who had considerable rank and file support, the Majority Socialist leadership proved more clear thinking and resolute. They continually negotiated with the Independents in an effort to maintain working-class solidarity and keep the Independents form joining with the Communists. They also worked to create a coalition with the other pro-Weimar parties, the Democratic and Catholic Center Parties. The early leaders, Paul Hirsch, Albert Südekum, Wolfgang Heine and Ernst Heilmann, all fought for significant reform but wished to avoid radical measures.

The Prussian coalition decided early on to break any linkage between the Prussian cabinet and the Weimar cabinet. This decision helped to maintain the dominance of coalitions based on parties supportive of parliamentary democracy within Prussia while that effort met with much less success at the national level. The People's Party and the Center Party remained much closer to the political center and much more supportive of democratic processes and values at the Prussian state level than they did nationally. In union with the Social Democrats, they provided a firm structure for republican principles in Prussia.

Until the outbreak of the Kapp coup attempt, the non-socialist coalition partners thought that the greatest danger to the stability of the new state came from the radical left in the form of the Independents. However, the Kapp Putsch proved this assessment wrong and revealed the radical right as the greater threat. On March 13, 1920 the Erhardt Brigade, a rebellious military unit, marched into Berlin as part of the first serious rightist attempt to destroy the Republic and seize power. This brigade, a *Freikorps* unit that had fought in the Baltic under Captain Hermann Erhardt, had refused orders to demobilize. It was greeted in Berlin by the civil servant Wolfgang Kapp and General Walther Lüttwitz who proclaimed a new government of national unity. The Social Democratic leadership proved unable to get regular military units to engage the Erhardt Brigade. Although General Walther Reinhardt, the Prussian Minister of Defense, was willing to use troops against the rebels, his effort failed. Instead of looking to Reinhardt, most troops took their cue from General von

Seeckt, the Army Chief of Staff, who told the Social Democratic leaders that troops would not fire on other troops. President Friedrich Ebert and his cabinet fled to Dresden and then to Stuttgart where they called on their supporters to stage a general strike. Prussian trade unionists responded to the strike in large numbers while civil servants struck a neutral pose waiting to see if the coup succeeded. The strike was extremely effective in bringing transportation and commerce to a standstill. Within four days, convinced they could not govern, Kapp and Lüttwitz fled Berlin.

The failure of the Putsch was largely the result of working-class action. It emboldened the Communists to believe that left-wing revolution was again possible, and a uprising of about 50,000 radical workers in the Ruhr now threatened the government. Ironically, Ebert now turned to General von Seeckt to put down this uprising which he did with dispatch using regular army and *Freikorps* units who had no reservations about firing on workers. Against these enemies, von Seeckt acted decisively and even managed to control the *Freikorps* troops. Virtually none of the officials in the military, police or civil service who refused to act against the Kapp forces were ever disciplined. The Prussian leaders, all firm supporters of the Ebert government, did however realize the necessity for significant reform of the civil service and for a more extensive reorientation of their police (which will be discussed separately).

The Kapp Putsch had benefitted from a miscalculation by members of the Prussian cabinet who had underestimated the threat of the radical right. This belief was shared by many Prussian Social Democrats who had once been comrades of the former Spartacists and current Communists. Convinced that only the leftists were a danger, the Prussian leaders neglected significant reform of the civil service which was considered conservative but supportive. The Kapp Putsch demonstrated the unreliability of Prussia's old civil service in the face of a threat from the right and provoked significant changes:

> [T]he ministries' failure to act decisively in this area seriously undermined the viability of the new form of government in the first year of its existence. Conversely, when the new rulers did undertake energetic reforms after the Kapp Putsch had exposed

> their earlier mistakes, the Prussian civil service helped the state to become the democratic bulwark that it was during the crisis-ridden years of the 1920s.[3]

The Prussian leaders were determined to create a democratic society. Based in the heartland of the former Hohenzollern monarchy and struggling against centuries of Prussian tradition, they faced a formidable task. A government of printers and metal workers had replaced emperors and aristocrats. From the pool of workers and Social Democrats, some new civil servants emerged to support the government. The reformed Prussian civil service contributed to a much more republican and stable democracy than the national government enjoyed. Rudolf von Thadden observes that: "Throughout the upheavals of the Weimar period, Prussia was indeed to serve as a counterweight to a politically unbalanced Germany."[4] The Prussian government, in contrast to the national government, dealt firmly and severely with the forces of the radical right after the Kapp Putsch and thereby prevented them from becoming a significant political force in Prussia from 1921 to 1929.

Having reformed the civil service, the new leaders confronted other traditional institutions as well. One of the trickiest questions which plagued the new Prussian government was its relationship with the churches which were a pillar of German society. While there had been constant complaints about declining church attendance and growing secularity among the German population at the end of the nineteenth century, churches still contributed strongly to setting the moral tone of the society and shaping the values and *Weltanschauung* of most Germans. Dealing with the churches represented a significant challenge to the new leaders, particularly the Socialists. Since Prussia was the largest of the Weimar states and one in which the Socialists played such a large part, the state-church issue was presented there in high relief.

Two particular aspects of the question stand out. One concerns government relations with the Catholic Church in light of the fact that the Catholic Center Party was a vital part of all Weimar coalitions and of the Prussian state government as well. This relationship, in part, explains the substantial negotiations that led to a Concordat between the Prussian government and the Roman

Catholic Church. The agreement seems particularly significant in the context of a Socialist-dominated government. However the Social Democrats recognized that a successful coalition government required good relations with the Center Party. They were also inspired by the spirit of co-operation created by a Concordat in Bavaria. Thus Prussian Social Democrats were willing to work with Cardinal Pacelli, the future Pope Pius XII to negotiate a formal relationship.

Governmental relations with the Protestant Churches were in many ways even more problematic. These churches had never been political in the same sense that the Catholic Church had been because its leaders had never felt the need to do so since the dominant Protestant Churches had always functioned as auxiliaries to the state. While the level of church monetary support was never high and they were significantly understaffed, church leaders nonetheless felt that they were part of the ruling elite. With the end of the monarchy and the creation of a new state, everything appeared to change for the leaders of the Protestant Churches. They believed that they had lost their favored status and feared the actions of a state dominated by Socialists.

Church leaders rallied their rank and file to agitate for favorable treatment in the Constitution. Two factors aided them in this process. The leaders of the Social Democratic Party were more often pragmatic politicians than dogmatic socialist ideologues. Secondly the Social Democratic Party was dependent on the co-operation of the Catholic Center Party as a major coalition partner both at the national and state level, thus making it more sensitive to religious issues. The irony here is that the Protestant leadership had longstanding negative feelings about the Catholic Church and its political movement in Germany. Thus, although the Protestants benefited as a result of the religious program of the Catholic Center Party which they considered sound, they still rejected the Center Party because it was Catholic. The Constitution produced by the National Assembly was a much more positive document in those provisions of prime importance to the Protestant leadership than they feared it might be. As J. R. C. Wright asserts:

> The Protestant Church had every reason to be pleased with the Weimar Constitution. The November fears of a hostile programme

> of separation of church and state were dispelled. Church privileges were confirmed while state control of the church was reduced. The SPD was justified in arguing that this had produced a situation in which the church was free of the state, but the state was not free of the church.[5]

Since the churches had been treated generously in the transitional period from monarchy to republic and in the Constitution, the possibility emerged for an accommodation between the Protestant Church and the leaders of the new state. The test case came in the Old Prussian Union, a large church organization, formed by a union of the Lutheran and Calvinist Churches. Almost all the leaders of this Prussian Church were on the conservative side of the political spectrum; Helmreich reports that seventy to eighty per cent of the Protestant clergy were conservative. Thus the saying he quotes: "The church is politically neutral, but it votes German National."[6] The most supportive group of Prussian Union clergy, represented by the theologian Kapler, attempted to establish a productive relationship with the Republic. These churchmen tilted towards republican leaders such as Gustav Stresemann. However, they lacked Stresemann's enthusiasm for the Republic. They were *Vernunftrepublikaner* (republicans by virtue of reason) who found the Republic to be the lesser of evils among the realistic governmental systems that existed at the time.

The resistance of even the more supportive church leaders was the residue of lingering hostility from earlier socialist attacks on religion in general and church leaders in particular. Protestant leaders were responding to what Social Democrats had said about the churches and their interests. In J. R. C. Wright's words "The SPD press frequently made fun of Christian festivals, attacked state subsidies for the churches and church social work, and opposed denominational schools ..."[7] Once again the Social Democrats were hurt by a substantial gap between their rhetoric and their practice. Many people judged them by their more extreme rhetoric and concluded that their more conciliatory actions were the result of opportunism at work. Protestant leaders assumed that the moderation which the Social Democrats showed towards the churches when they came to power had been brought about by the influence of the Catholic Center Party. This assumption was only in part true because the Social Democrats had always been more moderate in practice than in rhetoric and inclined to accommodate various interests. The Protestant Churches grudgingly accepted the benefits offered but showed little gratitude towards the Catholic Center Party even though they attributed some of their favorable treatment to its relationship with the Social Democrats.

In spite of the attempt by some moderate Protestant leaders to work with the new Prussian government, many Protestant leaders often articulated political attitudes which were truly out of sympathy with republican ideals particularly on the issues of anti-Semitism and National Socialism. Protestant leaders were disturbed by what they saw as the moral deterioration of society under the Republic. They saw German culture in a life or death struggle for survival. As Wright comments:

> Another threat to German 'Kultur', in Protestant eyes, was Jewish influence. Paul Althaus, the Protestant theologian, criticized 'völkisch' theories but maintained there was a 'Jewish danger.' … It was not a question of racial or religious anti-Semitism, 'but only of the threat of a … demoralized and demoralizing, urban intellectual class which is represented by the Jewish race.[8]

Protestant leaders who were appalled at the signs of "decadence" that they saw on the streets of cities, in the theaters and cabarets attributed this to alien, often Jewish, forces at work. Much of Protestant clerical anti-Semitism of the Weimar period was moderate in intensity in contrast with the the virulent racist anti-Semitism of the Nazis. However, the long-term exposure of large numbers of Germans to moderate anti-Semitism, particularly when articulated by respected church leaders, inoculated them against the more virulent kind of anti-Semitism. The effect did not make them resistant to it, but rather prevented a reaction and ultimately increased their susceptibility.

Leaders of the Old Prussian Union believed that both the state and the society had lost actual and moral authority, and that values had become totally distorted. As one leader put it, "A state, in which the authority of government has gone over to the broad masses; a family in which … children command parents …; a society, in which the forces of tradition … are scorned and destroyed etc., are subordinated to expediency and thereby also opposed divine will. These types of perversion destroy their organisms."[9] This condemnation not only reveals a hostility to the Republic but to basic ideas of democracy itself and to many of the values of the new more liberal Weimar society.

The attitudes of the church leaders also reflected their strong sense of traditional hierarchy and reverence for titles, aristocratic bearing and academic degrees. Without the trappings of royalty or at least aristocracy and without other symbols of distinction which commanded respect, the new leaders were demeaned and judged to be suspect in the eyes of many churchmen and others. Many were troubled that a saddler (Friedrich Ebert) had replaced the Emperor as the head of state and that the new first lady had also been a worker. Even workers themselves sometimes had difficulty regarding the new leaders with respect. The Prussian state leaders, particularly the Socialists, were now in charge of a state which had been the symbol of monarchy and aristocracy. In addition to meeting the demands of running a government, they had to prove the validity of their credentials for doing the job.

Otto Braun, former printer and long-time Social Democrat, was the most important of the Prussian leaders of the Weimar era. Braun proved to be an effective coalition politician and a pragmatic leader. His first position in the new Prussian government was as Agriculture Minister. He briefly served as Minister President of Prussia in 1920, and then became Minister President again in 1921, a position he held with one brief interruption until the summer of 1932. Braun led two kinds of coalition governments (the so-called Weimar Coalitions) of Social Democratic, Catholic Center and Democratic Party representatives and broader coalitions which included members of the People's Party as well.

One of the key moves that Braun engineered was separating the fate of Prussian cabinets from that of the Weimar government and thereby providing Prussia with greater stability. Throughout the upheavals of the Weimar period, Prussia was indeed to serve as a democratic counterweight to a politically unbalanced Germany. Whereas Reich governments changed constantly and lost their parliamentary–democratic basis by 1930, Prussia demonstrated remarkable political continuity which it was to maintain right up to 1932. As Von Thadden put it, "It was not an exaggeration when Prussia was described as the 'bulwark' of democracy in the German Republic."[10]

Braun led Prussia through the crisis year of 1923 during which his state demonstrated its unswerving loyalty to the Weimar government and the principles it represented. These principles were threatened when, in response to right and left-wing uprisings, the dislocations of inflation, and foreign occupation of the Ruhr, President Friedrich Ebert declared a state of emergency under Article 48 of the Constitution and gave General von Seeckt provisional dictatorial powers. In states like Saxony and Thuringia, army officials took control. However, in Prussia the emergency was administered by the regular civil service under democratic rule.[11] When Hitler and the Nazis attempted to overthrow the government of Bavaria by a Putsch on November 9, 1923, Braun and his Minister of the Interior Severing mobilized the Prussian police in case they would be needed to defend the Republic. Otto Braun watched with dismay as Erich Zeigner, the Social Democratic Minister President of Saxony, became a virtual prisoner of his Communist coalition partners and armed groups of workers, called *Proletarische Hundertschaften*, patrolled the streets of Dresden and Leipzig.[12] He reluctantly acknowledged the need for national intervention by a Reich Commissioner and military force to bring the situation under control in Saxony.

Braun worried about what action if any the army would take in the wake of the Hitler Putsch in Bavaria. He remembered that General von Seeckt had refused to use army troops against the rebellious *Freikorps* in 1920 during the Kapp Putsch when he had declared that, "the Reichswehr will not shoot at the Reichswehr." He expressed surprised satisfaction when von Seeckt moved against rebellious "Schwarze Reichswehr" troops under Major Buchrucker in Küstrin at the beginning of October and acted forcefully to make sure that Bavarian Reichswehr units remained loyal to the Weimar government during the Hitler Putsch in November. Braun concluded that von Seeckt read the political signals and realized that, in spite of the crisis, there was more support for the Weimar government in 1923 than he had thought there was in 1920.[13] Thus von Seeckt had followed his reading of the political winds and had surprised Braun.

During the period from 1924 to 1928 which represented the so-called "golden age" of the Weimar Republic, Otto Braun and his coalition government continued to govern Prussia. While Germany was generally stable at this time, Prussia was still more stable politically than was the Republic as a whole. A center-right coalition dominated the Weimar government even though the Social Democratic Party was the largest party in the Reichstag and had been the strongest supporter of the Republic. In contrast in Prussia, the Social Democrats led a center-left coalition, and Social Democrats held the dominant positions.

The election of 1930 brought huge gains for the National Socialists and substantial losses for the Weimar coalition parties. The sharp swing to the right of the German Nationalist Party made pro-republican majority government problematic. President Hindenburg appointed Heinrich Brüning of the Catholic Center Party as Chancellor. Brüning remained Chancellor until 1932 when he was replaced by Franz von Papen. Brüning never commanded a legislative majority and ruled by decree using the emergency powers of President Hindenburg to develop and attempt to carry out a program. These Brüning years can be seen as the end of parliamentary democracy and the beginnings of a new type of government: a presidential dictatorship with legislative sufferance. Brüning's use of these powers could have been stopped, and he could have been toppled if the Social Democrats who refused to support him directly had used the legislative powers of the Reichstag to end the rule by decree. However, for two years, the Social Democrats failed to oppose Brüning who was at best an unenthusiastic republican who retained monarchist sympathies and considered co-operation with the National Socialists.[14]

The decision by the Prussian leaders to make their cabinets and leadership independent of the national leadership enabled Braun to lead a stable pro-Weimar coalition which retained a majority in Prussia until 1932. In 1932, however, President Hindenburg appointed Franz von Papen as Chancellor. It was at this point that the election of General Hindenburg in 1925 began to have truly ominous results for the Republic. Clearly if Wilhelm Marx had been elected President of Germany in 1925, he never would have appointed von Papen as Chancellor nor would he have made the subsequent appointments of Kurt von Schleicher or Adolf Hitler. Certainly had Otto Braun been President, he never would have made this appointment.

Franz von Papen had come from the right-wing of the Catholic Center Party but, by the later twenties, had moved into the

Nationalist orbit. He was fundamentally anti-republican, had no popular base of support and owed his position to the circle around President Hindenburg. Von Papen introduced a right-wing regime which was sympathetic to the National Socialists, openly opposed to the republican parties, and extremely hostile to left-wing groups. His negotiations with the National Socialists alarmed Braun who had always vigorously opposed them as declared enemies of republican principles.

The critical challenge to republican rule came for Braun and Prussia with a major transit workers' strike in Berlin in July 1932. The Communists and National Socialists were both supporting the strike. The Prussian police were hard pressed to handle the agitation and disorder, but they were a dedicated and effective force and were coping with the crisis. However, on July 20, 1932, the central government of Franz von Papen moved to seize the Prussian state government. Von Papen acted under authority of an edict signed by President Hindenburg and counter-signed by himself as *Reichskanzler*. The edict called upon Braun to surrender his government to a Reichs Commissioner appointed by von Papen. Braun was faced with a dilemma: should he accede to the demands of von Papen or should he resist?

Braun had been willing to see Prussia merged into a democratic republic. He had declared: "Prussia must die so that the Reich may live. We shall realize Prussia when we are able to achieve a unified Reich."[15] Although supporting Prussia's integration into a democratic republic, he was not willing to see it submerged into von Papen's rightist state. Braun warned that all forces had to be marshalled if Germany was to be kept from degenerating into a fascist dictatorship. Similar sentiments were expressed by Carl Severing and Albert Grzesinski who had been Braun's Ministers of the Interior and the principle creative spirits behind the Prussian police. Severing had been such a vital part of the Braun regime that the term "Braun-Severing government" was often used.

The supporters of the Braun government and of republicanism in general brought suit against the Reich for its takeover of Prussia. By this action, republican faith in due process was put to the test. This group went into court in an effort to overturn von Papen's action and, thus, to preserve the constitutional basis of the Republic. This celebrated case was tried at Leipzig in October, 1932.

Some republicans such as Albert Grzesinski, who was the Police President of Berlin in July 1932, maintained that the conflict should have been settled in the streets several years earlier and should never have come to the courts.[16] Historians such as Koppel Pinson have agreed.[17] The reasons why the Braun forces chose the courts rather than the streets for their confrontation reveal their understanding of the nature of republican rule. Essentially, there were three reasons for their choice: a commitment to liberal-democratic ideology; a belief that there was a qualitative difference between von Papen and the National Socialists and that therefore von Papen might be used against the greater threat; and a calculation that overwhelming force was on the other side.

The first of these factors is, in many ways, the most complex. The republican leadership was by background and inclination unsuited for the kind of violent action that might have been substituted for an appeal to the courts. They were committed to the ideals of justice and due process. They believed that, in the free market place of ideas, truth would win out. Overriding all these considerations was republican devotion to rule by law and an essentially bourgeois need for order. These characteristics were evident to republicans, themselves. Friedrich Stampfer, a socialist newspaper editor, recognized that the principle republican bulwark, the Social Democratic Party, "was for decades a party of peaceful evolution, of reasonable and balanced consideration, of understanding without force. If it had given the signal for violent action, it would have attempted to appear what it indeed was not."[18]

Although violent resistance was unthinkable, the Social Democrats did not hesitate to use force when they were the elected administration in Berlin or Weimar because they believed that force was the monopoly of legally-constituted authority. Ebert and Sheidemann had used force in a very dramatic fashion as early as January 1919 in dealing with the Spartacist Revolution. In 1923, the Social Democratic President had used troops against left-wing revolutionaries in Thuringia and Saxony and most decisively against Max Holz and his revolutionary forces in Hamburg. Braun and Severing used their police very effectively in Prussia earning the wrath of both left and right-wing extremists. The Social Democratic leaders who had risen from the working class through the ranks of the trade union and party bureaucracies to political power believed that they were part of the establishment and the status quo and could not see themselves in the position of revolutionaries.[19] Thus, this belief reinforced their rejection of violence against those in power. In this situation, as Stampfer himself saw it, Social Democrats have "no tendency to bloody adventure."[20]

The reluctance of the Social Democrats to oppose legally-constituted authority no matter how distasteful had not developed only with the von Papen regime's drastic action; it had been clearly evident at earlier times when violent resistance was not even a consideration. This reluctance to oppose constituted authority had characterized the relationship between the party and von Papen's predecessor Heinrich Brüning. Brüning's policies, particularly his economic programs, were austere, deflationary, authoritarian and burdensome for the working classes. Nonetheless, the Social Democratic Party refused to oppose Brüning, a decision which cost them the loyalty and fervor of many working people. To many of the workers concerned mainly with economic issues, the differences between Brüning and von Papen were insignificant. Therefore, they responded with indifference to Braun's appeals for support against the anti-democratic forces of von Papen. They were unwilling to support the party in its political struggles when the party had not supported them in their economic struggle. The fact that the Social Democrats had already forfeited much popular support was one of the reasons for Albert Grzesinski's conclusion that July 1932 was probably too late for resistance.

In spite of the loss of support of a considerable number of workers, many contemporaries and later critics believed that, if Braun and Severing had wanted to resist forcefully, they had the capacity to do it. Younger and vigorous socialist leaders such as Kurt Schumacher and Willy Brandt advocated a fighting policy.[21] Koppel Pinson, a prominent emigré historian, who was both an on the spot and retrospective observer, saw a basis for meaningful action.[22] These observers pointed to the effective Prussian police, the *Reichsbanner* (socialist para-military organization), the labor unions and youth organizations as sources of fighting strength. They also believed that Braun and Severing would have received help from other German states and municipalities.

Braun and Severing denied the claims that effective armed

resistance was possible. Severing advanced a six-point argument to support his position.[23] He claimed that National Socialist sympathy of a minority within police ranks made reliance on their unified support impossible. Furthermore, had they been unified, Severing believed they would have been no match for the Reichswehr. The *Reichsbanner* could not be counted upon to supplement police power because they had virtually no weapons. Six million unemployed negated the possibility of the repetition of a general strike similar to the one that had foiled the Kapp Putsch in 1920. The power of the working class was further weakened by the adherence of a significant number of workers to the program of the Communist Party. In the name of a future Communist Germany, they were willing to see the socialist government of Prussia and the entire Weimar Republic fall before the forces of right-wing nationalism. Severing then argued that if, in spite of these handicaps, the socialists had decided to resist actively, they would have alienated the other pro-Weimar parties, namely the German Democratic and the Catholic Center Parties, because these groups were overwhelmingly committed to due process through the court system. Having cited these factors, Severing argued that the burden of resistance would have been costly and unsuccessful. His conclusion: "You have no right to be brave at the expense of your policemen."[24]

Braun agreed and argued that resistance would have had only symbolic significance which was not worth the sacrifice of life. He also questioned the objective of resistance. Would it be to overthrow the national government of President Hindenburg? How could that be considered a democratic act when the President was elected by over fifty per cent of the people?

On the surface, these arguments seem convincing, but did they mean that a democratic minority had no recourse against authoritarian or totalitarian actions when taken by a leader, even one who had majority support? Braun's comment raises the question of whether there was a popular base for republican government in Germany in 1932. Arnold Brecht, a major political thinker and active civil servant prior to World War I and continuing through the Weimar period, argued that by 1920 the Weimar Republic had lost its majority and never regained it.[25] If there was not a majority for democracy, then the Hitler state, when it emerged from the ruins of Weimar, was a truer expression of German political sentiment than any alternative might have been.

Whether or not there was a large popular base for republican government or whether armed resistance was either appropriate or viable for the republican elements in Germany, there was also the question of the effect of a major act of resistance, successful or unsuccessful, on the future of the German people and on world reaction to Germany. Braun concluded in retrospect that, at best, it would have been an unsuccessful civil war like that which took place in Austria in 1934 between right and left-wing forces.[26] The better prepared and armed right-wing elements won a bloody victory and a right-wing dictatorship emerged. However, perhaps even an unsuccessful act of resistance would have clearly demonstrated to Germans and non-Germans alike the character and courage of the pro-republican forces and would have formed the basis for later resistance and post-National Socialist era rebuilding. Whatever the possibilities might have been, the government of Braun and Severing rejected the pathway of resistance and instead turned to the courts to decide Prussia's lawsuit.

The case itself was tried in October 1932 before the German Constitutional Court at Leipzig. The collection of lawyers representing the parties involved contained many of the leading lights in German law. These lawyers realized that, in addition to the specific issues involved in these proceedings, the case was also about democracy, republicanism and the shape of Germany's political future. Carl Schmitt was the key lawyer for the von Papen national government, and Hermann Heller represented the Social Democratic Party, which had dominated the deposed Prussian state government. They manifested in their arguments, careers and beliefs many of the fundamental conflicts which had characterized and precipitated the fall of the Republic.[27]

Carl Schmitt was a prominent legal theorist and scholar by the time of the seizure of Prussia. He had progressively moved from writing intellectual history and political theory to producing political criticism and propaganda. In the late twenties, he had defended the notion of presidential dictatorship and, in theoretical terms, had shown clear evidence of preference for "totalitarian democracy." He was a devastating critic of pluralistic liberalism, parliamentarianism, and individualism. He began his political involvement as a Catholic political theorist but, by the late 1920s, he was drawn to the *Tatkreis*, a group of conservatives and right-wing radicals who shared hostility to parliamentary government. Schmitt had developed a friend-foe theory of politics in which opposition to the enemy formed the cement of political unity, and the willingness to kill the foe was the sign of a unified community. His goal was the creation of unity in a homogeneous community led by a strong and decisive leader unhindered by interest group, "debating society" legislators.

Schmitt's decision to defend the von Papen government was significant in itself. Schmitt essentially agreed with Braun that the von Papen government represented the destruction of the Republic. However, destruction was precisely what he wanted. Therefore, by serving the von Papen government, Schmitt was striking a blow against republicanism.

On the other side in this legal battle, Hermann Heller came closest to Schmitt in orientation and ability. Indeed, they were bitter rivals. Heller was a match for Schmitt in terms of the breadth of his learning and the range of his interests. However, they were worlds apart politically. Heller was a convinced socialist and republican.[28] He was aware of the dangers of Fascism and worked to warn the public of those dangers.[29] While critical of the lack of wide-ranging basic reform within the Republic, he defended it in the face of right-wing attacks. Heller was an active member of the Social Democratic Party and a supporter of Otto Braun and Carl Severing in Prussia.

The major arguments in this case were a combination of interpretations of the law and of the actual historical situation. Schmitt argued that law and order had broken down in Prussia and that the state could no longer maintain its obligation to keep the peace. Therefore, intervention by the President was both mandated by the Constitution and required by what he described as chaos on the streets of Prussian cities particularly Berlin. He then accused the Braun government of violating the constitutional provision subordinating state policy to national policy. He argued that the Prussian government was undermining national policy because the government of von Papen was sympathetic to the patriotic forces such as the Stahlhelm and the National Socialist movement and hostile to the Communists. He claimed that Braun's government was hostile to nationalist movements and sympathetic to the Communists. Furthermore, he argued for the greatest possible latitude in the exercise of presidential power during this time of crisis and pointed to the extensive use of this kind of power by President Ebert in 1919, 1920 and particularly in 1923.

Hermann Heller argued in rebuttal. He challenged Schmitt's description of the actual situation in Berlin. He acknowledged the difficulties of coping with the transport workers' strike and the aggression of both Communists and National Socialists. However, he claimed that the Prussian police were controlling the situation and that national intervention was not necessary. He defended the hard line that the Prussian government was taking towards the extreme nationalist movements arguing that they were pledged to destroy the Republic. He challenged the idea that the Braun government had been in any way sympathetic to the Communists and described continual conflicts between them and the Prussian police. Finally he argued that the von Papen government was exceeding constitutional prerogatives in their use of presidential emergency powers.

In many ways, the case is more significant as an ideological debate than for its practical effects. By the time the decision was rendered, Adolf Hitler was Chancellor of Germany and Hermann Göring was Minister–President of Prussia. However, this process which signalled the death of the bulwark of the Weimar Republic provides an important record of the perspectives and events of the late Weimar period. Heller's description of the actual situation in Prussia was more accurate than that of Carl Schmitt. Yet, Schmitt's arguments about the use of presidential powers had a strong ring of truth about them. Socialists and moderates had realized that President Ebert was stretching emergency powers in questionable ways in the period from 1919 to 1923, but they admired and trusted Ebert and sympathized with his objectives. However, as they learned in 1932, the sacrifice of principle to expediency can have unexpected and undesired future consequences. With the dissolution of the Prussian state government, republicanism had been dealt a fateful blow and the Nazis were one step closer to power.

Notes

1 Dietrich Orlow, *Weimar Prussia 1918–1925: the Unlikely Rock of Democracy*, Pittsburgh, 1986, p. 50.

2 *Ibid.*, p. 52

3 *Ibid.*, p. 115.

4 Rudolf von Thadden, *Prussia: the History of a Lost State*, trans. Angi Rutter, Cambridgeshire, 1987, p. 68.

5 J. R. C. Wright, *Above Parties: the Political Attitudes of the German Protestant Church Leadership, 1918–1933*, London, 1974, p. 19.

6 Ernst Christian Helmreich, *The German Churches under Hitler: Background, Struggle and Epilogue*, Detroit, 1979, p. 77.

7 Wright, *Above Parties*, p. 53.

8 *Ibid.*, p. 54.

9 Daniel R. Borg, *The Old-Prussian Church and the Weimar Republic: a Study in Political Adjustment, 1917–1927*, Hanover, New Hampshire, 1984, p. 107.

10 Von Thadden, *Prussia*, p. 68.

11 Orlow, *Weimar Prussia*, p. 235.

12 Otto Braun, *Von Weimar Zu Hitler*, New York, Europa Verlag, p. 132.

13 *Ibid.*

14 Heinrich Brüning, *Memoiren 1918–1934*, Stuttgart, 1970.

15 Quoted in Hans Joachim Schoeps, *Preussen: Geschichte Eines Staates*, Berlin, 1966, p. 291.

16 Albert Grzesinski, *Memoirs*, original manuscript with handwritten corrections, Paris, January, 1933, Bundesarchiv, Koblenz, p. 3.

17 Koppel Pinson, *Modern Germany*, New York, 1954, pp. 470–5.

18 Friedrich Stampfer, "No Armed Resistance,"*Frankfurter General Anzeiger*, June 8, 1932, p. 2.

19 Carl Schorske, *German Social Democracy 1905–1917: the Development of the Great Schism*, Cambridge, Mass., 1955.

20 Stampfer, "No Armed Resistance," p. 3.

21 Lewis J. Edinger, *Kurt Schumacher: A Study in Personality and Political Behavior*, New York, 1965, p. 41; Willy Brandt, *In Exile: Essays, Reflections and Letters 1933–1947*, Philadelphia, 1971, p. 100.

22 Koppel Pinson, *Modern Germany*, New York, 1954, p. 470.

23 Karl Severing, *Mein Lebensweg*, Cologne, 1950, Vol. II, p. 579.

24 *Ibid.*, p. 182.

25 Arnold Brecht, *The Political Education of Arnold Brecht: an Autobiography, 1884–1970*, Princeton, New Jersey, 1970, p. 184.

26 Braun, *Von Weimar*, p. 410.

27 J. W. Dietz (ed.), *Preussen Contra Reich von dem Staatsgerichtshof*, Berlin, 1933, transcript with page numbers illegible.

28 Hermann Heller, *Sozialismus und Nation*, Berlin, 1925.

29 Hermann Heller, *Europa und der Faschismus*, Berlin, 1931.

5

Bavaria: reluctant republicans

Bavaria was among the last states to join the newly formed German Empire in 1871. The kingdom had a long and glorious history and was reluctant to surrender to the domination of Prussia, to the Prussian Chancellor Bismarck and to its Protestant Hohenzollern monarch. Bavaria's Catholic Wittelsbach kings could trace their lineage back to the ninth century and looked at the Prussian royal family, who first began their rise to power in the seventeenth century, as upstarts. Reluctantly bowing to the realities of modern power state politics, the Bavarians joined the new German nation in 1871. They did, however, fight to retain their royal family, their army and as much of their spirit of autonomy as they could. The Bavarian view of the world, conditioned by its history, would affect the evolution of the state during the Weimar years as well.

Bavaria was the second largest state in the Republic. While Germany as a whole was about 62 per cent Protestant and approximately 32 per cent Catholic, the situation in Bavaria was almost reversed. It was 69 per cent Catholic and 28 per cent Protestant. Bavaria's Catholicism and the conservatism of its Catholics were keys to the character of the state during the Weimar years. The BVP (the Bavarian People's Party) was the state Catholic party, and it dominated Bavarian politics. In the initial phase of the Republic, it was affiliated with the Catholic Center Party (*Zentrum*), but it often functioned independently. Later it considered itself to be a totally separate party. What made the BVP so unique during the period from 1919–33 was its frequent opposition to the

Republic combined with its resistance to Nazism.

Weimar Bavaria encompassed eight million people and was one of the most rural of the German states. At the end of the Weimar period 31.5 per cent of its population, as compared with 21 per cent of the entire German population, was engaged in agricultural pursuits. Bavaria was less highly industrialized than the rest of Germany, and many of its industrial and craft workers worked in small and medium-sized businesses.[1] The building trades and consumer goods industries were the key industrial segments of Bavarian economic life. Many craft workers operated home style workshops common in earlier periods. Many of these workers and their families lived in poverty. While there were major industrial corporations such as BMW automobile works in Munich and MAN machine works in Augsburg and Nuremberg, small scale production characterized Bavarian industrial activity. Industries, such as textiles, clothing, food production and toys, depended upon a large number of trained crafts people with a high percentage of female workers. Bavaria had few large cities. Only four cities had over 100,000 people. Munich with its population of 735,000 was by far the largest city, followed by Nuremberg with 410,000, Augsburg with 177,000, and Würzburg with 101,000.

In spite of its conservative rural character, in the period of near chaos at the end of 1918, Bavaria seemed to be in the forefront of a leftist revolutionary wave. In the winter of 1918–19, Bavaria was ruled by a small group of radical independent leftists headed by Kurt Eisner. Eisner and his company of poets and playwrights were idealists who hoped to create a socialist state quickly. They had stepped in to fill the vacuum created by the rapid departure of King Ludwig III and his ministers during the chaos. In their enthusiasm, they had misjudged their level of popular support and lacked any practical political skills to implement their vision.

Eisner had been born in 1867 to a middle-class Jewish family. He attended a Gymnasium in Berlin and studied *Germanistik* (German studies) and philosophy at the university level. In many ways, his background was similar to that of Karl Marx, but his own view of the world was more closely influenced by Kant and romantic idealism. Eisner was a much gentler and less confrontative figure than Marx, but he had served nine months' imprisonment in 1897 on the charge of lese-majesté for an article critical of

Kaiser Wilhelm II. In his invitation to Gustav Landauer to come to Munich to participate in the 1918 revolution, Eisner talked of his need for help in "changing the souls of men."[2] At a major celebration in November at which Eisner spoke, his speech followed the playing of Beethoven's *Leonore Overture*. Eisner declared, "Life itself should be a work of art, and the state itself the greatest work of art."[3] In contrast to the working-class socialists, he was more a utopian intellectual than a practical politician.

Eisner was also a democrat. When he put his popularity to a test by holding elections, he suffered a serious loss. In contrast to a revolutionary like Lenin who would not accept the unfavorable results of an election, Eisner accepted his defeat. Whereas Lenin argued that he and his Bolsheviks would have to rule by force until the people could be educated to recognize the truth of his policies, Eisner was unwilling to depend on force. He was prepared to yield his power to the winners of the election, the Majority Social Democrats. As Eisner prepared to step down, he was assassinated by a disgruntled young aristocrat, Count Arco-Valley, who blamed him and the socialists for Germany's defeat in the war. Following Eisner's death in February 1919, the more radical of his followers moved to suspend the results of the election and turn Bavaria into a *Räterrepublik*, a state ruled by councils of workers and intellectuals. However, the radicals offended the conservative Catholic Bavarians by calling for an end to monogamous marriage and, in the words of Erich Mühsam, pharmacist apprentice turned writer and cabaret performer, for "a republic based on councils combined with a sexual revolution."[4]

Johannes Hoffmann and the Majority Social Democrats, who had actually won the election, tried to rule. Their effort was first verbally challenged and then forcibly thwarted by the radical leftist forces. The Hoffmann cabinet fled from Munich in April, and Eisner's followers declared Bavaria a Soviet Republic. This brief radicalization of the state was brought to a bloody end in May by the army and units of the *Freikorps* who dislodged the radical leaders by storming Munich and summarily executing many. This "white terror" may have cost as many as 1100 lives. The confrontation was one-sided. The "Soviet" forces were led by Ernst Toller, a playwright with no previous military command experience. The army and *Freikorps* forces were experienced fighting units. Beppo Römer's *Bund Oberland Freikorps* had recently returned from fighting against Polish forces in Silesia.[5] The leftists were defeated and order was restored. The Hoffmann cabinet returned briefly in May, but new elections brought a sharp shift to the right.

Beginning in May 1919, Bavaria was ruled by conservatives. It became the spawning ground for the most extreme rightist groups in Germany including Adolf Hitler's Nazi Party. The existence of strong rightist sentiments in Weimar Bavaria was demonstrated as early as 1919 when Count Arco-Valley received over 15,000 congratulatory telegrams upon his arrival in prison to serve a sentence for his assassination of Kurt Eisner.

After the radical left was crushed in 1919, three strong interrelated passions asserted themselves to dominate Bavarian politics. One of these was a strong feeling of Bavarian autonomy and a resistance to the power of the central government. A second was anti-Prussian sentiment which had deep roots in Bavarian history but had intensified at the end of World War I and in the immediate post-war period. The third was rabid anti-Marxism, based on strong economic and religious convictions. When fed by real left-wing uprisings, this sentiment rose to panic proportions. It encouraged the acceptance of unsubstantiated and often wildly exaggerated conspiracy theories. Bavarians, always desirous of maintaining what they considered their distinctive Bavarian national character, also came to believe that they would need to be crusaders protecting Germany from her internal enemies. For a period of time particularly concentrated around 1923, some Prussian conservatives, frustrated by Social Democratic dominance of their own state, surprisingly came to share that assessment and to look to Bavaria as the bulwark of conservatism.

The period of Eisner's rule and the declaration of a Soviet state in Bavaria contributed to the already strong anti-Semitic sentiment. Although Jews were a small part of the Bavarian population and had little economic influence, they did play a highly publicized role in the revolutionary period. According to the *Encyclopedia Judaica*, "In Bavaria Jews played an even more significant role [than in Prussia]: the head of the revolutionary government was a Jew, Kurt Eisner, and the majority of the Soviet-type government set up after Eisner's murder consisted of Jewish intellectuals (Eugen Leviné, Gustav Landauer, Ernst Toller, etc.)."[6]

In his comprehensive satirical novel *Erfolg* (Success), the popular Weimar author, Lion Feuchtwanger, described Bavaria in the early twenties, noting the extreme concentration of attention and hostility directed towards the Jews. Feuchtwanger's Hitler-like character Rupert Kutzner declares, "The international ring of Jewish financiers was trying to destroy the German people as a tubercular bacillus tries to destroy a healthy lung. Everything would be all right again and in its proper place once the parasites were eliminated."[7] Hatred of the Jews was a motivating factor among the violent young man who emerged from the army and *Freikorps* groups to form the secret murder societies called the Feme. Feuchtwanger accurately describes the level of their thinking and their violence and brutality in a parody of their songs:

By night I lie with my dear in bed,
By day I strike the Hebrews dead,
And so I grow lusty and well fed,
My colors are black and white and red,
[Nationalist Colors of the flag of the monarchy][8]

Feuchtwanger was one of the sensitive observers who recognized the high level of irritation, frustration and anger in Germany in the twenties. He knew that these feelings led to short tempers, rudeness and a proclivity towards violence. He concluded that Bavarians manifested this behavior pattern most clearly. In a parody of scientific research, he reported: "The Board of Studies of an American Institute for Applied Psychology took statistics from people chosen as far as possible from the same classes of society, and found that in every thousand, four in China were discourteous, eighty-eight in Scandinavia, 124 in England, 204 in America, 412 in Germany, and 632 in Bavaria."[9]

While instability and crisis plagued all of Germany between 1920 and 1923, the Bavarian state government was hostile to and unco-operative with the national government. Numerous radical right-wing *völkisch* movements developed and agitated to win converts among Bavarian voters who tended to support one of three blocs of parties: the Socialist and Communist left; the Catholic BVP; and a group of bourgeois and special interest parties, chief among them the *Bauernbund* (BBB) or Peasants' League. Bavaria proved to be a fertile spawning ground in the early 1920s for the *völkisch* movement.

The term *völkisch* was first applied to a movement in the early nineteenth century which witnessed the development of German nationalism and the struggle against France. The term signified a bonding of all people who spoke German and were committed to German culture regardless of the area of Germany or, for that matter, Europe they inhabited. This movement was cultural, historical, linguistically-based and designed to rally German national feeling. Beginning with a strong anti-French bias, it became anti-Jewish and in general xenophobic. By the later nineteenth century, it had become dominated by racial biological theory and anti-modernist sentiment.

The extreme crisis of November 1923, which saw inflation reach catastrophic proportions and left-wing rebellion in the states of Saxony and Thuringia, also witnessed the attempt by Hitler, General Ludendorff and the National Socialists to take over the government of Bavaria in what came to be called the Munich Beer Hall Putsch. Their intention was then to march on Berlin in imitation of the March on Rome through which Mussolini and his Fascists seized power in Italy. Political meetings in the major cities in Germany took place in large beer halls which could hold several thousand people. Each political group usually had one or two beer halls in which they met. The Munich Beer Hall Putsch of November 9, 1923 began in the Bürgerbräu, the frequent meeting place of the Nazis.

On that evening, Hitler and a group of his followers attempted to convince the Bavarian state strongman, Gustav von Kahr, to join their conspiracy. Von Kahr had been appointed Special State Commissioner by Bavarian Prime Minister Dr Eugen von Knilling who was worried that unrest evident in Saxony and Thuringia would spread to Bavaria. Von Kahr had himself been Bavarian Prime Minister after the leftist forces were crushed in 1919 and was a more extreme opponent of the Weimar government than was von Knilling. He was also a much stronger personality and dominated the state. As an enemy of the Republic, he first considered co-operating with Hitler's plan. However, General von Seeckt, as overall military chief, made it clear that he would not tolerate the insurrection which had been rumored for some time. Von Kahr was convinced that Hitler's plan could not succeed and the next day decided to resist .

Von Kahr also had a different vision for the future of Germany than did Hitler. While they shared a common hostility to democracy, their goals were quite different. Hitler envisaged a *völkisch* dictatorship while von Kahr wanted a return to monarchy. Hitler and his forces also had a national outlook while von Kahr was first and foremost a Bavarian patriot. The situation was described in a report that Hellmut von Gerlach, a democrat and a pacifist sent to the Carnegie Institute for International Peace in New York: "On the next day von Kahr and his friends reversed themselves in spite of their promises of the previous night. They acted under the influence of ex-Crown Prince Ruprecht of Wittelsbach. This reversal was based on a deep antipathy between the Bavarian legitimists and the pan-German fascists, ..."[10]

The German army also vacillated between support for Hitler's aims and defense of the legitimate government. While von Seeckt's central army command had issued orders to the Bavarian forces to stop any uprising, they were reluctant to intervene themselves in Bavaria. This reluctance contrasted with their enthusiastic intervention in Saxony and Thuringia where the revolutionary forces came from the left. In an effort to deal with the threats to the government from the left and the right, President Ebert with the support of the Reichstag had granted temporary but extensive dictatorial powers to General von Seeckt. Von Seeckt oversaw military intervention in Saxony and Thuringia and the removal of their left-wing state governments. While he was firm with the Bavarian military, he was much more restrained in his actions towards the right-wing Bavarian government. This policy decision was clearly more reflective of ideological considerations than of an accurate assessment of the relative dangers of each of these insurrections. The well-informed democrat General Schoenaisch estimated the arms situation and concluded that the weapons in the hands of the Bavarian rightists compared to those in the hands of Saxon leftists were in the ratio of 20 to 1.[11] The problems with Saxony had also just developed while Bavaria had consistently taken a posture of resistance to national policies. As Gerlach reported in July 1922, "the Law for the protection of the Republic had not been recognized in Bavaria. Bavaria is the most reactionary and therefore the most monarchist part of Germany."[12]

While von Kahr did resign after the failure of the Beer Hall Putsch of 1923, Bavaria's government remained in the hands of extreme conservatives for the remainder of the life of the Republic. In fact, as Orlow points out, Bavaria had served as a beacon for conservative forces as early as 1920:

> Indeed, after the Kapp Putsch, the radicals looked with considerable interest to developments in Bavaria to further their Prussian and national aims. The Escherich Organization (Organisation Escherich, or Orgesch), a brainchild of the Bavarian forestry official Escherich, posed as a strictly civilian instrument of law and order, but it was in reality a successor organization to the Erhardt Brigade which had been the primary military unit involved in the putsch.[13]

This organization, like Consul which also contained many former members of the Erhardt Brigade, would also play a role in the Feme violence. In contrast to the Prussian police, the unreformed Bavarian police served as a right-wing bastion as well.

Bavarians watched with interest the separatist movements which developed during the early crisis period, perceiving them as potential destabilizing forces. With French encouragement and support, separatist movements arose in parts of the Rhineland. None of these movements showed real signs of substantial indigenous support, but they did present an additional challenge to the new government. Bavarian opponents of the Republic offered encouragement to the separatists and used their threat to extract more autonomy from the Weimar government than the constitution writers had envisioned.

After the resignation of Gustav von Kahr, Dr Heinrich Held emerged as the leading political figure in Bavaria. He had headed the Bavarian People's Party legislative delegation in the Bavarian Landtag.[14] He was a conservative Catholic and participated in the negotiations which led to the signing of the Concordat between the government of Bavaria and the Vatican. Held was a friend and confidant of Cardinal Pacelli, the papal nuncio who became Pope Pius XII. During the years from 1924 to 1933 when he was Bavarian Prime Minister, the influence of the Catholic Church was strong. This alignment made the state resistant to educational reform and to changes in the abortion and homosexuality laws and conservative on women's issues. Held considered all forms of socialism to be "godless" and made little distinction between Communists and Social Democrats. While he was a constitutionalist, he always interpreted the Constitution to favor the states at the expense of the central government.

Yet Held's Catholic conservatism did not appeal to all Bavarians on the political right. Support for the National Socialist Party grew in influence particularly among young Protestant men. Bavarian Protestants resented the influence of the Catholic Church in the state and the predominance of the Catholic Bavarian People's Party. Protestant regions of northern Bavaria, which had split their vote in the early 1920s between liberal and various *völkisch* parties, became strong bases of support for the Nazis.[15] In the rural Protestant districts, support from Protestant pastors also aided the Nazis. These pastors often presented Nazism as a crusading force against the growing decadence of the Republic.

The Bavarian People's Party remained dominant in Bavaria, in spite of the Nazi gains in Protestant areas, because of the huge preponderance of Catholic voters. It had been associated with the national Catholic Center Party but had constituted itself as a separate entity when the national party had supported a Prussian state proposal to dissolve all states in favor of a centralized government. As the largest section of the national Catholic Center Party once the Bavarians had withdrawn, the Prussian Center Party moved towards a deep commitment to pro-Republican coalitions while the Bavarian People's Party moved in the opposite direction. It became increasingly right-wing, and allied itself with other anti-republican forces.

However, the anti-Catholicism of General Ludendorff and the overwhelming Protestant anti-Catholic protest vote which the Nazis received limited the possibility of close co-operation between the Bavarian People's Party and the Nazis during the early 1920s. Heinrich Held's constitutionalism, his Catholicism and his conservative distrust of the mass politics of the Nazis made the Bavarian government even less sympathetic to the National Socialist movement in the last years of the Republic than it had been earlier. Held did not see Hitler, as had earlier Bavarian leaders, as a tool who could be used to fight the Republic and advance Bavarian state aims.

Held and many other Catholics were most fierce in their antipathy towards Communists and Social Democrats whose important differences they often did not recognize. They were strongly influenced by Cardinal Faulhaber of Munich who Pope Pius XI praised as one of the leading figures in the Church's battle against Bolshevism.[16] At the same time, Held also took seriously the warnings of one of the best known Catholic publicists of the Weimar period, Friedrich Muckermann, who declared that the Nazis were a form of "brown Bolshevism", and were a threat to the Catholic church.[17] The message of Muckermann and Held had an effect on Catholic Bavarian voters right up to 1932. In the Reichstag election of July 1932, seventeen Bavarian rural districts with overwhelmingly Catholic populations gave the Nazis fewer than 15 per cent of the vote. All Catholic constituencies fell well below the Reich average Nazi vote of 37 per cent.[18]

In spite of their resistance to National Socialism, the lack of co-operation between BVP leaders and the Weimar coalition served to weaken the Republic. Their support for Hindenburg and their general militarism, their resistance to social reform and their anti-Semitism certainly undermined republican principles and programs and thus aided the Nazis in their quest for power. The positions taken by many among the more conservative Catholic clergy also served to promote hostility to republicanism, and contributed to anti-Semitism.

Bavaria consistently asserted its claim to as much authority as it could get away with. Its leaders were hostile to republicanism and consistently made life difficult for the central government. They were initially more sympathetic to Chancellor von Papen than they had been to other Weimar Chancellors since he had belonged to the most conservative wing of the Catholic Center Party for much of his political life. However, the seizure of Prussia in July 1932 alarmed Held and other Bavarian leaders and lost von Papen their support. Although these leaders had been hostile to Otto Braun and the Prussian Social Democrats, they were frightened by the specter of the assault that von Papen had carried out against a state government. The Bavarians judged that the Prussians were, in part, paying for their failure to assert state autonomy fully against the claims of the central government. Yet they still supported the claims of the deposed Prussian leaders. Bavaria joined in the legal suit concerning the seizure of Prussia in support of Otto Braun and his cabinet. What position would the Bavarians have taken had Prussia decided to resist the takeover by force?

Notes

1 Ian Kershaw, *Popular Opinion*, Oxford, 1983, pp. 13–16.

2 Stephen Lamb, "Intellectuals and the challenge of power: the case of the Munich 'Räterrepublik,' " in Phelan (ed.), *Some Weimar theories* ..., p. 145.

3 *Ibid.*

4 *Ibid.*, p. 149.

5 George Mosse, *The Crisis of the German Ideology*, Madison, Wisconsin, 1954, p. 45, p. 229.

6 "Germany," *Encyclopedia Judaica S.V.*, Jerusalem, 1971, p. 483.

7 Lion Feuchtwanger, *Success*, trans. Willa and Edwin Muir, New York, 1984 (1930), p. 196.

8 *Ibid.*, p. 598.

9 *Ibid.*, p. 208.

10 Karl Holl and Adolf Wild (eds), *Ein Demokrat kommentiert an Weimar: die Berichte Hellmut von Gerlachs an die Canegie Friedenstiftung in New York 1922–1930*, Bremen, 1973, p. 99.

11 *Ibid.*, p. 97.

12 *Ibid.*, p. 56.

13 Dietrich Orlow, *Weimar Prussia 1918–1925: the Unlikely Rock of Democracy*, Pittsburgh, 1986, p. 21.

14 Geoffrey Pridham, *The Nazi Movement in Bavaria*, New York, 1973, p. 21.

15 Kershaw, *Public Opinion*, pp. 25–6.

16 Horst W. Heitzer, "Deutscher Katholizmus und Bolshevismus gefahr bis 1933" *Historische Jahrbuch*, Jahrgang 1993, p. 356.

17 *Ibid.*

18 Kershaw, *Popular Opinion* ..., p. 25.

6

The Prussian police experiment

The birth of the Republic created an atmosphere of crisis and exhilaration in which perceptions of the present and expectations for the future varied radically across the gamut of political opinion. For the conservatives who had been content with the old regime, the events of 1919 and 1920 were an unmitigated disaster. However, the republican and radical leftists found elements of hope and cause for optimism in the midst of the tragedy of the war. Yet, even the optimists had widely differing views of the future. Expectations of what would arise out of defeat varied from Kurt Eisner's socialist utopia to Otto Braun's less grandiose concept of a representative constitutional government which would protect the rights of its citizens and offer them opportunities for successful employment, thereby decreasing the glaring inequalities in wealth and improving the quality of life for the broad masses.

Because neither Eisner's vision nor Braun's program was finally realized, the Weimar Republic is too frequently studied as a failure and a transitional phase between the Second and Third Reich. Institutional failures certainly played a major role in the Republic's history. The judiciary, the army, the churches and the universities all contributed to the perception that the Republic failed to create a viable society. Yet the failure of the Republic did not necessarily signify the failure of all its institutions. While much can be learned from the failures of Weimar, its hidden success stories reveal the possibilities the new state presented.

The police, for example, played a significant role in the drive to create a stable society which would permit Weimar institutions to function effectively. The Social Democratic leadership made a substantial effort to create a different type of police force consistent with the needs of a democratic state. The question that confronted them was whether the police force they created could effectively support the principles of the Republic.

Efforts to reform the police encountered obstacles from the start even within the parties of reform. At the end of World War I, while the Social Democrats emerged as the strongest political force within Germany, major disagreements in orientation within their ranks were destined to result in debilitating conflict. The Majority Socialists, the largest and most moderate section of the pre-war Social Democratic Party, were steeped in the revisionism of Eduard Bernstein and closely connected to the trade union movement. Their leadership, mainly composed of men who had risen through the trade unions and the party bureaucracy, had become successful in their own terms and had developed a stake in the status quo. These men were not very receptive to the sweeping ideas for major social and economic reform that their more radical colleagues, the Independent Socialists (USPD) and the Spartacists advocated. They argued that an attempt to enact radical reform measures too quickly would undermine the opportunity to work with moderate bourgeois political parties such as the Democratic Party and the Catholic Center. They were criticized by the radical left-wing lawyer Alfred Apfel among others who attacked the Social Democratic leaders for their failure to change or dismantle many of the society's institutions: "They all seemed to have forgotten everything that Karl Marx in theory and Lenin and Trotsky in practice had taught them. They had not the courage to assume the responsibility of turning what they had been preaching for many years into practice at last."[1]

By contrast to the resistance to political and economic change characteristic of the national government, the institution of the police stands out as an area of substantial reorientation which offered encouragement to the reformers. The changes were made at the state level, particularly in Prussia, where the political responsibilities of the police underwent significant transformation. Prussia, along with the first Weimar government, was led by Majority Socialists. However, the Prussian socialists were the most vigorous of all the reformers. Otto Braun and Carl Severing, the leading political figures in Weimar Prussia, and their police officials made a substantial effort to create a radically different type of police force: a force committed to republican principles and the protection of civil liberties. This police force was expected to battle against both left and right extremism, to protect public figures, to deal with street demonstrations, and to foil any attempt to overthrow constituted authority. The years during which this Prussian police force functioned were times of frequent political instability thus providing a definitive test for a police force. Much of the assessment of police performance is implicit in the perceptions and responses of extremist forces on both sides of the political spectrum who continually confronted authority and in the publications of individuals and groups within the ranks of the police themselves.

The Weimar political leadership was divided in 1919 over the question of whether to create a unified national as opposed to a federated police structure. Those arguing for a unified structure touted its efficiency as an organizational pattern; the one most likely to avoid duplication and overlap. Most of the Social Democratic leadership believed that a national organization would be committed to republican principles undeterred by particularist interests and anti-republican sentiment such as existed in Bavaria. They were also wary of the stability of leadership in states like Bavaria where the extremism of the radical left at the end of the war had been followed by the extremism of the conservative right in dominating the political climate. In many ways, the Bavarian experience was similar to the situation in many American southern states following the defeat of the Confederacy when the radicalism of the carpet-baggers was replaced by the reactionary nature of the Ku Klux Klan. On the other hand, representatives from most of the states led by Baden and Bavaria raised the specter of governmental tyranny that might result from a national police force. They advocated state control as the best protection against violations of republican principles.

Yet special interests and motivations were not always clear-cut. For example, Otto Braun who became the dominant leader in Prussia during the Weimar years supported the idea of a national police force in spite of ostensible state interests. Modern police theory would tend to substantiate the claim of the Social Democrats that a centralized police force and democracy are compatible.

As George Berkley states, "Centralization ... is in many ways more consistent with democratization than in opposition to it. First, it permits and encourages such practices as standardization, advanced education, crime prevention, public relations, trade unionism, representatives, and perhaps most important of all, impartial treatment."[2] The initial debate was resolved by the Allies who had oversight power after Germany signed the Versailles Treaty. The French General Nollet, head of the Allied Control Commission, ruled that a national police force would be unacceptable to the commission because it could be used too easily as a smoke screen for developing military forces in violation of the Versailles Treaty.[3]

Once the question of the national versus federal nature of the police force was resolved in favor of a federal system, other factors awaited clarification, particularly the assignment of responsibility for the political police functions required by the national government. These functions included the protection of government officials, the combatting of terrorism, control of extremist groups and the prevention and control of crowd violence. Prussia, the site of the federal capital at Berlin and the largest of the federal states, was necessarily a focus for the issue of political police responsibility. The first Weimar cabinet decided that the Prussian police would provide protection for the national government in addition to performing their state functions. Therefore, the composition and development of the Prussian police force took on national significance in spite of the federal system.

The first attempt at Prussian police re-organization included a separate force, the *Sicherheitspolizei* (Security Police, Sipo or green police) to perform political functions. Many of the members of this force came from the *Freikorps*, the paramilitary organizations created to fight on the eastern front after the collapse of the regular army in the last days of the war. The military character of this force, its uniforms and organization alarmed the occupation authorities, particularly General Nollet, who worried that the new police might be used as a front for rearmament and recruitment of military forces in excess of the numbers allowed under the treaty.[4] The General and his fellow officers did not look into the philosophical program of the new unit or into the leaders who were organizing it but responded instead to appearances. In 1920, in response to Allied protests, Weimar officials constricted the

Sicherheitspolizei, diminished their military character, and changed their green uniforms to blue ones. However, these changes did not satisfy the objections of General Nollet and the Allies, and in 1921 the *Sicherheitspolizei* were disbanded.

The elements of the *Sicherheitspolizei* were incorporated into a new organization, the *Schutzpolizei* or *Schupo,* which combined criminal and political police work. The false start and the confusion created by the transformation contributed to an unsteady beginning for this republican police organization. Ironically, the difficult time that the civilian politicians had in creating an effective police force which could fulfill political functions contributed to President Ebert's reliance on the unreformed army and even on *Freikorps* units in the first hectic days of the new Republic. Eric Hobsbawm claims that the events of 1848 on the European continent reached revolutionary proportions because no civilian police force existed, thereby necessitating reliance on the army for crowd control.[5] This assessment raises speculation on how different events might have been in the period of transition from monarchy to republic if there had been effective civilian police power. Hobsbawm contrasted the lack of revolution in England which had civilian police, particularly in London, with the situation on the continent.

If we are to judge the Allies' concerns about German police fairly, we must consider that the ranks of the Prussian police were to reach nearly 60,000 by 1926 and that these forces were to have unusual armaments by American and English police standards such as hand grenades, machine guns and armored cars. Certainly there was a basic need to monitor these forces since Germany was mandated to have a regular army of only 100,000 men. However, if the Allies were interested in promoting republican ideals and institutions in Germany, it would have been worth their while to understand the nature of the new police, the Republic's need for them and the differences between these forces and the regular army.

The *Schutzpolizei,* born in international controversy, immediately encountered turmoil and significant political and economic discontent within their precincts. The new force had to deal with growing inflation, right-wing assassinations and left-wing revolution in addition to their normal police business. The major disorders of this period would have been a challenge to any police force, even one with a long period of development and established traditions. For a new force, these challenges verged on the overwhelming. After the relatively tranquil period of the mid-twenties, the police again faced major economic and political instability. The Weimar Prussian police program itself evidenced the ways in which the police coped with these problems, the measure of police commitment to republican values and their success in defending those values.

The underlying assumption that a radically different kind of police organization could be democratic in its orientation and committed to the defense of the Republic was highly original and open to attack. The discussion itself was extremely complex because there were many different definitions of the term "democratic" and many different ideas about the role of a political police force within any society. In the introduction to his history of the police, Paul Riege quotes the expression symbolic of the Restoration, the period following the defeat of Napoleon in 1815: "*Nach Gott kommt gleich die Poliziei*" (After God, come the police).[6] The political police were, according to Riege, as old as ancient Egypt. They were recreated in modern times as the "haute police" under Louis XIV.[7] Yet, their existence did not presuppose tyranny but could represent the legitimate need of a society for self-defense. The Weimar leaders, particularly police officials such as Bernhard Weiss, hoped to prove that a political police force could actually protect republican institutions from extremists and prevent an undemocratic minority from thwarting the will of the majority. Riege concluded that the Weimar police were a great success:

> The presentation of the history of the police in the Weimar Republic is incomplete if we do not consider the fact that this police force acquired a special significance for the state and the people which has seldom been the experience of such a force ... These Weimar *Schutzpolizei* were in fact the best that any state could ask for. The best sons of our people who had gone earlier as volunteers to the German army now entered the police profession. Young police officers, celebrated world-wide in the police academies, demonstrated both in their units and in individual service the highest achievement and the best deportment. With only minor exceptions they were not corrupted by political pressure or invective. They remained true and reliable at their difficult task.[8]

Riege's comments represent a needed antidote to the uncritically negative view of Weimar institutions which has characterized much of the scholarship dealing with the period.[9] Also among the few positive commentators, the American writer, George Berkley, praises the republican loyalty of the police but even he questions their effectiveness.[10]

The quality of police recruits, to which Riege alluded, was one of the first manifestations of the changes that the Prussian Social Democrats introduced and resulted from a new method of recruitment. During the monarchy, the overwhelming number of policemen came from rural peasant families which were likely to be conservative in their political orientation. Carl Severing, representing the Prussian Social Democratic leadership, wanted to change the orientation by recruiting as many young men as possible from blue collar, trade union, Social Democratic families. He contended that these families represented the most progressive and democratic stratum in the country.[11] Young men from these families had not traditionally chosen careers in the police. Under the monarchy, workers had looked upon the police as a reactionary force and more particularly as the enemy of the working class and the defender of propertied capitalists.

Severing's belief that trade union workers were the most progressive and democratic element in Germany holds up well under investigation. These workers were committed to representative institutions and individual freedoms and most resistant to the viruses of nationalism and anti-Semitism.[12] His concerns about the nature of the policemen themselves are echoed in contemporary American judgments on police orientation: "A democratic police force requires democratic policemen. Organizational structures and systems operations by themselves will not suffice."[13]

Severing confronted the dilemma of recruitment from the working class in the face of their traditional antipathy towards the police. The problem was a circular one: how could he change the image of the police until the type of recruit had changed? Yet how could he attract a new type of recruit until the nature of the police had changed? Severing had two hopes for dealing with this dilemma. First, public relations would stress that the new government represented all the people and the police would do so as well. Second, the economic difficulties following the end of the war would expand the pool of candidates who applied for police jobs to include members of the working class. The campaign was partially successful and, although even during the twenties most of the police still came from rural villages, more of a balance was created. The Prussian police under the Weimar Republic contained a larger percentage of policemen from urban working-class backgrounds than ever before.

Once the recruiting mechanisms were in place a steady influx of recruits developed who were young, between the ages of twenty and twenty-two, and in excellent physical condition. They were to serve twelve years of active police duty and then be transferred to other positions within the police or the civil service. In a study which compares Prussian and American police during the 1920s, James Richardson comments on the age and fitness of the Prussian police who were younger and in better physical condition than their American counterparts.[14] They were thus physically able to do battle and win control of the streets when and where that was necessary.

The background and preparation of police administrators was varied, but those chosen were clearly men of ability as exemplified by two of the leading administrators of the Berlin police force, Albert Grzesinski and Bernhard Weiss. Grzesinski was a metal worker for thirteen years before becoming a union secretary in Offenbach and Kassel.[15] He was a member of the Social Democratic Party and in 1919 an undersecretary in the War Ministry. During the unsettled period preceding the establishment of the Republic, he served on a workers' council in Kassel where he opposed the extreme leftist elements of the USPD and the Spartacists. In 1921 and 1922, he served as Commissioner for Special Employment in the National Labor Ministry. In 1922, he became a state police official which was his first involvement with the police. After two years, he became Chief of the Berlin police and, a year later, he was appointed Prussian Minister of the Interior, a position that he held until 1930 when he returned to the Berlin force where he remained until the government of Prussia was nationalized. He was also politically involved as a city commissioner of Kassel during the early 1920s and a member of the Prussian state legislature.

Bernhard Weiss came from a middle-class Jewish family and was a university-trained jurist. In the pre-war period, he was one of the very few Jews to become a judge. In spite of his position and his age – he was thirty-four when the war broke out – he volunteered for active service and received the Iron Cross (first class). When he returned from the war, he entered the Criminal Division of the police. After holding the position of Deputy Chief of the Criminal Division, he organized and led the political operations from 1920 to 1924. In 1924, he was transferred back to the Criminal Division as Director. In 1927, he became *Regierungsdirektor* and Deputy Police Commissioner, the position he held until July 20, 1932. His political sympathies were of a German-national variety, but he was a fierce defender of the Republic and the Social Democratic-dominated government of Prussia. In *Polizei und Politik* (*Police and Politics*) published in 1928, he defended the need for a political police in a democratic state.[16]

Although Grzesinski and Weiss came from radically different backgrounds and held different political views and party associations, they shared a passionate commitment to republican principles and to the creation of a police force that was compatible with a democratic society and a representative parliamentary government. They were determined enemies of the Communists and the National Socialists. In his memoirs, Grzesinski accused the Communists of subverting the Republic. Weiss was forced from his position as head of the political police in 1924 because of a raid he planned and carried out on the Soviet trade mission. Yet, both men frequently confronted the National Socialists in the streets and in the courts. They were dismissed when the government of Prussia was seized by the arch conservative Chancellor Franz von Papen in 1932, and were forced to flee from Germany to avoid arrest by the Nazis in 1933. They were frequent targets of the Nazis' leading propagandist Joseph Goebbels and both brought him into court on charges of libel. Although quite different, they represented a type of police official that was consistent with the view of the police projected by Otto Braun and Carl Severing.

Some critics of the Weimar police experiment argued that the quality and orientation of the administration and rank and file would not be the result of recruitment policy because function rather than origin was the decisive factor in determining police attitudes and actions. Leon Trotsky, the co-leader of the Bolshevik Revolution in Russia was the classic proponent of this thesis and argued that a policeman in a capitalist state was always conservative and authoritarian.[17] However, the Prussian police leaders believed that there were radically different styles of policing which were predominantly the result of the personality and training of the policemen rather than the economic organization of the society, an opinion shared by many modern students of police behavior.[18]

Putting their faith in the power of education, the Prussian Social Democrats designed a police training program which stressed even-handed justice and concern about preserving representative institutions and individual civil rights. Inculcating the idea of equal treatment for everyone was an uphill battle in a society where the general attitudes would have supported a police who based their tactics on the premise that, "What they deserve depends on what they are."[19] They presented the new orientation in lectures, discussions and readings drawn from the disciplines of history, sociology, and political and legal theory. They stressed liberal theory emphasizing writers like Immanuel Kant and John Stuart Mill and more contemporary thinkers like Max Weber, Friedrich Naumann, Eduard Bernstein, Harold Laski and G. D. H. Cole. The major leaders of the Social Democratic Party, including Otto Braun, Carl Severing, and Otto Wels, addressed the police recruits.

A public relations effort reinforced the educational program to acquaint the public with the new goals and methods of the police, particularly in the areas related to their political function. Public response to the performance of the police provides the parameters for the evaluation of these aspects of the police experiment. Although there is no uniform public, the reactions, charges and counter-charges of various interest groups representing different parts of the political spectrum taken together can present a balanced picture.

A successful merger of republican principles and political police exigencies centered on the issue of impartiality. The major test of the even-handedness of the police was their response to right-wing extremism. When evaluating police forces, the assumption is that their sympathies lie with the right. In the case of Weimar Germany, this bias would have been manifested in police partiality to the Nationalist and National Socialist forces. Few questions have been raised in retrospect about the willingness of the police to do battle with Communist extremists even though that issue was used as a justification for the seizure of Prussia in 1932. While bearing in mind the unequivocal treatment of leftists and taking into account the assumption that the police leaned to the right, the relationship between the police and the right becomes the litmus test of their commitment to republican values. The need to balance criticism and evaluation today echoes the need for even-handedness and balanced response which confronted the Prussian police from the time of their inception. Only through such an orientation, could they have hoped to reflect the values of the society they were pledged to defend.

The early years of the *Schutzpolizei* provided a complex setting where confrontations with left and right-wing radicals tested the republican orientation of the police. Communist and right-wing agitators flourished, and the level of violence was very high in a population where millions of men had lived under battle conditions. The major test of the police was their ability to deal effectively with all extremist violence. Left and right-wing opponents charged the police with discriminatory action and brutality. This criticism testifies to the political orientation of the police and their success in dealing with political radicalism.

In assessing criticism from the right, one of the most valuable and unique sources is the notebooks of Police-Major Eldor Borck who was a career officer in the Prussian police. Major Borck was a member of the German Nationalist Party and a representative in the Prussian Landtag (the state legislature). In his notebooks, he collected letters, essays, newspaper articles, and speeches that he had written. He also collected writings and cartoons produced by others dealing with police matters and with the proceedings of the Landtag. Borck's testimony is particularly useful in evaluating the assertion of many critics of the Weimar police that they were more than willing to harass and do battle with the Communists but did not react equally firmly to groups on the right.[20] Borck charged that the police were dominated by leftists and, in his most extreme utterances, declared that they were an auxiliary of the *Reichsbanner*, the Social Democratic paramilitary organization. In questions that he put to cabinet ministers before various Landtag sessions and in his own speeches and writings, he made his views abundantly clear. His writings and the writings of those with whom he sympathized convey a sense of the basis of right-wing discontent with the police. He criticized the police leadership at both administrative and political levels and political associations, particularly the *Verein der Polizeioffiziere Preussens* (Association of Prussian Police Officers) and the *Reichsbanner* (pro-Republic paramilitary organization) in their relation to the police.[21]

Major Borck's "enemies list" within the political and police hierarchy included Otto Braun, Carl Severing, Albert Grzesinski, Bernhard Weiss and Jenossse Zörgiebel. One of the thrusts of his criticism was that the leadership wanted to politicize the force by extending left-wing influence throughout its organization. He was hostile to all aspects of the three-part program of police reform instituted by the Social Democrats. He viewed the campaign to recruit among urban blue collar families as a deliberate effort to politicize and radicalize the force. In contrast, he argued that the rural peasantry, which had been the major source of police in the past, was the most wholesome and moral stratum of society, and he lamented the transfer of emphasis in recruiting policy. The education program which the leadership inaugurated and which was designed to promote republican ideals was an anathema to him. He argued that police training should be technical, perhaps moral but never political. Public relations, the third aspect of the police program, also came in for attack. He charged that the writings of Minister of Interior Severing and police Vice-President Weiss did not provide any service either to the police or the public but instead served only as a forum for the dissemination of the left-wing ideas of the leadership itself which were not shared by most of the rank and file. However, an analysis of the voting patterns of the Prussian police carried out by Joseph Goebbels in 1930 shows that Borck was clearly wrong about this issue. The largest number of police voted Social Democratic, and the overall orientation of the rank and file was clearly towards the moderate left.[22]

Borck's criticism testifies to his conclusion that a basically leftist leadership was attempting to corrupt and seduce an essentially nationalist police rank and file. He claimed that the leadership was overwhelmingly composed of Social Democrats who were determined to undermine the traditional basis of German society. He charged that they were opposed to nationalism and submissive to republican politicians and trade union leaders. In his most extreme criticism, he accused the new police leadership of attempting to make the force an auxiliary of leftist political parties.

Borck was especially critical of the *Schrader Verband*, the organization of lower police officials, and questioned among other things the effect of a police union on discipline. However, while this organization clearly worked to promote the interests of its police members, its commitment to the Republic and to discipline was quite clear. One of the most explosive issues that the organization discussed was how it should deal with captured right-wing terrorists who were likely to be treated far too leniently by the conservative and nationalist judiciary. There was some sentiment within the organization to suggest to members that, where the evidence was clear, these terrorists should receive summary justice, that is, they should be shot resisting arrest. However, the weight of opinion was clearly against this tactic. Those arguing against it stressed their commitment to discipline, due process and individual civil rights.

In spite of Borck's accusations of anti-rightist bias, some recent critics accuse the Social Democratic leadership of unwillingness to remove anti-republican elements from the higher levels of the Prussian police who seemed to have the same right-wing orientation as many in the judiciary.[23] The case of Colonel Heimannsberg has been used to prove this point but, in fact, testifies to the strength of republicanism in the police. Colonel Heimannsberg was, in many ways, a classic representative of the middle of the road policeman who was unswervingly loyal to the Republic but was disliked by extreme elements on the left and the right. Heimannsberg strongly believed in the Republic and the role the police ought to play in protecting it. However, he did not believe in union organization among the police or in the display of overt support for political parties. These attitudes were responsible for the conflict that developed between Heimannsberg and the *Schrader Verband* and were the basis for the call by some politicians for his dismissal. They have also been used to illustrate the unreformed nature of the police.

Nevertheless, there is strong evidence that Heimannsberg was worthy of his position. He always did his job effectively and never hesitated to lead his men against extremists. He was also very popular with his men. When crisis came in July 1932 and the Social Democratic state government of Prussia was about to be taken over by the right-wing nationalist central government, Colonel Heimannsberg considered leading armed resistance on behalf of the Prussian state, a point which speaks of his basic commitment to the Republic and his lack of sympathy for the political right. Heimannsberg's ideas and actions undermine the argument that he represented the inability of the political leadership of Prussia to remove anti-democratic elements from the police.

Critics also point to the case of Colonel Levitz who clearly exhibited right-wing sympathies. Levitz had strong support from Borck and nationalist organizations such as the *Stahlhelm*. The *Schrader Verband* argued for his dismissal on the grounds that his views were antagonistic to the development of republican values by the police. However, he did his job, and the civil libertarians among the republicans feared that to remove him would raise the specter of the total politicization of the police. Certainly this argument can be disputed, but it is a liberal not a reactionary argument.

The National Socialists had no doubts about the political stance of the Prussian police. Their feelings were clear from the S.A. man on the street, up through the leadership to Joseph Goebbels and Adolf Hitler. Their complaints and attacks focused on police response to street fighting particularly in Berlin and provide another test in the assessment of the impartiality of the Prussian force.

Based on police reports and newspaper accounts and pictures, the Prussian police actually spent far more time on the streets of Berlin battling Communists than National Socialists. However, this phenomenon was a result of the tactics of the radical groups themselves and their appraisal of their own strength rather than of the inclinations of the police.[24] The Communists had a clear-cut policy of baiting the police and starting street battles. They judged that their Berlin strength was very great, and this confidence encouraged their defiant and aggressive posture. The National Socialists, on the other hand, avoided direct street confrontations with the police. They always felt insecure about their relative strength in Berlin thus contributing to a more reserved policy on street fighting. "The Nazis, in contrast, were never preparing for open conflict with the armed police. Unlike the Communists, they lacked the massive support of a well-defined segment of the Berlin population and could not stage an uprising in one or more parts of the city."[25] Therefore, the apparent profusion of police actions against the Communists as compared to the fewer actions against National Socialists resulted from the greater provocation presented by those on the left.

Nevertheless, the frequent complaints in National Socialist newspapers such as *Der Angriff*, the challenging questions in the Prussian Landtag by National Socialist representatives and their Nationalist colleagues and even direct complaints from Adolf Hitler to President Hindenburg indicate that the Nazis felt persecuted by the police.[26] Leading Nazis like Joseph Goebbels kept up a constant attack on police officials such as Grzesinski, Weiss and Zörgiebel. In one of his polemics, Goebbels concluded that over sixty per cent of the police were outspokenly Marxist thus explaining their brutal treatment of the National Socialists.

Simultaneously, the Communists also attacked these police officials accusing them of being right-wing tools of the capitalists and, therefore, hostile to Communists. In left-wing pamphlets aimed at the police such as *Der rote Gummiknuppel: Zeitung für die Interessen der unteren Polizeibeamten* (*The Red Billy Club: Newspaper for Rank and File Policemen*), the Communists constantly complained about their treatment at the hands of the police. They accused many of the police leaders of being rightists, and, at the same, they agreed with the Nazis about the strong influence of the Social Democratic Party on the police. Since the Communists regarded the Social Democrats as their enemies and called them social fascists, they regarded Social Democratic influence as just as bad as conservative or Nazi influence. Both groups claimed that many police were secret members of the Social Democratic paramilitary organization, the *Reichsbanner*.[27] Yet the Communists frequently accused Police Commissioner Zörgiebel of attacks on members of the *Reichsbanner*. The fact that both the Nazis and the Communists felt hostile to the Prussian police is strong evidence of the moderate pro-republican orientation of most of Prussia's police and also of their effectiveness.

In the early 1930s, the Prussian police struggled with rapidly rising Nazi and Communist movements which carried out some of their political struggles on the streets. In 1932, Nazis and Communists combined on the streets of Berlin in support of a transit workers' strike in an attempt to topple the Prussian State Government headed by Otto Braun. Hard-pressed though they were, the Prussian police were still able to control the situation. However, the anti-republican Chancellor Franz von Papen claimed otherwise when he seized control of the Prussian state government on July 20, 1932. Many in the police leadership and among the rank and file believed that the seizure was the real death knell of republicanism in Germany and were willing to resist it by force. The highest leaders of the state government and the police decided against armed resistance. However, in the debates about the possibility of armed resistance, many police showed a fervor in their support for republican government that was not to be found among a significant number of those representing many other institutions such as the schools, universities, civil service, army and certainly the judiciary.

There is a serious question about whether those committed to republican government and humane democratic institutions and values can impose republicanism by force on a majority composed of the hostile and indifferent. The Prussian police did not desert the Weimar Republic. They fulfilled the greatest hopes of the leaders who created a democratic police force. Their history is indeed a Weimar success story which unfolded in intensely challenging episodes none greater than the Feme crimes which plagued Germany between 1919 and 1923.

Notes

1 Alfred Apfel, *Behind the Curtain of German Justice*, New York, 1935, p. 54.

2 George Berkley, *The Democratic Policeman*, Boston, 1969, p. 22.

3 "General Nollet to Reichskanzler Dr Wirth," Bundesarchiv, Koblenz, March 11, 1920, R 431/2691.

4 *Ibid.*

5 E. J. Hobsbawm, *The Age of Revolution 1789–1848*, Cleavland, 1962.

6 Paul Riege, *Kleine Polizei-Geschichte*, Institut Hiltrup, 1959, p. 27.

7 *Ibid.*, p. 29.

8 *Ibid.*, p. 39.

9 See, for example, the essays in Theodore Eschenberg (ed.), *The Paths to Dictatorship*, trans., John Conway, New York, 1967.

10 Berkley, *The Democratic Policeman*.

11 "Carl Severing-Report Der Minister des Innern," Berlin, Bundesarchiv, Reichskanzlei, April 17, 1920, R 431/2689.

12 *Ibid.*

13 Berkley, *The Democratic Policeman*, p. 23.

14 James F. Ricardson, "Berlin Police in the Weimar Republic: a Comparison with Police Forces in Cities of the United States," in George Mosse (ed.), *Police Forces in History*, London, 1975, p. 83.

15 Albert Grzesinski, *Memoirs*, original manuscript with handwritten corrections, Paris, January, 1933, Bundesarchiv, Koblenz, p. 3.

16 Bernhard Weiss, *Polizei und Politik*, Berlin, 1928.

17 Leon Trotsky, *Germany*, London, 1970.

18 William K. Muir Jr., *Police: Streetcorner Politicians*, Chicago, 1977.

19 James Q. Wilson, *Varieites of Police Behavior*, Cambridge, Mass., 1986, p. 36.

20 Eric D. Kohler, "The Crisis in the Prussian Schutzpolizei 1930–1932," in Mosse, *Police Forces in History*.

21 Some representative examples are Eldor Borck, "Reichsbanner, Jüstiz und Polizei," *Berliner Lokal-Anzeiger*, August 24, 1926; "Letter to Stahlhelm," December 10, 1928; "The Value of Armed Force – Speech before the Prussian Landtag," March 10, 1929, in the Eldor Borck Collection, Bundesarchiv, Koblenz.

22 Joseph Goebbels, "Schupwähler und NSDAP," *Der Angriff*, No. 17, 1929, unpaginated.

23 See for example Eric D. Kohler, "The Crisis in the Prussian Schutzpolizei, 1930–1932," in Mosse, *Police Forces in History*.

24 Hsi-Huey Laing, *The Berlin Police Force in the Weimar Republic*, Berkeley, California, 1970.

25 *Ibid.*, pp. 95–6.

26 "Telegram from Adolf Hitler," Bundesarchiv, Koblenz, R431/2693.

27 Jakob Toury, "Jewish Aspects as Contributing Factors to the Genesis of the Reichsbanner Schwarz-Rot-Gold," *Leo Baeck Institute Yearbook*, 1992, XXXVII, p. 237.

7

The Feme and the Weimar judiciary

The first crisis phase of the Republic between 1919 and 1923 was epitomized by the political violence called Feme. This development stood in stark contrast to the atmosphere before the war. Pre-war Germany gave few hints of the conflicts that were to characterize the Weimar Republic. Wilhelmine society was committed to law and order and the protection of property and persons as an absolute social and legal value. Thus political violence had been generally condemned, regardless of the victims. This protective umbrella included Jews and socialists in spite of their unpopularity among many segments of the population. The policy of the monarchy was reflected in decisions made by judges, who were among the staunchest defenders of these principles, and enforced by police who were equally committed to these precepts. Anti-socialist or anti-Semitic violence or, for that matter, inflammatory speech or writing was dealt with harshly by the police and the judiciary. While many were anti-socialist and anti-Semitic themselves, they did not countenance any behavior that might have led to an attack on life or property.

Certainly the unprecedented violence and the enormous number of casualties of the war transformed the psychological climate. It is possible that, as H. Stuart Hughes has argued, western attitudes towards human life itself were changed.[1] Sigmund Freud feared that hatred and violence generated by the war would take generations to subside.[2] For Germans, these effects were compounded by a defeat they did not expect and could not understand, by a peace treaty they regarded as grossly unfair, and by a chaotic economic and political situation which they compared with the relatively stable Bismarckian and Wilhelmine eras. Bitterness, insecurity and an adversarial view of the world engendered by war propaganda all contributed to the creation of an environment receptive to political violence that would have been unheard of in the pre-war period.

The perpetrators and justifiers were radically transformed people. Chancellor Joseph Wirth of the Catholic Center Party acknowledged this change in attitude when he wrote in a letter dated April 8, 1922: "The conceptual confusion is already so great that good, pious people coming from the best circles place little value on the lives of murder victims if they are Poles or traitors, that is traitors as defined by the Ludendorff people [Nazis and other radical right-wing groups]. This definition includes all members of the present government."[3] The prominent Weimar jurist Otto Kahn-Freund, comparing Germany and England, said that Weimar Germany was "a society in which the conflictual element was more palatable, more visible to the eye. I am also convinced that it was objectively stronger."[4] Kurt Tucholsky, a left-wing satirist, commented upon arriving in France in 1924 that he could be more relaxed in a place where, if you bumped into someone on public transit, they "didn't regard it as a stain on their honor that could only be settled by blood."[5]

Thus, the breakdown of human values and legal objectivity contributed to the eruption of political violence which became one of the hallmarks of Weimar Germany. It was a factor in the instability of the Republic and contributed to its failure and to the success of Adolf Hitler. A significant component of the political violence prevalent in Weimar Germany has been labelled "Feme" sometimes written "Fehme" of even "Vehme."

The modern "Feme" movement took its name from a secret fraternity founded during the Middle Ages by men who believed that their society was corrupt and unjust and that they alone represented the "true" society which existed only as an idea to be realized some time in the future. In the name of this future Utopia, the members of the Feme created their own law, held secret trials and rendered judgments which they then carried out. Although most of the verdicts were death sentences, occasionally a punishment of severe beating or torture was mandated. The Weimar groups who resurrected the name "Feme" also believed that they represented the "true" state. Each group had its own idea of the nature of that state, and the model varied from Wilhelmine Germany to the medieval Hohenstaufen Holy Roman Empire or even to a state unlike any that had ever existed. The thread common to all Feme groups was the conviction that their enemies were evil and illegitimate. The term "Feme" was also applied in the Republic to different types of violence. Emil Julius Gumbel, a mathematician and the major contemporary commentator on the Feme, documented almost four hundred murders and several thousand assaults which he labelled as Feme crimes.[6]

Essentially there were three phases to the political violence. First, murders and assaults were committed in the midst of the revolutionary actions of 1919 and reflected the right's reaction to left-wing uprisings. Second, attacks followed closely on the heels of the suppression of the revolutions and were again part of the spontaneous reaction of the right against those they regarded as members of the revolutionary left. This type of assault bubbled up during the early years of the Republic whenever left-wing activity intensified. Assaults planned in cold blood and carried out by members of murder clubs and other secret organizations constituted the third type of Feme violence. While these acts occurred largely in the period from 1920 to 1924, their effects reverberated throughout the fourteen-year history of the Weimar Republic and laid the foundation for the climate of violence which contributed to its collapse. The nature of the Feme crimes, the victims and the perpetrators reveal the attitudes and institutional problems which created a culture of political violence and thwarted the development of a stable democratic society during the Weimar years. The response of the largely unreformed judiciary who tried the Feme cases also contributed to the crisis confronting the Republic.

The first wave of violence came during the Spartacist Revolution in Berlin and the rule of the left-wing workers' councils in Bavaria. Troops sent into Berlin under a deal worked out by the Social Democrat, Gustav Noske, and General Groener, the representative of the army, were indiscriminate in their shooting of workers. They failed to distinguish the radical from the moderate and the armed from the unarmed. The most blatant example of such action was the killing of seven unarmed individuals who sought shelter in the offices of the Social Democratic newspaper

Vorwärts. Similar events took place when the army moved into Bavaria to topple the socialist republic which had been declared after the assassination of the idealist intellectual Kurt Eisner who briefly dominated the state's left-wing movement.

The suppression of armed resistance did not end the violence. Army troops and members of the semi-official *Freikorps* murdered the leaders of the uprisings. They hunted down the Spartacist leaders Karl Liebknecht, who was shot while still in custody, and Rosa Luxemburg who was beaten and murdered while being transported and whose mutilated body was found in a canal months later. Acts of retribution aimed at leftists were also carried out in Munich initiated by Eisner's murder. The right-wing aristocrat Count Arco-Valley had assassinated him when he was on his way to resign his position after his faction had lost a popular election to more moderate socialists. While these more spontaneous acts of violence were concentrated in the explosive period of 1919, they did not totally disappear after that. There were repeated manifestations of such violence during the Kapp Putsch in 1920, labor unrest in the Ruhr in 1921, and abortive left-wing uprisings in Hamburg, Saxony and Thuringia in 1923.

Even though Gumbel, the principle compiler of statistics on the Feme, included the spontaneous acts of counter-revolutionary violence among his statistics, the name Feme was more generally applied to cold-blooded, calculated acts of violence. The victims of such violence included among those killed, the major governmental figures Matthias Erzberger and Walther Rathenau, the Independent Socialist leader Hugo Haase and the Bavarian Deputy Karl Gareis. Philipp Scheidemann, the Social Democrat and the proclaimer of the Republic, and the left-wing publicist Maximilian Harden were among those assaulted. These acts were carried out by members of secret societies as part of a plan to purge Germany of its enemies.

In his book *Vier Jahre Politische Mord*, Gumbel identified fifty-nine secret societies. Some of them masqueraded as gymnastic groups, sporting clubs or associations of civil servants. Among the more publicized of these organizations were Consul, Orgesch, the Brandenburgischer Heimatbund, and a group called General Wrangel's Messmates. Their membership was composed of young men, most of whom were from aristocratic families, and the overwhelming number were junior officers during the last year of the war. Among those who commanded the most attention were Count Arco-Valley, Cadet Ernst von Salomon, Major Buchrucker and Lieutenants Gunther, Rossbach and Schultz. Count Arco-Valley's murder of Eisner provided an inspiration for many of the later crimes. Major Buchrucker was the head of the *Arbeitskommando* (official labor battalions), which had connections with Consul. Lieutenant Rossbach commanded a *Freikorps* group which provided members and was actively involved with many of the secret societies. Lieutenant Schultz was accused of being the leader of the Schwarze Reichswehr (Secret Army). Lieutenant Gunther and Cadet Ernst von Salomon were members of Consul and participated in the murder of Walther Rathenau. The Feme groups identified Prussia, the seat of the national government, as a hotbed of traitorous leftism and targeted it for many of their attacks although most of their home bases were in Bavaria.

Feme nationalists did not accept Germany's defeat in the first world war as a military phenomenon but saw it as the result of betrayal by enemies at home. The same traitors had accepted the Treaty of Versailles which Feme members regarded as a "Diktat" that no true German could accept or attempt to fulfill in any way. Ernst von Salomon articulated a typical Feme rallying call when he declared: "We must make an end to *Erfüllungspolitik*, to the policy of co-operating with the West"[7] There was a vague revolutionary content to the programs of these groups as well: "But we did from the very beginning desire basic change, a national revolution that would free us from the material and ideological supremacy of the West as the French Revolution had freed France from its monarchy."[8] No issues of social justice or distribution of wealth were contained in the objectives of the Feme groups. They mixed elements of *völkisch* ideology with their nationalism and concluded that the enlightenment and parliamentarianism were alien to the German folk soul. They compared the ideal of the communal *Gemeinschaft* of the German people to the materialistic and alienated *Gesellschaft* of foreign intruders and aimed to establish the former while destroying the latter.

Their program hinged on the elimination of their enemies, and its blatancy was epitomized in the slaying of Matthias Erzberger, the leader of the peace wing of the Catholic Center Party during World War I. He was the sponsor of the "Peace Without Annexations Resolution" which passed the Reichstag in 1917, and he articulated the legislators' commitment to negotiate a just peace which would protect Germany's vital interests but include no territorial gains. He had also agreed to participate in the armistice negotiations and believed that Germany had to try to meet the Versailles Treaty obligations while working to moderate the terms. For his pacifism and moderation, he was hated by the young men who peopled the Feme groups. On January 26, 1921, he was seriously wounded by the student and former junior officer, Ottwig von Hirschfeld. Erzberger slowly recovered from his wounds. Hirschfeld received an eighteen-month sentence for his crime but, after several weeks of treatment in a psychiatric hospital, was released. On August 26, 1921 at a vacation resort in Baden, Erzberger was attacked again, this time fatally. His two young assailants, Schultz and Tillessen, were members of Consul. They fled to Bavaria and then were able, with the help of Bavarian officials, to leave the country and find sanctuary in Hungary which refused to extradite them.[9]

The political assassination that produced the strongest reaction in Germany was the murder of the sitting cabinet minister Walther Rathenau. He was killed in his automobile while on his way from his home in Grünewald to his government office on July 21, 1922. His assassins fired automatic pistols and threw a hand grenade into his car. In a plenary session of the Reichstag, the Reichstag President (Speaker of the House), the Social Democrat Paul Loebe, declared that a right-wing murder organization had been responsible for the assassination and expressed his fear that the Republic was in trouble.[10] The German Chancellor, Joseph Wirth, of the Catholic Center Party, argued in an impassioned speech that the agitation by the right had created a murderous atmosphere in Germany. Ending his speech by pointing to the right section of the Reichstag, he proclaimed, "There sits the enemy, where Mephisto dribbles his poison into the wounds of the people, there is no doubt this enemy is sitting on the right."[11]

The assassinations of Matthias Erzberger and Walther Rathenau attracted international attention as did additional information about other potential targets of Feme violence. An article in *The New York Times* from July 1, 1922 discussed the Feme organization Consul, which it described as carrying on a campaign of terror in Hamburg and Berlin. It characterized the terrorist group as a "murder and bomb squad" led by Lieutenant Warnecke on instructions from the Munich organization. The article commented on potential victims: "Twelve leading politicians, editors and financiers of Jewish extraction were marked for assassination, among them Theodore Wolff, editor of the *Berliner Tageblatt* and Max Warburg, banker of this city."[12]

Following Wirth's speech and the growing attention focused on Feme violence by left-wing critics of the Republic and elements of the international press, the Reichstag began a process which led to the passage of the Law for the Protection of the Republic aimed at dealing more effectively with political assassins. This law set up special courts and mandated severe penalties to deal with attacks on state officials and other acts of insurrection. For a brief moment, a significant percentage of the citizenry of Weimar Germany and a majority of its leaders seemed determined to stop the terrorism. Harry Kessler, a contemporary commentator, saw the reaction to the Rathenau assassination as a cause for optimism about the future of the Republic: "The bitterness against Rathenau's assassins is profound and genuine. So is firm adherence to the Republic, a far more deeply rooted emotion than prewar monarchical 'patriotism' was."[13] On July 17, two of Rathenau's assassins were trapped in Saaleck Castle by the police, and, sensing that their situation was hopeless, they committed suicide.

Kurt Tucholsky was far less sanguine than Kessler about the deep-felt reaction to Rathenau's murder. In one of his many cynical writings, he has one of his characters, Herr Wendriner, a Jewish businessman, react to the ten-minute cessation of phone service which communication workers carried out as a small tribute to Rathenau. Initially, Herr Wendriner has positive things to say about Rathenau and deplores the assassination, but within a few minutes, he demands that phone service be restored so he can get back to work. "Operator! The longest ten minutes I ever saw. It they're on strike one minute more than ten, I've got a good mind to send in a complaint."[14] Tucholsky's Herr Wendriner essays have been called anti-Semitic, although Tucholsky was of Jewish origins himself. However, the intent of the essay was to suggest that the intensity of feeling for the Republic and its leaders was weak and superficial even among those people who should have been its strongest supporters.

Tucholsky, who was especially critical of Weimar judges, was constantly frustrated by what he believed was the lack of outraged reactions on the part of the republic's supporters against the politicized justice of the Weimar period. Certainly the regular courts were not harsh in dealing with Feme assailants. Even the special courts created under the Law for the Protection of the Republic were not particularly effective as a major legal process in 1924 demonstrated. Twenty-four former members of the Erhardt Brigade, a *Freikorps* unit, were accused of belonging to Consul, the group which planned Erzberger's murder among others. The court concluded that there was no evidence of either a conspiracy to carry out acts of murder or the existence of some sort of a murder centre from which assailants were sent out.[15]

The activities of young officers like those placed on trial in 1924 raise one of the most serious issues concerning the Feme attacks: the question of the relation of these groups to the regular army and to politicians. Throughout the twenties, rumors circulated about the existence of a secret army funded by the regular army. Articles in the press and testimony at several trials kept this issue alive. Some of the suspicions centered on the *Arbeitskommando* (labor battalions). Under the Treaty of Versailles, these units were allowed to carry out the necessary work of reconstruction. Legally, the labor battalions were non-military groups and were not permitted to possess arms. However, the Prussian State Police had gathered clear evidence as early as 1920 that the *Arbeitskommando* did have weapons.[16]

The issue came to public attention in 1923 when members of these battalions were involved in a series of violent acts including several murders as part of an abortive coup attempt at Küstrin.[17] These crimes remained public issues throughout the entire life of the Republic, surfacing in major trials in Landsberg in 1926 and Stettin in 1929. The Landsberg Trial was actually the third such process of 1926, but it was the first one to receive publicity. Two earlier cases, one in Schwerin and one in Berlin, had been held in closed sessions with no publicity under the pretext that secrecy was required to protect the "safety of the State." This rubric was often used to protect the military or groups connected to it and sometimes to harass journalists or anyone else investigating areas such as illegal armaments or treaty violations.

At the Landsberg and Stettin trials, government officials, including the Minister of Defense Otto Gessler, denied that the

Arbeitskommando constituted a Schwarze Reichswehr. Gessler explained that the arms in their possession were the result of their searches for hidden weapons belonging to other groups and that the *Arbeitskommando* planned to turn them over to the government.[18] However, testimony given at Landsberg by *Arbeitskommando* leader Major Buchrucker, himself, called these explanations into question. In response to Minister Gessler's claim that the only contact these groups had with arms was their attempt to confiscate them, Major Buchrucker declared: "Officially these battalions were trying to locate arms, but this was only a pretext to save them from possible charges of treason. The real purpose of these organizations was quite different. The Minister of the Reichswehr knows what it was."[19] Thus, testimony and physical evidence indicated that Feme groups who constituted a secret army received help from the regular army sympathetic particularly to the anti-leftist activities of the Schwarze Reichswehr.[20]

The 1923 Feme murders in Küstrin and the implications of a secret army became central again at Stettin in 1929 in the trial of members of the *Freikorps* group led by Lieutenant Rossbach. He had become a *Freikorps* commander after being a junior officer at the end of the war. He ignored orders to dissolve his battalion in 1920, and the group was implicated in the 1923 murders. Although Lieutenant Rossbach was arrested at that time, he was not convicted. New evidence brought members of his group to trial six years later when Army Commander General Hammerstein delivered expert testimony charging that the Rossbach organization was illegal and was part of a Schwarze Reichswehr.[21]

Hammerstein asserted that Rossbach and his group had no official standing and was in no way legally associated with the army.[22] The lawyer for the defense attempted to demonstrate that the Rossbach group was indeed sponsored by the armed forces and had been acting in the national interest. He produced a letter from General Weber, former Commander of the Second Reichswehr Division at Stettin, which indicated that he had known of the existence of these battalions, and that they had always been available for his use.[23] On rebuttal, General Hammerstein denied any knowledge or any recognition of these groups and claimed that, if General Weber's statement was true, he had deceived the army command including the Commander in Chief, General von

Seeckt.[24] These claims and counter claims testify to the fact that, even in the last years of the Republic, it was not clear whether Feme violence had, in some sense, been officially sanctioned. They reveal the deep divisions within the institutional heart of the Weimar state.

In 1923, the Prussian police arrested twenty members of the secret society called General Wrangel's Messmates which purportedly had army connections. Plans were found on these men for the rescue of Lieutenant Rossbach and for the murder of Otto Braun, the Prussian Minister President, and Carl Severing, the Prussian Minister of the Interior.[25] Braun and Severing were among the Reich officials who did not attempt to cover up Feme crimes. As early as April 29, 1920, in reply to a question by Deputy Steinbrink in a Prussian Landtag question and answer session, Severing said: "It is quite true that at Duisberg, Mulheim, Essen and other places, a number of people have deliberately been shot by soldiers and members of *Freikorps* groups."[26]

In spite of some unequivocal statements like Severing's, it is difficult to assess the real level of involvement of the military, the civilian government and political party leaders with the Feme groups. In contrast to the area of illegal rearmament where complicity clearly reached to the top because all Weimar leaders shared the conviction that the terms of Versailles Treaty were unfair, knowledge about the secret army appears to have been more limited. While all Weimar leaders publicly condemned the Feme murders and almost all deplored the excesses of the labor battalions, these groups were supported by elements of the military and by some civilian government and party leaders. When he was arrested for participating in the Rathenau assassination, Lieutenant Gunther was carrying letters from many significant figures including General Ludendorff, and the Nationalist politician Karl Helfferich.

Once Feme members committed crimes and were caught by the police, they were placed in the hands of the judiciary. The left-wing lawyer Alfred Apfel looked on in disgust at the favoritism many of the courts showed towards anti-republican army officers: "And again and again it is German justice that holds the stirrup for these spur-clinking aristocrats and accepts the bigoted viewpoint of an army major as a better standard than the clauses of the constitution, the provisions of which the judges each and all swore to uphold when they took their oath of office."[27]

Certainly the young men who comprised the Feme groups received sympathetic treatment from the judges they faced in courtrooms during the Weimar years. In spite of the differences in age, background and education, they shared a great bond of sympathy in outlook and goals even though the judges were, in Fritz Ringer's terms, elite "mandarins" while the Feme assailants had no established position within the society.[28] Both groups rejected the Republic and had their own concepts of an idealized state to which they aspired. British legal observers who, as members of the control commission, had the opportunity to watch the Weimar judges, wrote, "The knives of the murderers were concealed under the robes of the judges."[29]

Judges had always been an influential force in German society. In the period before the First World War, they constituted a prestigious and important segment of the leadership of the Empire. The structure of the judiciary and their method of training and selection were fixed in 1879 and were not significantly changed until 1933. Lawyers and candidates for the judiciary were among the one per cent of the population who received three years of university training. This training often took students to various parts of the country since most travelled from one university to another during their years of study. The three years of university study were followed by three years of practical legal training during which the students also travelled. The products of this six-year educational process developed a more national and more homogeneous *Weltanschauung* than any other group within the nation. Candidates for the judiciary followed a separate track from those pursuing other careers in law, and this separate tracking also contributed to the general uniformity of views developed by judges.

Their crucial role in the legal decision-making process was analyzed by Carl Schmitt, who became a leading legal theorist during the Weimar era while also active as a practicing lawyer and political propagandist. In *Gesetz und Urteil*, Schmitt addressed the central question of the criteria for justice in a legal decision. He concluded that, in pre-war Germany, a legal decision was just when it could be understood by "the other judge," a cross-sectional representative of the standardly trained jurist.[30] This corps of magistrates constituted an elite confident of its own ability. They were sufficiently independent to make judgments designed primarily to satisfy their own colleagues.

Judges came from middle and upper-middle class backgrounds and enjoyed the prestige of inclusion in the small stratum of university-trained professionals in the society. Some critics argue that senior civil servants attached to the foreign service and other ministries had more prestige than did judges because a few Jews were allowed in the Wilhelmine judiciary while none were allowed in other departments.[31] The appointment of a small number of Jews to the judiciary was an historical anomaly. However, the observations of these critics reflect that, under most conditions in Wilhelmine Germany, the presence of Jews was perceived as an indication of diminished prestige. Judges were, in fact, clearly members of the elite class. They were politically conservative and nationalistic and strongly anti-socialist and anti-Semitic. Although they had an extremely independent position and a theory of jurisprudence which tended to reinforce their independence, their values did not conflict with those of the Emperor and the aristocracy. Therefore, the judges represented a bulwark that worked to protect the status quo in Wilhelmine Germany.

The structure of the courts reinforced the power of the judiciary. Germany did not use a jury system, and defendants faced one judge, a panel of judges or sometimes a mixed group of judges and trained lay people. In these mixed panels, there were always as many judges as lay people, and the opinions of the judges always carried the greatest weight. Thus, judges dominated the German legal system, in a way that was impossible in English and American systems where juries balanced the decision-making process.

When the Republic was created, the new leaders did not move to reform the judiciary in accordance with republican principles. They were committed to liberal pluralism and believed that the judiciary should be independent and politically neutral. They were also aware that the conservative political forces were committed to the judiciary and that an attempt at substantial modification risked alienating the more moderate members of these groups with whom the leaders of the middle of the road republicans hoped to work. The decision not to reform the judiciary left the Republic with a fifth column within government circles which contributed substantially to the undermining of the new state. In an insightful analysis, Tucholsky perceived the threat of the judges to the Republic:

> When the Republic was created these same judges held over from the monarchy found it impossible to transfer their allegiance to the new organization of the state. Thus they entered into opposition and began to serve their own independent ideas of what they desired the state to be. They created a private law and subverted the public law of the Republic by refusing to administer justice in an equal manner to all people. In a sense the judiciary confused itself with the state and served its own interest instead of the whole society.[32]

Thus, the judges represented a Feme of their own which served their unique vision of the state while they looked upon the leaders of the Weimar government as illegitimate usurpers. As Gotthard Jasper points out, the concept of the politically neutral judge bore little relation to the realities of Weimar justice.[33] In a study which appeared in 1926, a leading judge who was president of a major court concluded that a breakdown of the politics of the judges would show that five per cent were republican, fifteen per cent were reactionary and eighty per cent were waverers, *schwankende*.[34] However, when the term *schwankende* was further defined, it meant judges who, while not members of a particular political party, could still be identified politically as national-conservative. There were four hundred members of The League of Republican Judges, but twelve thousand in The Conservative League of German Judges.[35]

The political orientation of the judiciary became a critical factor in the rendering of just decisions in cases involving political violence. Gumbel's detailed documentation of the treatment of left and right-wing assailants clearly indicates the extreme bias that characterized the administration of German justice during the Weimar years. Table 1 illustrates the point graphically.[36]

Judges, in contrast to the Prussian police, made decisions predicated upon defendants' political affiliations rather than upon the nature of their actions. They gave stiff sentences to left-wing revolutionaries in the worker's rebellion in Bavaria, for example, condemning one defendant to death and 2,209 to long terms of imprisonment. Most of these sentences were actually served. Out of a total of 6,080 years of imprisonment imposed, 4,400 were served.[37] By contrast, of those who participated in the Kapp Putsch, only one leader was sentenced, and he was given a minimal term. When challenged on the question of inequality of treatment, judges claimed that they were mainly punishing leaders. However, if that were the case, the workers rebellion in Bavaria had 2,200 leaders while the Kapp Putsch had one.[38]

Table 1: *Political murders and penalties*

	Left	*Right*
No. murders	22	354
Death penalties	10	0
Severe punishments	17	1
Average sentences	15 years	4 months

The judges also posited a more serious legal/theoretical justification for their actions. Building on an analysis put forward most clearly by Schmitt in the immediate post-war period, they constructed a theory of guilt which suited their purposes and would have ominous implications for National Socialist law. Schmitt had stated that guilt was political rather than psychological, philosophical or theological.[39] He argued that defendants were guilty if they acted in a way that was inconsistent with the goals of the state and the purposes of the collective will of the people. The extent of the guilt was determined by the value to the state of the person or object damaged by these actions. Schmitt quoted one of his own teachers of legal theory:

> The value of the protected object must be determined directly by the constitutive significance of its role in the state's purpose. That is as far as it [the significance of the object] concerns the jurist. Naturally it follows that the more valuable the object to be protected, the greater the damage caused by the divergence between the individual and the state's purpose therefore the greater the guilt.[40]

Weimar judges, following this line of reasoning, felt empowered to sentence left-wing defendants to much heavier punishments than right-wing defendants by arguing that what or who they damaged was of greater value. Even the standard of value they used was not consistent with that of the Weimar Republic. Instead it was predicated on an idealized construct of a state served by many judges and by Feme assailants.

These distinctions, based on the political convictions of judges who were only theoretically neutral, were in evidence in cases of all degrees of seriousness. A defendant who slandered the Republic by calling it a *Rauberrepublik* (Robber Republic), a familiar left-wing epithet, received four weeks in prison, while a defendant who called the Republic a *Kommunist Judenrepublik,* a common right-wing epithet, received a small 70 Mark fine.[41]

The nature of Weimar justice was manifested as early as the "Geiselmord" trial which took place in Munich in September 1919, in the earliest days of the Republic. The defendants were charged and found guilty of the murders of Kurt Eisner and Gustav Landauer. Count Arco-Valley, Eisner's young aristocratic assassin, was sentenced to five years imprisonment, much of which he did not serve. Landauer's murderer was sentenced to serve only five weeks in prison. As an indication that judges were not alone in their disregard of traditional rules of justice, when Count Arco-Valley arrived in his prison cell he was greeted by 15,000 sympathetic letters and telegrams.[42]

While Kurt Eisner and Gustav Landauer could have been identified as revolutionaries, although they were willing to surrender power when they lost an election, other victims had played no active political role in the revolutionary period at all. Maximilian Harden typified the Feme victim who was not a politician but an intellectual. His case graphically illustrates the politicized nature of German justice. The members of the Feme believed that left-wing intellectuals, particularly Jews, were poisoning the moral atmosphere of Germany just as republican politicians were poisoning the political atmosphere. Prominent figures, such as Albert Einstein, appeared on their hit lists. However, unlike Harden, Einstein was given warning and travelled to the United States until the initial danger passed. Harden was a left-wing, but extremely independent writer. He had spent much of his career as a critic of the Wilhelmine monarchy and an advocate of reform. He was in his sixties by the time the Republic was created but continued to criticize what he perceived as a lack of serious reform in the new state. The right condemned him as a radical and a Jew. In 1922, Consul set out to enforce a death sentence on Harden. Three assassins went to his home in the Moabit suburb of Berlin and assaulted him intent on beating him to death. The attackers were scared off by Harden's neighbors and, although seriously injured, he survived the assault.

The Prussian police made short work of the investigation and brought the three defendants to trial. As in many cases of this nature, the facts were not in question. The assailants employed a political defense strategy; they claimed that Harden's outspoken attacks on everything they considered sacred – the army, the aristocracy, the church, and the corporate structure – were sufficient provocation to justify the attack. The judge also allowed Harden's Jewish origin to be mentioned as part of the defense argument, provoking Harden's response that it was not yet against the law to be a Jew.[43] The defendants were treated with respect while Harden and the police officers were not. The sentences imposed were the minimum allowable under the law. Harden made a statement to the court at the end of the trial which bore the sound of prophecy: "Then take care that all men who were born as Jews receive the yellow patch and that they not be allowed to publish magazines and books. But you will not be able to control this terror! Do you not see how far it establishes itself in the courtroom?"[44] In spite of the blatant bias in the Harden case and many others, the police, particularly in Prussia, continued to arrest Feme perpetrators, highlighting the contrast between the attitudes and performances of the unreformed judiciary and the reformed police. The great majority of judges throughout all of the German states exhibited an unreformed perspective, while the police varied from the most strategically vital and most reformed Prussian police to the least reformed Bavarian police.

The drama of this conflict and the growing polarization of justice was played out again in police headquarters and courtrooms in Saxony in the 1925 Helling-Haas-Schröder murder trial. In this case, Helling was the murder victim and the clues pointed to Schröder. However, a much less likely suspect, the Jewish industrialist Haas, was arrested based on pressure by judicial investigators, and judicial officials were determined to indict him.[45] At that point, a major conflict developed as the Saxon police, supported by the evidence of their independent investigations, intervened on behalf of Haas charging that anti-Semitism was the motive for the action being taken against him.[46] The prosecutors maintained their position and charged the police with attempting to impugn the independence of the judiciary. They clung to this stance until Schröder confessed to the crime.

The Feme and Schwarze Reichswehr cases were the most extreme manifestations of the bias of the Weimar judiciary. They demonstrated the crucial role played by judges in a state which was predicated on the rule of law. Ironically, the Republic entrusted the interpretation of its law to judges who were at war with the Republic itself. These judges served their own vision of a true state rather than the actual existing legally constituted government.

The judges were the most extreme example of civil servants who were committed to their own view of the state while also promoting their own power at the expense of that of the elected officials. Jane Caplan's characterization of the civil service under Weimar and Nazi Germany captures these inclinations: "... the civil service – itself a powerful social institution – aimed to retain and reauthorize the excessive power of bureaucratized over political and social structure."[47] Thus, when many parts of of the civil service, particularly the judges, were convinced that they could not shape the new state in their own image or control it sufficiently, they became a revolutionary force determined to destroy the status quo. Many Weimar judges were convinced that they were following a concept of *recht* (right or justice) rather than *gesetz* (law). This ephemeral concept of justice provided them with a rationale to serve their own political orientation and impose those views on the nation. Indeed, the knives of those who would ultimately destroy the Republic were also under the robes of the judges.The violent young men in the Feme found their way into the paramilitary formations of the Nazi Party, the SA and the SS, during the mid-twenties. They were able to use violence in their street politics as another way to fight for the true state that they felt they would bring into being. Given the relative prosperity and order of the middle Weimar years, however, they recognized the need to suppress some of the violence which had defined their Feme activities. It was necessary to sublimate it and use it in less sensationalistic ways than the assassinations of the early twenties. Certainly people like Hermann Göring and Ernst Röhm, among the most violent men in the generally violent Nazi movement, attracted many of the young men who had been part of the Feme movement. When the depression again fomented chaos in Weimar Germany, these former Feme members could fight in the streets and unleash their violent behaviour more publically.

Notes

1 See H. Stuart Hughes, *Consciousness and Society: the Reconstruction of European Social Thought, 1890–1930*, New York, 1954.

2 Sigmund Freud, *Thoughts on War and Death*, London, 1953.

3 Reichskanzler Joseph Wirth, "Memorandum", Bundesarchiv, March 4, 1922, R431–2692.

4 Roy Lewis and Jon Clark (eds), *Labour Law and Politics in the Weimar Republic, Otto Kahn-Freund*, Oxford, 1981, p. 195.

5 Quoted in Harold Poor, *Kurt Tucholsky and the Ordeal of Germany*, New York, 1968, p. 119.

6 Emil Julius Gumbel, "Archival Material", Leo Baeck Institute, New York; *Zwei Jahre Mord*, Berlin, 1921; *Vier Jahre politischer Mord*, Berlin, 1922; *Verräter verfallen der Feme*, Berlin, 1929; *Lässt Kopfe rollen*, Berlin, 1932.

7 Ernst von Salomon, *Fragebogen*, Berlin, 1949, p. 45.

8 *Ibid.*, p. 53.

9 Cuno Horkenbach (ed.), *Das Deutsche Reich von 1918 bis Heute*, Vol. I., Berlin, 1930, p. 131.

10 *Ibid.*, p. 144.

11 *Ibid.*

12 "Banker and Editor on hit list", *New York Times*, July 1, 1922, p. 3.

13 Harry Kessler, *In The Twenties: The Diaries of Harry Kessler*, trans. Charles Kessler, New York, 1971, p. 184.

14 Harry Zohn and Karl F. Ross, (eds and translators), *What if-? Satirical Writings of Kurt Tucholsky*, New York, 1967, p. 24.

15 Horkenbach, *Deutsche Reich*, p. 202.

16 Carl Severing, "Report der Minister des Innern," Bundesarchiv, Reichskanzlei, April 17, 1920, R 431/2689.

17 See Carl Mertens, *Die deutsche Militärpolitik seit 1918*, Berlin, 1926.

18 Otto Gessler, "Schwarze Reichswehr? Ja oder Nein," *Berliner Tageblatt*, December 23, 1926.

19 Bruno Ernst Buchrucker, "Otto Gessler? Ja oder Nein," *Vorwärts*, December 24, 1926.

20 Martin Sabrow, "Reichsminister Rathenau ermordert," *Die Zeit*, June 26, 1992, p. 3.

21 Bertold Jacob, "Bemerkungen," *Die Weltbühne*, 64, 1929, p. 601.

22 *Ibid.*, pp. 603–4.

23 *Ibid.*, p. 610.

24 *Ibid.*

25 Emil Julius Gumbel and Erich-Otto Volkmann, *Weissbuch Uber die Schwarze Reichswehr, Deutsche Liga für Menschenrechte*, Berlin, 1925, p. 49.

26 Carl Severing, "Kleine anfragen und antworten", Prussian Landtag, Borck Collection, Vol. I, Bundesarchiv, Koblenz.

27 Alfred Apfel, *Behind the Scenes of German Justice: Reminiscences of a German Barrister, 1882–1933*, London, 1935, pp. 107–8.

28 Fritz Ringer, *The Decline of the German Mandarins: the German Academic Community 1890–1933*, Cambridge, Mass., 1969.

29 *Das Nürnberger Juristenurtiel*, January 1923, p. 43.

30 Carl Schmitt, *Gesetz und Urteil- Eine Untersuchung zum Problem der Rechtspraxis*, Berlin, 1912.

31 See Lewis and Clark, *Labour Law*, Introduction.

32 Quoted in Harold Poor, *Kurt Tucholsky and the Ordeal of Germany*, New York, 1968, p. 119.

33 Gotthard Jasper, "Justiz und Politik in der Weimarer Republik," *Vierteljahrshefte Für Zeitgeschichte*, 30. Jahrgang, 2 Heft, April 1982, pp. 167–205.

34 *Ibid.*, p. 172.

35 Lewis and Clark, *Labour Law*, p. 37.

36 Gumbel, *Verräter verfallen Der Feme*, p. 134.

37 Ingo Müller, *Hitler's Justice: The Courts of the Third Reich*, trans. Deborah Lucas Schneider, Cambridge, Mass., 1991, p. 12.

38 *Ibid.*, p. 13.

39 Carl Schmitt, *Über Schuld und Schuldarten – Eine terminologische Untersuchung*, Breslau, 1910, p. 51.

40 *Ibid.*, p. 54.

41 Kurt Kreiler (ed.), *Traditionen deutscher Justiz: Politische Prozesse 1914–1932*, Breslau, 1973, p. 194.

42 Heinrich Hannover and Elizabeth Hannover-Drück, *Politische Justiz, 1918–1933*, Hornheim-Merten, 1968, p. 109.

43 Maximilian Harden, *I Meet My Contemporaries*, trans., William Lawton, Freeport, New York, 1968, p. 68.

44 Quoted in Harold Poor, *Kurt Tucholsky*, p. 119.

45 Gerhard Kramer, "The Influence of National-Socialism on the Courts of Justice and the Police," in Maurice Beaumont, John H. E. Fried, Edmond Vermeil (eds), *The Third Reich*, New York, 1955, p. 603.

46 *Ibid.*, p. 609.

47 Jane Caplan, "National Socialism and the State", in *Reevaluating the Third Reich*, New York, 1993, p. 108.

8

The Weimar Bauhaus

While the Weimar Republic is often viewed primarily as a failure and as a prelude to Nazi Germany, Weimar culture has been singled out as a phenomenon of unusual creative richness, originality and diversity. Weimar Germany was on the cutting edge of developments in the visual arts, architecture, theater, literature and film. However, many of its intellectuals, particularly those on the left, have been castigated for their merciless critique of the Republic's shortcomings and their lack of praise for the freedom and opportunity it provided for creativity and experiment. Few artists and intellectuals were willing to say, in its day, what the writer Henry Pachter later said in an autobiographical fragment:

> It is a matter of historical justice to say that, for all its shortcomings, the Weimar Republic was one of the freest states that ever existed, that it afforded the working classes greater opportunities for collective improvement than any other European state at the time, and that its cultural life was determined by progressive minds more effectively than at any other time in German history.[1]

In characterizing himself and other Weimar artists and intellectuals, Pachter sheds additional light on the atmosphere that made such creativity possible:

> We did not suffer, we were not alienated. Each of us lived in his own crowd; each was a priest of some cult or a functionary of some church. In no period of German literature or art were creative spirits so well adjusted to their environment, audiences so eager to

accept whatever artists presented as the latest chic of their own sensibilities.[2]

Certainly there is much truth in what Pachter says. Yet the Weimar Republic that Pachter describes as being so free sent the editor and essayist Carl von Ossietsky to prison for exposing the illegal rearmament program and prosecuted the satirist Kurt Tucholsky and the artist George Grosz for their criticism of the unreformed military. Republican leaders also gave in to right-wing violence and banned showings of the film version of Erich Maria Remarque's *All Quiet on the Western Front*. While Weimar artists could be incredibly creative, their work was not always accepted; and those who tried hardest to play a vital role in the reform of society and to be one with the people were often harassed and their efforts rejected. The flight of so many of the most creative of the Weimar intellectuals and artists which accompanied the Nazi takeover in 1933 was a blow to German cultural production from which the nation has never recovered.

The struggles of many German artists to play a role in the new state, the conflicts within the artistic community about what that role should be and what type of art would best play that role manifested the most dynamic qualities of Weimar life. While the history of Weimar culture has been told better than most other aspects of the Republic, study of the early evolution of one cultural institution reveals the conflicted idealism and ingenuity of the age. The Bauhaus was created as a paradigm of Weimar vision, yet the story of its struggles up to its ejection from the city Weimar in 1925 can serve as a microcosm of the creativity and tensions of Weimar culture and, in many ways, of the Republic itself.

On December 23, 1918 in Berlin, the young architect Walter Gropius wrote to his friend and art patron, Karl Ernst Osthaus:

> I came here to participate in the revolution. The mood is tense here, and we artists have to strike while the iron's hot. In the *Arbeitsrat für Kunst*, which I have joined, there's at present a congenially radical atmosphere and productive ideas are being brought up.[3]

Gropius had been drawn to the center of this vortex by the forces of change which were convulsing Germany. Upon witnessing the November Revolution in Berlin, he declared: "This is more than just a lost war. A world has come to an end. We must seek a radical solution to our problems," while at the same time, Rainer Maria Rilke wrote a letter to a friend signing it "with ardent hope that mankind would for once turn over a new page."[4]

Intellectuals lost no time in joining the revolution. On the day of the proclamation of the Republic, the Council of Intellectuals, composed mostly of expressionist artists and writers, convened in the Reichstag building and demanded the abolition of all academic institutions, the nationalization of all theaters, and the immediate convocation of a world parliament. They declared that "art should be brought to the people, and the world should be changed through art."[5]

By December, this spirit had become more focused with the formation of the *Arbeitsrat für Kunst* (Working Council for Art). Gropius, council chairman, declared: "The arts must be brought together under the wing of a great architecture [which is] the business of the entire People."[6] His vision is also implicit in the catalogue essay for the *Exhibition of Unknown Architects* (sponsored by the *Arbeitsrat für Kunst* in Berlin in 1919) which united architecture with society's ideals and declared it to be "the crystallized expression of man's noblest thoughts, his human nature, his faith, his religion".[7]

In his December letter to Osthaus, Gropius revealed his nascent plans for the future which would be expressed first in *Arbeitsrat* proposals:

> I am working on something entirely different now, which I've been turning over in my head for many years – a *Bauhutte*! With a few like-minded artists ... I ask you to keep quiet about it until I have spoken with you face to face, otherwise the idea, which requires gentle discretion, will be trampled in the economic turmoil before it's able to live ...[8]

The council called for all artists to unite. It urged the dissolution of royal academies and state museums while calling for government assurances that art would be guaranteed a future in the new Republic. It advocated reforms in art education that would foster children's expressive tendencies rather than "correct" formal achievements.[9]

While Gropius was formulating his ideas for revolutionizing the teaching and practice of art, the forces of the past which had not been banished were undermining the general optimism of late 1918. In fact, they were very much a factor in the new government as it struggled to establish a middle path between reaction and revolution, both of which seemed to be leading to chaos. The crushing of the November Revolution was a blow to many artists. Rilke voiced the new disillusionment that engulfed left-wing intellectuals: "Under the pretense of a great upheaval, the old want of character persists", and Count Harry Kessler commented at the 1919 May Day celebration that: "The festivities gave the impression of national mourning for a revolution that misfired."[10]

Thus, the stage was set for a struggle of oppositions: of revolution and reaction, of creativity and repression, of idealism and practicality, of innovation and tradition. Toni Stolper, an observer, characterized the tensions that defined the nature of the Weimar Republic: "The Republic was marked by creativity in the midst of suffering, hard work in the midst of repeated disappointments, hope in the face of pitiless and powerful adversaries."[11] He could just as well have been describing the history of the Bauhaus, Gropius's invention and one of the defining institutions of this immensely creative but conflicted period.

Like the Republic, the Bauhaus did not emerge full-blown in 1919. Gropius's idea for a *Bauhutte,* an artists' guild, did not materialize of its own volition. It was, in fact, the result of theories, plans and real programs with which artists, architects, and craftsmen had been experimenting for more than half a century. These efforts developed in the atmosphere of dramatic industrial expansion. By the middle of the nineteenth century, industry threatened to make the craftsman obsolete, and the process was already well underway. While craftsmen struggled against the tide of progress, artists had grown remote from everyday reality in classicized academism and romantic detachment. Both groups began to wonder if hope for their futures might lie in a union of effort and a sharing of insights and skills.

The formation in 1903 of the Wiener Werkstätte (Viennese Workshop) to design, produce and market high-quality domestic objects was an early and successful effort to unite art and craft. The results of this collaboration were simple and sophisticated translations of the "innate moral strength" of good design and craftsmanship into commodities with commercial appeal.[12] The efforts by the Wiener Werkstätte to resolve the tension between artistic vision and materialistic demands were intensified in Germany where anxiety about the quality of German industrial products was matched by the anxiety of displaced German craftsmen. In an effort to satisfy consumer demands at the lowest cost, German manufacturers had abandoned standards of craftsmanship, and their products had suffered in quality rendering them inadequate to compete in the international market.

The evolving efforts to resolve the tensions between art and crafts under the pressures of industrialization played themselves out most clearly in Germany in the arena of art education. Many of the key artist/players were also professors in art academies or in schools of applied arts. Gropius recognized the centrality of education in the creative process when he formulated his ideas for the Bauhaus in 1918, and he reiterated that view fifty years later at the opening of the exhibition *Fifty Years of the Bauhaus* in Stuttgart in May 1968:

> When the Bauhaus was founded I had already come to the conclusion that an autocratic, subjective learning process choked off the innate creative tendencies of talented students ... I concluded that the teacher must beware of passing on his own formal vocabulary to the students and that he must rather allow them to find *their own way*, even if they were detoured ... Artists at the Bauhaus attempted to find an objective common denominator of form – in a way to develop a science of design; this has since been expanded in countless schools in various countries. Such a foundation of general, superpersonal formal laws provides an organic and unifying background for various talents.[13]

Questions concerning the goals and effectiveness of art education in Germany had been hotly debated in the late nineteenth century. They reflected uncertainties about the relationship of "fine" and "applied" art training, particularly within the context of industrial demand, and about the position of art academies and trade schools in the educational hierarchy which had become consolidated under the state after unification in 1871. These legitimate issues had been carried to an ominous extreme in Julius Langbehn's *Rembrandt als Erzieher* (*Rembrandt as Educator*, 1890) in which the author first conflated identification with nature and identification with national culture through folk art and then concluded that German culture was being destroyed by science and intellectualism, particulalry that produced by Jews. Germany's only hope of salvation, in Langbehn's scenario, was regeneration through art and the rising to power of great nordic artistic individuals as leaders and teachers in a new society.[14]

In a more democratic spirit, Alfred Lichtwark, director of the Hamburg Kunsthalle, was involved in reforms of the city's Kunstgewerbeschule (school of applied art), in the practical education of women, and in the preservation of local art and culture. In 1887, he founded the Art Education Movement to consolidate art education in relation to the welfare of the individual and the state. He believed that art should be central to life and education and that, if the eye were trained as the intellect is trained, the problems of German industry would be solved. The barriers between the producer and the product, the product and the consumer would disappear as all recognized genuine quality.[15] His ideas inspired the best in German design and art training before World War I.

The efforts to revitalize craft and industrial production through the reformulation of the relationships between fine and applied art and between art and industry were most graphically played out in the city of Weimar. The pre-1919 city of 40,000 had been an "art town", the home of Bach, the Cranachs, Goethe, Schiller, Herder and Liszt. The town's income at the turn of the century was primarily from agriculture and several small, mainly craft-based industries. The art academy, established in 1860, became the Hochschule für bildende Kunst in 1910, and Max Beckmann, Hans Arp and Hans Richter studied there. In 1902, the Belgian architect and educator, Henry van de Velde, was invited by the Grand Duke Wilhelm Ernst of Saxe-Weimar to advise him on ways to revitalize the crafts and industries of the city. By 1904 he was appointed professor at the new Grand Ducal Kunstgewerbeschule that he had created. He designed the new buildings for the school including weaving, ceramics, book-binding and precious metals workshops and a new but independent fine arts academy which opened in 1907 on the same site.[16] In spite of his successes, van de Velde was resented as a Belgian and an avant-gardist in the face of growing xenophobia and nationalism at the outbreak of war. His position became untenable by 1915; he left and the school closed.

Even the demands of war could not totally distract from the

pressing need to provide training for those who would determine the visual culture of the future and the form of German industrial products. The effort to formulate a new methodology for concretizing visual experience and for characterizing the relationship between the creator and the object created would become the defining work of the institution which came to be called the Bauhaus. In 1915, the goal seemed somewhat more limited as the Weimar State Council set out to replace Henry van de Velde and to reorganize the state's Kunstgewerbeschule.

The Grand Duke summoned Walter Gropius to an audience to discuss his taking over the school. Gropius's name was one of three that van de Velde had submitted as a potential replacement for him when he left. Already an accomplished architect, Gropius was descended from a long line of artists and architects. Gropius's great uncle Martin was an architect and the designer of the Kunstgewerbe (Crafts) Museum in Berlin. His father, who was also named Martin, was principal of the Kunstgewerbe Museum and the director of education in Prussia.[17] Gropius convinced the Grand Duke and the Weimar State Council that his vision of an art school combining the Kunstgewerbeschule and the academy was both innovative and reasonable. This new institution would train artist-craftsmen to create product designs as prototypes for manufacturing which would thrust German industry into the forefront of modern design. The Council agreed to fund the new institution.

The atmosphere in the city in early 1919 was both chaotic and exciting. The newly constituted National Assembly relocated there because of the city's liberal cultural and political associations in contrast to the autocratic associations with Berlin, the center of the Hohenzollern monarchy and the conservative Prussian tradition. The militancy of the November Revolution was also in evidence. In January 1919 more than one thousand Weimar workers demonstrated against the reactionary forces responsible for the murders of Liebknecht and Luxemburg, while the following month protestors against unemployment confronted the National Assembly.

In the middle of this agitation, the Bauhaus was born, and it carried with it the marks of its birth in the form of its idealism and its imperative to reconcile differences in order to survive. Gropius's call to arms was first articulated in April 1919 in the

Programm des Staatlichen Bauhauses in Weimar, the Bauhaus Manifesto:

> Let us create a new guild of craftsmen, without the class distinctions that raise an arrogant barrier between craftsman and artist. Together let us conceive and create the new building of the future, which will embrace architecture and sculpture and painting in one unity and which will rise one day towards heaven from the hands of a million workers, like the crystal symbol of a new faith.[18]

After the rallying call of the manifesto, Gropius had to confront the realities of implementing the ideals he had presented: how craft and fine art training would be directed to achieve the new architecture; how distinctions between fine art and craftsmanship would be abolished; how a cross-disciplinary approach would be structured within a guild system of training and examination; how the "priority of creativity" and the "freedom of individuality" could be reconciled with "strict study discipline."[19] Gropius's exhortation: "Architects, sculptors, painters, we must all turn to the crafts!" echoed the call of the *Arbeitsrat für Kunst*, but its revolutionary implications had to be conflated with the conventions of the craft tradition.

Gropius's intentions, as expressed in his statements and reflected in his actions, would change over the period of his tenure as Bauhaus director. However, his general statement of the goals of the curriculum articulated in "Theory and Organization at the Bauhaus" comes as close as any to being a summary of the Bauhaus vision:

> The culminating point of the Bauhaus teaching is a demand for a new and powerful working correlation of all the processes of creation. The gifted student must gain a feeling for the interwoven strands of practical and formal work ...[20]

The hopes of the students rested on the Bauhaus program. Gropius laid out its theoretical organization initially consistent with the concept of unifying craft and fine art instruction. It was to be composed of three major parts: the preliminary course (*Vorlehre* or *Vorkurs*), the workshops (*Werklehre* and *Formlehre*), and the architecture course. The preliminary course included in one semester, elementary instruction in problems of form combined with practical experiments with different materials in beginners' workshops. Successful completion of the course was necessary for admission to study in one of the workshops. The apprenticeship program was comprised of three years of craft instruction in the chosen workshop with advanced instruction in form. It would result in a Journeyman's Diploma of the Chamber of Crafts (*Gesellenbrief der Handwerkskammer*) and a Diploma of the Bauhaus depending on the student's performance on the examination of the Chamber of Crafts. Instruction in architecture, not fully implemented at Weimar, was to include practical participation in the construction of buildings and independent architectural training in the Bauhaus Research Department. The result would be the Master's Diploma of the Chamber of Crafts and a Diploma of the Bauhaus, again contingent on test performance. The entire curriculum would be accompanied by a practical course on "the fundamental relationships of sound, color and form designed to harmonize the physical and psychic qualities of the individual."[21]

To carry out the workshop program, every apprentice and journeyman would be taught by two masters, a craftsman and an artist working in close co-operation. The purpose of craft instruction was to develop manual dexterity, not as an end in itself, but as preparation for the handling of machines in factories. All students would be trained in all aspects of a craft to avoid the division of labor which leads to alienation, and to prepare them to use their craftsmanship to revitalize industry. The purpose of form instruction, in close contact with manual training, was to provide a new co-ordination of means of construction and expression. Rules of rhythm, of proportion, of light value, of full and empty space, accompanied by practical training based on observation and representation of nature, would form a new unity.[22]

The student's initiation into the Bauhaus program would occur in the preliminary course. Its methodology became a sign to participants and to outside observers of the philosophy and operation of the Bauhaus as a whole. It provided a six-month trial period in which to liberate the student's creative power and to provide an understanding of nature's materials and of the basic principles underlying creative activity in the visual arts. Theo van Doesburg described it as concerning "the student's whole personality, since it seeks to liberate him, to make him stand on his own feet, and makes it possible for him to gain a knowledge of both material and form through direct experience."[23]

Students responded enthusiastically to their first encounter with the Bauhaus. Johannes Driesch wrote home: "... The whole place is fabulous anyway: one big family, teachers and students. Bauhaus people can do everything, are allowed to do everything, and get everything ... And above all the classes! ... I'm telling you, I haven't worked like this for ages! ..."[24] By the end of the first year, the student population consisted of two hundred Germans, fourteen Austrians, three Germans from Baltic countries, two Sudetan Germans, and two Hungarians. They ranged in age from seventeen to forty although most were in their early twenties. Two thirds were men of whom one half had served in the army. While the students had to support themselves, Gropius persuaded the Weimar Ministry of Education to cancel tuition fees, and students who produced saleable goods in the workshops were given financial support.[25]

Public support meant public interest in how the school was working: what the students produced and how the teachers taught. Many people were uneasy about the alliance of art and craft and suspicious of the new methods brought by avant-garde artists. Early conflicts between the school and the city and within the Bauhaus community itself centered around the controversial figure of Johannes Itten whom Gropius had invited to the Bauhaus, at the suggestion of his wife Alma Mahler, primarily to teach the *Vorkurs*. Through art projects and visual and physical exercises which stressed the tactile qualities of materials, Itten hoped to expand his students' sense of their own creative potential, and, to some extent, he succeeded. However, he did little to develop their understanding of form or structure and the discipline needed to move beyond the most basic expressive stage of art-making. Furthermore, his own eccentric demeanor encouraged unconventional behavior in his students. He and his followers, often wearing outlandish clothing such as monks' habits and conducting their own mystical ceremonies, not only alienated other students and faculty members, but shocked the staid Weimar citizens and officials who wondered if public funds were being well-spent at the Bauhaus.[26] Gropius tried to moderate Itten's role, Itten refused to compromise, and Gropius asked for his resignation.

Itten's intransigence was consistent with his personal commitment and style. Gropius's stance, however, reflected a change in his posture from the emotional expressiveness of the 1919 Bauhaus Manifesto, with its emphasis on the linkage of art and crafts, back to the more pragmatic vision of his pre-war dialogue with the Weimar State Council in which he had stressed the relationship of art and industry, a position which had found favor with government officials and manufacturers. He was also motivated to establish the semblance of order and direction and to nullify the negative public image that Itten had created. Gropius argued that: "The Bauhaus could become a haven for eccentrics if it were to lose contact with the work and working methods of the outside world."[27]

With Itten's departure, the roles of Paul Klee and Wassily Kandinsky became central to the Bauhaus program of instruction in form. Klee had come to Weimar in Jaunuary 1921 to teach a self-contained course on color, form and composition as part of the over-all preliminary course and to be master of form in the book-binding and glass-painting workshops. Kandinsky came the following year also to teach within the preliminary course and as master of form in the wall-painting workshop. Gropius saw in their participation the public validation of his assertion that the Bauhaus was committed to the unity of art and industrial design. Their names carried weight in the cultural community, and they offered real insight into the language of pure visual form.

Like many faculty members and students at the school, Klee saw the Bauhaus initially in the revolutionary context of the time. He wrote to his artist-friend Alfred Kubin in 1919: "The idea of the new art school was to further the ideals of a communist community [because] the art of the individual is a capitalist luxury. This new art will then be absorbed into handwork where it would blossom freely. For there are no more academies, only art schools for handworkers."[28] However, Gropius had come to realize that politics would be fatal to the school and vehemently denied any political allegiance: "If the Bauhaus becomes a playground for political games, it will collapse like a pack of cards. I have always stressed this, and watch like Cerberus to keep politics of any kind out of the school."[29] Once in Weimar, Klee, too, avoided social and political issues including Bauhaus debates.

In both Klee's and Kandinsky's approaches at the school, art was not considered as an end in itself. Neither artist gave painting classes in Weimar. Instead, art was viewed as part of a "triumverate with science and industry" which achieved a synthesis in design.[30] That synthesis began with an analysis of the simplest geometric shapes and progressed systematically to more complex compositions of three-dimensional solids.

Color was studied in relation to the aims of the workshops. Kandinsky's treatice, *Point and Line to Plane*, a 1926 Bauhaus publication, was an expansion of the "science of art" concept which he taught in his wall-painting workshop. He concluded that theory had to replace intuition in the creation and interpretation of art: "The progress achieved by systematic research will give birth to a dictionary of elements that, developed further, will lead to a 'grammar' and finally to a theory of composition that will overstep the boundaries of the individual arts and refer to 'Art' in general."[31] In this work, Kandinsky abandons the mysticism which had inspired his earlier painting in favor of "mathematical expression" common to all the arts. He explained that, "Interest in mathematical expression tends in two directions – the theoretical and the practical. In the former, it is the logical that plays the more important role; in the latter the purposive."[32] While Itten had sought empathy with materials as the basis of the design process, Klee and Kandinsky searched for a more rational experience of form and color. The challenge remained to apply these ideas to actual designs for craft and industrial production.

However compelling the issues of visual theory might have been, the key to the ultimate success or failure of the Bauhaus design program rested on the products of the workshops. In that arena, the effort to reconcile art and craft, craft and industry, was played out. The workshops were also key to Gropius's hope of financial independence for the school. He calculated, based on commissions that van de Velde had recorded during his tenure at the Kunstgewerbeschule, that fees for prototype designs for industry and sales of products could eventually make the school independent of outside support.[33]

However, given the enormous fluctuations in the German economy and quixotic public support for the Bauhaus, the search for outside income became less a matter of financial independence and more a struggle for survival. Frustrated by the school's inability to teach because of a lack of equipment, Gropius wrote urgently to the Thuringian Cultural Ministry stating: "We cannot work without materials and tools! If help does not come quickly I am pessimistic about the existence of the Bauhaus. Many [students] must or want to leave it because they cannot work"[34] Gropius's pleas went unanswered, and, in July, Oskar Schlemmer, whom Gropius was trying to recruit, wrote to his wife about conditions at the school: "[The Bauhaus] is bitterly opposed by the reactionaries. They want to do much but can do nothing because there's no money and they therefore end up playing games ... Many people are leaving ..."[35]

Gropius had to create workshops that would turn out saleable objects at a high enough price to help support the costs of the school. In the final analysis, the real source of income had to come from licences and royalties on industrial prototypes. The key was to make the workshops initially profitable through luxury crafts, but ultimately to work towards industrial design.

Gropius's first effort to reoriente the craft/industry focus involved the metal workshop which was, as described in the original prospectus, to train blacksmiths, locksmiths and founders. When it opened in 1919, it stressed goldsmithing and silversmithing in an effort to maximize profit through luxury goods. Itten, Schlemmer, and Klee were the form masters between its opening and 1923 along with various master-craftsmen. A student remarked that the workshop "turned out spiritual samovars and intellectual door-knobs."[36] With frequent personnel changes, "the domain of each artist was revised repeatedly, so that not even the master-craftsmen always knew with which form master they were supposed to work."[37]

The arrival of Christian Dell in 1922 brought order and direction to the metal workshop within the craft format. Dell had worked with van de Velde in the Wiener Werkstätte tradition.[38] He demonstrated how different forms could be made from a flat sheet of inexpensive metal combined with silver, ebony, and other fine materials. The students developed designs from the simple geometric forms they studied in the preliminary course. Dell's understanding of the craft process and his sympathy with the materials significantly raised the standard of quality of the output of the metal workshop. However, these objects, at their best, had a limited market in the buyer of luxury goods. It took the arrival of Laszlo Moholy-Nagy the following year to complete the reorientation of the workshop to mass-production prototypes.

There were outside pressures which also contributed to the the change in workshop focus. Weimar craftsmen felt threatened on all sides. With the end of the war and the political revolution, Weimar had become the capital of Thuringia and had absorbed the industries of nearby Erfurt, Mülhausen and and Nordhausen. It was no longer simply the "citadel of the crafts."[39] Faced with industrial competition, craftsmen became increasingly resentful of Bauhaus handcrafts which they viewed as unfair publicly-financed competition. Gropius countered their objections by arguing that the sale of Bauhaus designs (as royalties) for mass-produced objects did not compete with the handcrafts. Unfortunately, his explanations generally went unheeded. He complained: "The short-sighted attitude of the craftsmen's organizations in Germany was one of the greatest obstacles the Bauhaus encountered. Instead of recognizing the Bauhaus as a natural link between craft and industry, they fought it, and feared it as a new factor likely to accelerate that decline of the crafts which had resulted from twentieth century industrial development."[40]

Seeing the financial opportunity that industry offered while also trying to mollify craftsmen, Gropius presented a statement at the Bauhaus in February 1922 which he heralded as a major break with the past but which reiterated earlier goals while subtly suggesting a shift in emphasis towards industrial design:

> The Bauhaus has begun to break with the previous conventional kind of academic training which taught students to become little Raphaels and pattern-designers ... The Bauhaus has quite consciously aimed to replace the principle of the division of labor by returning to collaborative work in which the creative process is perceived to be an indivisible whole ... True craftsmanship must first be revived if young people are to understand the entire, developing process of the activity of design. But this does not mean that the machine and industry must be rejected ... If the creatively gifted person had a factory with all its machines at his disposal, he would be able to create new forms, different from those produced by hand and whose new possibilities cannot be anticipated before the time for them has come.[41]

Gropius had to contend with opposition to his plans from within the Bauhaus as well as from outside. Gerhard Marcks who had come in 1919 as the master of form in the pottery workshop, responded to the director's memorandum two weeks later:

> One cannot derive an entire philosophy from the dispute about the machine aesthetic. The existence of the machine cannot be denied, but it should not be overestimated. Give it its due and no more ... Whoever wants to help the engineers, metal-workers, potters, joiners, etc. should become one himself, i.e. he should immerse himself in the object and not the theory ... Each apprentice has to become what none of us is: master of form and workshop master in one person.[42]

By the Fall of 1922, the antipathy within the school was beginning to affect even its most loyal members. Lionel Feininger, Gropius's closest friend and confidant and the designer of the cover for the Bauhaus Manifesto, wrote to his wife asking: "Tell me, honestly, how many are there in the Bauhaus who really know what they want to achieve or who are strong enough to make something of themselves through painstaking work?"[43] Within a month of this query, things began to change dramatically. In October, Theo van Doesburg organized a Constructivist Congress at Weimar, in some ways as a challenge to what he perceived as the irresoluteness of Gropius and the Bauhaus. The participants constituted a wide spectrum of avant-garde orientations from constructivists to dadaists including El Lissitzky, Hans Richter, Hans Arp, Tristan Tzara, and Lucia and Laszlo Moholy-Nagy. The group's rallying call, articulated by Lissitzky, echoed with the sounds that had been heard in Weimar since 1919: "The new art is formed, not on a subjective, but on an objective basis. This, like science can be described with precision and is by nature constructive. It unites not only pure art, but all those who stand at the frontier of the new culture. The artist is companion to the scholar, the engineer and the worker."[44]

At the time of the Congress, Gropius was already negotiating to bring Moholy-Nagy to the Bauhaus. Gropius had seen his paintings in a Berlin gallery, and their clarity, objectivity and abstraction had appealed to him. However, some students had ambivalent feelings about the new master. Paul Citroën had reservations even while recognizing the innovative approach he would bring to the school:

> None of us who had suggested Moholy liked his Constructivism. This 'Russian' trend created outside the Bauhaus, with its exact,

> simulatively technical forms was disgusting to us who were devoted to the extremes of German Expressionism. But since Constructivism was the newest of the new, it was – so we figured – the cleverest move to overcome our aversion and, by supporting Gropius's choice of one of its creators, incorporate this 'newest' into the Bauhaus system ...[45]

Citroën did not look upon Mohly-Nagy's modernist vision as a potential inspiration for personal transformation as Itten's students had viewed him, but rather perceived the new master as a prestigious addition because of his reputation.

In spite of the initial reservations that greeted his arrival, Moholy-Nagy's efforts to reform the metal workshop were substantial as he worked to move from a craft to an industrial-design orientation. His rhetoric, written for the Bauhaus catalogue in 1938, reflects his egalitarian and utilitarian approach: "When Gropius appointed me to take over the metal workshop he asked me to reorganize it as a workshop for industrial design ... Changing the policy of this workshop involved a revolution, for in their pride the gold- and silversmiths avoided the use of ferrous metals, nickel and chromium plating and abhorred the idea of making models for electrical household appliances or lighting fixtures ..."[46]

While craft objects continued to be produced in the metal workshop alongside potential prototypes for lighting fixtures and other mass-produced objects, a transformation in the students' orientation began to manifest itself. The key term "form and function" appeared in student as well as faculty statements. Wilhelm Wagenfeld, a metal workshop student, expressed the textbook wedding of the theory of form and the production of a concrete object:

> Form and function must always attain a clear, unambiguous design in which function has produced the form ... The relationship between the various parts of a [tea] service should not be announced by means of formal similarities. The formal resolution of each object should rather reflect its function and thus emphasize its dependence on the other objects ... In this way the formally dynamic appearance of the pots arose.[47]

Gunta Stölzl, a student in the weaving workshop in the early 1920s and later its director in Dessau, traced the evolution of her workshop which was similar to the new consciousness Wagenfeld described:

> In 1922–3 we had an idea of living fundamentally different from that of today. Our ideas could then still be poems fraught with ideas, flowery decoration, personal experience ... [Then] we noticed how pretentious these independent single pieces were: cloth, curtain, wall-hanging. The richness of color began to look too autocratic to us, it did not subordinate itself to the home. We made an effort to become simpler, to discipline our means and to achieve a greater unity between material and function.[48]

Stölzl and Wagenfeld further testified in their statements to changes in the preliminary course and the *Formlehre* which, with greater stress on the analysis and synthesis of form and color in a rationalist context, had prepared them to approach industrial design with greater clarity of vision and the formal means to achieve that vision. The reform of the preliminary course had also become the responsibility of Moholy-Nagy whom Gropius made its director. Josef Albers, the first Bauhaus student to be appointed to a teaching position as a "young master", was assigned to develop the preliminary course in the study of materials while also assuming the position of workshop master in stained glass. Both masters taught complementary but independent courses since Moholy-Nagy doubled the duration of the preliminary program to two semesters. Albers directed the first term and Moholy-Nagy, the second. Both courses emphasized "economy of materials and means" and replaced Itten's free-association experiments with exercises demonstrating structural, kinetic, and spatial articulation of materials.[49] Moholy-Nagy instituted a rigorous schedule which included the participation of Klee, Kandinsky and Gropius as well as Albers.

The course was fully functioning by Spring 1923, and student response was enthusiastic. While Moholy-Nagy focused on theoretical issues in painting, sculpture and later photography, Albers concentrated on the practical ramifications of theory. Lux Feininger, Albers's student, commented on the changes which his teacher had brought to the program: "The concept of the course itself ... was so drastically changed by Albers that nothing but the name remained [the same]."[50]

Albers's overarching goal in the first semester of the preliminary course was to prepare his students for later craft studies in the workshops. He devised problems for them using wood, metal, glass, stone, textiles and paint so that they could study relationships and differences to develop an understanding of the fundamental properties of materials and the principles of construction. He applied the lessons he had learned in his own work as a student to his teaching. He changed the course from a subjective to an objective approach to visual problems, from a view which exaggerated individualism to a more methodical and logical constructivism. The students' results reflected self-discipline rather than self-expression. They had to justify every decision and process involved in their experimental constructions as a designer must justify the reasons for every aspect of a design. His rigorous demands focused on economy of means and materials: "If in a form there is something that is not utilized, then the calculation has been wrong, for coincidence then plays a part and that is unjustified and unjustifiable".[51]

Albers and Moholy-Nagy produced collaborative assemblage sculptures to demonstrate the architectonic, not expressive, applicability of materials. This "objective" approach challenged the autonomy of the fine arts in general and the validity of painting and of individual creativity in particular. They used photography first to emphasize the formal elements in their constructions by recording them in abstract space under carefully modulated lighting conditions. Gradually, Moholy-Nagy became increasingly involved in photography and declared that "traditional painting has become a historical relic and is finished with."[52] Their stress on the creation and appreciation of art as a collective experience based in technology was consistent with contemporary thought outside the Bauhaus, particularly in the writings of Walter Benjamin.[53]

The belief that the artist played a direct and creative role in the regeneration of the crafts had been implicit in all the Bauhaus workshops – the form master (a painter or sculptor) was viewed as a more prestigious position than the workshop master (a craftsman or technician). However, as the emphasis changed from crafts to industry, the position of the artist became increasingly ambiguous. Feininger captured the growing tension between the painters and Moholy-Nagy:

> Only optics, mechanics and the desire to put the old static painting out of action. There is incessant talk of cinema, optics, mechanical projections and continuous motion and even mechanically produced optical transparencies, multicolored, in the finest colors of the spectrum, which can be stored in the same way as gramophone records ... Is this the atmosphere in which painters like Klee and some others of us can go on developing? Klee was quite depressed yesterday when talking about Moholy.[54]

Moholy-Nagy, in his own work, experimented with air-brushes and spray guns to achieve "machine-like perfection". He stopped signing his paintings and identified them with numbers and letters on the back of the canvas "like cars, airplanes and other industrial products". In 1924, his exhibition at the Sturm Gallery included "enamel pictures executed by industrial methods" which had been produced by ordering the panels and colors by telephone from a factory. In these works, the artist who had produced art without applying paint to canvas came very close to the designer who conceptualized a design without being involved directly in the manufacturing process. Moholy-Nagy had achieved Gropius's aim for the Bauhaus, the shift from art through craft to art through technology. He declared: "In our industrial age, the distinction between art and non-art, between manual craftsmanship and mechanical technology is no longer an absolute one."[55]

The change of focus from craft to industry and the ambiguous position of the artist in the creative process led to the reversal of the role of art at the Bauhaus. In 1923, Gropius had argued that:

> Modern painting, breaking through old conventions, has released countless suggestions which are still waiting to be used by the practical world. But when in the future, artists who sense new creative values have practical training in the industrial world, they will themselves possess the means of realizing those values immediately. They will compel industry to serve their ideas and industry will seek out and use their comprehensive training.[56]

However, in spite of Gropius's optimism, instead of the spiritual, or even the formal, aspects of art influencing industrial design, artists searched for the precision of the machine in their art. Even Klee and Kandinsky, who had taught that visual analysis derived from personal experience could contribute to workshop practice, sought ways to quantify and absolutize their work "scientifically". Oscar Schlemmer described a survey that Kandinsky had conducted to prove quantitatively the definitive relationships of primary colors and forms:

> Kandinsky once organized a questionnaire. A circle, a square and a triangle were printed on a sheet of paper, and one was asked to fill each out in red, blue or yellow. I didn't take part. The results, although I don't know the precise statistics, were: circle – blue, square – red, triangle – yellow. All the learned men agreed about the yellow triangle but not the others. In any case, I unconsciously always make the circle red and the square blue. I don't know enough about Kandinsky's explanations, only in rough terms: the circle is the cosmic, absorbing, feminine, soft form; the square is the active, masculine … Kandinsky constructs an entire edifice of teaching on this dogma: every curved line is part of a circle and must therefore be blue, every straight line red, every point yellow, varied into infinity. During his lectures only hesitant voices are raised. Why? …[57]

While Kandinsky's own work did not reflect this rigidity, students came away from his lectures confused, or at least amused. Xanti Schawinsky explained his understanding of Kandinsky's ideas:

> Actually I am dough. What kneads me is time. When I came to the Bauhaus six months ago, I was a facade decorated with little motifs. Today I am a red cube (red, as I then discovered, is boiling in itself). Everything became clear, the cube is damned simple. And it boils anyway. I believe every one who comes to the Bauhaus undergoes a transformation. But the internal temperature depends on the boiling point of the individual. And that's the entire crazy point … The demand for clarity grows increasingly powerful in us. What our masters serve up is not compatible with our flesh and blood. But we've become different people nevertheless …[58]

In a January 1924 memorandum to the Council of Masters, Gerhard Marcks also expressed doubts about the direction which the Bauhaus was taking:

> We must always remember that the Bauhaus is intended to be a place of education; that means that people with a certain amount of talent and personality are trained for tasks which suit them – in our field to achieve something fit to serve as a model. We believe

> that productive work is the right way to attain this end. But production must never be the only end. Otherwise, the Bauhaus will become the 101st factory among the 100 that already exist, in other words, a matter of total indifference ...[59]

The tumultuous atmosphere of the Bauhaus was exacerbated by political events in the outside world that reverberated through all aspects of German life. In January 1923, French and Belgian troops occupied the Ruhr and the elimination of a major source of government income from this rich industrialized area sent the nation's already struggling economy into a financial crisis. In March, Gropius appeared before the Thuringian Landtag to defend the finances and policies of the Bauhaus which were under intense scrutiny in the light of the general economic situation. Dr Emil Herfurth accused the school of extravagance for having two masters for every workshop, prestigious painters and a theater. Other critics said the school had established few links with the crafts while some said that no viable relationships with industry had been created.[60]

Gropius begged for more time and more support arguing that the school would be more self-sufficient if the government gave it commissions, that it took three years to train a student and therefore the school hardly had time to demonstrate professional accomplishments, and that, in spite of these limitations, the Bauhaus "idea" had already achieved world-wide recognition. Fortunately, the school had the support of Dr Max Greil, the Minister of Education who welcomed Gropius's proposal to create prototypes for industrial production. He argued "considering that the experiment has been under way for three years, it would be the greatest folly to break up its development and to abandon the incomplete experiment at the moment when the Bauhaus is able to demonstrate what it is capable of achieving."[61] Herr Tenner, the Landtag representative of the Communist Party, also defended the school in its change of direction from an emphasis on crafts to industry.

While this support saved the day in 1923, by the following year, the Nationalists had gained a majority in the Thuringia Parliament, and they were totally opposed to what they perceived as the left-wing radicalism of the school. In spite of Gropius's attempts to launch a pro-Bauhaus campaign, the opposition was unmoved. In December 1924, the Landtag cut the school's grants and limited staff contracts to a six-month renewal basis, effectively making continued operation impossible. The Council of Masters voted immediately to close the school as of March 1925.

An invitation from the Mayor of Dessau, Fritz Hesse, to move the Bauhaus to his city offered a reprieve for the school. A five-year contract for Gropius and a commitment of funds for a new building with dormitories and faculty housing as well as commissions for other government buildings (a labor exchange and a housing development) seemed the ultimate solution to the problems of the Bauhaus. However, the tensions and unresolved issues that had plagued the school through its tenure at Weimar simply moved with its equipment to Dessau.

The tandem teaching system, basic to the Bauhaus program but also the symbol of ambiguity and the flashpoint of conflict, was discontinued. Herbert Bayer, Marcel Breuer, Hinnerk Scheper, Joost Schmidt, and Gunta Stölzl, star graduates of the Weimar Bauhaus program who saw themselves more as designers than artists, were appointed to the faculty. The curriculum, particularly under the leadership of Hannes Meyer and Ludwig Mies van der Rohe, increasingly emphasized the training of architects.

The star artists whose excitement and prestige had lured students and supporters to the school initially, remained in a state of uncertainty. Nina Kandinsky, wife of the artist, recalled:

> In Dessau Gropius was strangely transformed. It was not only that his interest in the Bauhaus noticeably faded, but also that his views had worryingly changed. It suddenly became fashionable to think that architecture was superior to painting. Architects and painters began to fight each other. The architect Taut published a book in which he tediously attacked pictures hanging on walls. Gropius obviously thought this correct ... His incomprehensible attitude left a painful impression on the painters ... After the barrier between technologists and painters had become higher and higher, Kandinsky asked him, 'Why did you invite so many painters here if you are basically hostile to painting?' Gropius had no answer to this. They were talking different languages ...[62]

In spite of the on-going tensions and conflicts, the Bauhaus succeeded. Gropius's goal, to train artists and designers to produce visual objects that reflected the modern age, was achieved on a scale he could only vaguely imagine at the time and to which he alluded in his speech in Stuttgart in May 1968. Students, artists, architects and designers throughout the world and for decades after the school closed communicated in the language of forms invented at the Bauhaus. They created works, from paintings and sculptures to lamps and furniture, from typography and graphics to housing, schools and offices, that have characterized the modern environment.

The Weimar Bauhaus and its more splendid manifestation at Dessau, like the Weimar Republic which was its context, was motivated by idealism to believe that it could bridge gaps and reconcile differences that ran far deeper than its limited powers to overcome. Like the Republic, the Bauhaus was a battleground of conflicting ideas of progress, universality, individuality and art. The vehemence with which each of these ideas was advocated at the expense of the others ultimately weakened the structure that supported it and left that structure vulnerable to the forces of darkness committed to its downfall. In the Fall of 1932, the Bauhaus buildings at Dessau became a school to train Nazi Party functionaries.

Notes

1 Henry Pachter, *Weimar Etudes*, New York, 1982, p. 91.

2 *Ibid.*, p. 130.

3 Frank Whitford (ed.), *The Bauhaus: Masters and Students by themselves*, Woodstock, New York, 1993, p. 25.

4 Peter Gay, *Weimar Culture: The Outsider as Insider*, New York, 1968, p. 9.

5 Walter Laqueur, *Weimar, A Cultural History, 1918–1933*, New York, 1974, p. 110.

6 John Willett, *Art and Politics in the Weimar Period*, New York, 1978, p. 45.

7 Gillian Naylor, *The Bauhaus Reassessed*, New York, 1985, p. 55.

8 Whitford, p. 25.

9 Stephanie Barron, *German Expressionism 1915–1925: The Second Generation*, Los Angeles, 1988, pp. 13–14.

10 Count Harry Kessler, May 1, 1919, *Tagebücher*, in Gay, p. 10.

11 Toni Stolper, *Ein Leben in Brennpunkten unserer Zeit: Gustav Stolper, 1888–1947* (1960), p. 211, in Gay, p. 2.

12 Kirk Varnedoe, *Vienna 1900: Art, Architecture and Design*, New York, 1986, p. 87.

13 Eckhard Neumann, *bauhaus and bauhaus people*, New York, 1970, p. 19.

14 Naylor, p. 17.

15 *Ibid.*, p. 18.

16 Kenneth Frampton, *Modern Architecture: a critical history*, London, 1992, p. 98.

17 Naylor, p. 50.

18 Walter Gropius, "Programm des Staatlichen Bauhauses in Weimar" (Weimar, April 1919) in Neumann, trans., p. 9.

19 Naylor, p. 56.

20 Herbert Bayer, Walter Gropius, Ise Gropius, *Bauhaus 1919–1928*, Boston: Charles T. Branford, 1959, p. 28.

21 Gropius, "Theory and Organization of the Bauhaus" in Bayer, *et al.*, p. 24.

22 *Ibid.*, p. 26.

23 Theo van Doesburg, *Grundbegriffe des neuen gestaltenden Kunst* (1925) in Bayer, *et al.*, p. 34.

24 Johannes Driesch, "Letter to Lydia Driesch-Foucar" (Weimar, October 16, 1919) in Whitford, p. 42.

25 Bayer *et al.*, p. 18.

26 Neumann, p. 45.

27 Naylor, p. 82.

28 Rainer Wick, *Bauhaus Pädagogik*, DuMont Buchverlag, 1982, p. 216.

29 Walter Gropius, at conference of "Free Association of Civic Interests" (December, 1919) in Naylor, p. 60.

30 *Ibid.*, p. 88.

31 Wassily Kandinsky, *Point and Line to Plane*, Dessau, 1926, quoted in Naylor, p. 92.

32 *Ibid.*, p. 93.

33 *Ibid.*, p. 67.

34 Walter Gropius, "Letter to Thuringian Cultural Ministry, Weimar" (March 31, 1920) in Whitford, p. 46.

35 Oskar Schlemmer, "Letter to Tut Schlemmer, on a Train Between Leipzig and Dresden" (July 13, 1920) in Whitford, p. 42.

36 Naylor, p. 110.

37 Hans Wingler, *The Bauhaus*, Cambridge, Mass., 1969, p. 314.

38 Naylor, p. 112.

39 *Ibid.*, p. 83.

40 Bayer, *et al.*, p. 90.

41 Walter Gropius, "Bauhaus Memorandum" (Weimar, February 3, 1922) in Whitford, p. 134.

42 Gerhard Marcks, "Reply to Gropius's Memorandum" (Weimar, February 16, 1922) in Whitford, p. 135.

43 Naylor, p. 97.

44 *Ibid.*

45 Paul Citroën, "On the Arrival of Moholy-Nagy at the Bauhaus" (1946) in Whitford, p. 165.

46 Laszlo Moholy-Nagy, "From Wine Jugs to Lighting Fixtures" in Bayer *et al.*, p. 134.

47 Wilhelm Wagenfeld, "On the Work of the Metal Workshop" in *Junge Menschen* (1924) in Whitford, p. 176.

48 Gunta Stölzl, "The Development of the Bauhaus Weaving Workshop," *Bauhaus Journal* 5 (1931) in Whitford, p. 86, Naylor, p. 109.

49 Naylor, p. 101.

50 *Ibid.*, p. 100.

51 *Ibid.*, p. 155.

52 Moholy-Nagy, *Painting, Photography, Film* (Dessau: Bauhaus Book, 1925) English trans. (London: Lund Humphries, 1969), p. 45.

53 See Walter Benjamin, "The Work of Art in the Age of Mechanical Reproduction" in Walter Benjamin, *Illuminations* (English trans., 1955).

54 Moholy-Nagy, *Painting, Photography, Film*, p. 146.

55 Moholy-Nagy, *New Vision*, p. 79.

56 Walter Gropius, "Theory and Organization of the Bauhaus" (1923) in Bayer *et al.*, p. 29.

57 Oskar Schlemmer, "Letter to Otto Meyer-Amden" (Weimar, January 3, 1926) in Whitford, p. 80.

58 Xanti Scharwinsky in *Junge Menschen* (1924) in Whitford, p. 119.

59 Gerhard Marcks, "Memorandum to Council of Masters" (Dornberg, January 2, 1924) in Whitford, p. 183.

60 Naylor, p. 103.

61 *Ibid.*, p. 104.

62 Nina Kandinsky, *Kandinsky und Ich* (1976) in Whitford, p. 218.

9

Did the Weimar Republic have a Golden Age?

By the end of 1924, the Republic appeared to have survived its crisis and to have entered a period of stability. The second election of 1924 had seen movement away from the extremes and towards those parties that were more supportive of the government. The period from 1924 to 1929 is often called the "Golden Age", when Germany achieved international acceptance, the currency was stable and production and real income were on the rise. Feme murders had ceased, and neither left-wing uprisings nor right-wing coup attempts threatened the very existence of the Republic itself. This stability was purchased at the price of great vision, effort and sacrifice by many, perhaps most of all by Walther Rathenau. The symbol of stability during the middle Weimar years was Gustav Stresemann who built on the work of the murdered Rathenau. The lives of these two men created the possibility of the Golden Age.

Walther Rathenau was the son and successor of Emil Rathenau, the founder of the Allgemeine Electrizitätsgesellschaft (AEG) one of Germany's major electrical companies. It had developed during the period of rapid industrialization in the late nineteenth century. Walther Rathenau combined business acumen with scholarly interests and envisioned a future society where capitalists and working men could create a harmonious and prosperous society and eliminate the evils of poverty and crime. On the eve of World War I, Rathenau was a member of the monarchist, militarist, expansionist camp. However, because he was a Jew, his acceptance in these circles was limited.

During the war, Rathenau served his country with distinction by establishing the War Raw Materials Section of the War Ministry. This section worked to make sure that scarce war materials went to companies engaged in critical war production. The war experience inspired him to abandon his militarist and expansionist views and to convert to a belief in a truly democratic representative government for Germany. Based on this commitment, he helped to found the Democratic Party. Because of Rathenau's war record and international business connections, Prince Max von Baden called upon him to help to end the carnage of the war. Concluding that it was his patriotic duty, but forever damning himself in the eyes of the right-wingers, he agreed to participate in the armistice and peace negotiations along with Matthias Erzberger. As a negotiator at Versailles, he fought doggedly for his country's interests and reacted with indignation to the allied attempts to prosecute some of Germany's leaders as war criminals.[1]

In the early Weimar years, Rathenau participated in the government as Minister of Reconstruction and then as Foreign Minister. He recognized that improved relations with the western powers were key to Germany's future. However, he devised a risky strategy to achieve this objective in part by negotiating the treaty of Rapollo in 1922 with the outcast, Communist Russia, in order to pressure the French and British to improve their treatment of Germany. This strategy of raising the specter of a relationship between the two outcasts, Germany and Russia, produced an angry reaction on the part of the English and the French. However, it may have contributed to their more open policy towards Germany.

Rathenau was aware of the problems that the new Weimar state faced in becoming a stable democratic Republic. He said in early 1919, "Now we have a Republic, the problem is we have no republicans."[2] He himself had become one of those republicans and was, in spite of an introverted personality, a fierce advocate of republican positions. He functioned in an atmosphere of violence and hatred and was the target of virulent right-wing attacks in the Reichstag by nationalist politicians such as Karl Helfferich. Feme groups added to the drumbeat of abuse with songs, one of which concluded with the line, "Shoot down Walther Rathenau, that God damned son of a Jewish sow."[3] He refused extra security and became a victim of Feme assassins. The loss of Rathenau in

1922 was a blow to the Republic, but his work was carried on and developed much further by Gustav Stresemann.

Stresemann led two cabinets as Chancellor from August through November 1923, the most chaotic period in the life of the Republic. He also served as Foreign Minister at that time and retained that post when he resigned his position as Chancellor in November 1923. He remained Foreign Minister until November 1929. He had written a thesis on the beer-brewing industry and combined the experiences of a business and academic background. He began World War I as a devoted monarchistic with expansionist war aims, but, by 1918, he had become convinced, as had Matthias Erzberger, Walther Rathenau and intellectuals such as Max Weber and Friedrich Meinecke, that Republican government was necessary for Germany.[4] Stresemann, along with these and other leaders, had become one of the reasonable men and women of the Republic. There was a difference between these reasonable people and the *vernunftrepublikaner* (the republicans of reason), a term used to highlight the reluctant support of many for the Republic. The republicans of reason identified the Republic as the lesser of evils, as the best possible government under the circumstances. They were often half-hearted and unenthusiastic and always hoped for a better alternative. The reasonable men and women were those who believed that the Republic was a positive step forward for Germany. They were convinced that republican government could be, in the later words of Winston Churchill, a situation "where everything is settled for the greatest good of the greatest number by the common sense of most, after the consultation of all."[5]

Stresemann believed that statesmen and political leaders had to be able to look at the big picture and act for the entire community or nation. He recognized that those extreme nationalists and racists who accused the democrats of acting in narrow self-interest were themselves champions of the narrowest self-interest. They used the rhetoric of community to exclude, and they rationalized their own personal short-term self-interest under the guise of national or racial goals. Stresemann was also chagrined that so few of the political leaders of Germany were capable of acting with a broad national vision. Although reluctant to state his judgment publicly for political reasons, he acknowledged privately that it was the socialist leaders who were more often willing to compromise the particularist goals of their constituents for larger communal interests. Unfortunately when they did so, they paid a price for their actions at the ballot box and on the streets. Most leaders of other parties never made the effort. Yet, in spite of catering to the narrow interests of as many of their party members and voters as they could, party leaders saw the proliferation of even narrower regional and one-issue small parties as documented in the later voting record of the Republic. The Golden Age of co-operation and stability was ephemeral at best.

The plight of Weimar's reasonable supporters, as well as that of its reluctant supporters, critics and enemies, was closely observed by the diplomat, diarist, *bon vivant* and acquaintance of all the movers and shakers, Count Harry Kessler. Kessler was born in Paris in 1868, the son of a Hamburg banker titled by Kaiser Wilhelm I. His mother was the famous Irish beauty, Alice Bosse-Lynch. His early education in France and England was completed at the Universities of Bonn and Leipzig. He served as an officer in the Uhlan Guards regiment and then held diplomatic positions. He was widely known in political, artistic and cultural circles and recorded his observations and encounters in great detail in his diaries. His sympathies were with the left and the Republic. Gustav Stresemann and Walther Rathenau were two of Kessler's acquaintances, and he witnessed their struggle for the life of the Republic. He heard Stresemann's commemorative speech in January 1922 following Rathenau's murder in which Stresemann spoke about his compatriot with great warmth. Kessler commented, "Impressive was the way he underlined the duty of everyone to render service to the state as it is (i.e., the Republic) and not to persist in a convenient opposition."[6]

Stresemann, along with Rathenau, was a leading architect of the policy of fulfillment. They reasoned that if Germany made a good faith effort to meet the demands of the Versailles Treaty, relations with France and England would substantially improve and would lead to effective modification of the limitations and reparations provisions. However, he had problems selling this policy to the members of his own party, the German National People's Party, with part of the membership still unresigned to the existence of the Republic. Thus, Stresemann had to struggle even to keep his own party's support for the fulfillment policy. He also had to confront the great bitterness that accompanied the French occupation of the Ruhr following a modest default in reparations payments in 1923. The occupation led to a policy of passive resistance, unemployment, strikes, acts of local violence and eventually surrender to prevent a total economic collapse. Stresemann's attempt at a program of fulfillment created great hostility among those on the extreme right, and violent anti-Stresemann slogans such as "Death to Stresemann" were voiced among violent Nationalists.

Britain was more willing to be flexible in response to Germany's problems than was France, particularly under Raymond Poincaré. When the French administration changed, France also began to exhibit a greater willingness to negotiate modifications in schedules and payments. However, these changes of heart and policy came much more slowly than Stresemann had hoped. That they came at all reflects the overall validity of his policy. In spite of the fierce domestic opposition and foreign resistance, Stresemann persevered, and slowly he made progress towards his goals.

International help contributed to Germany's economic recovery and political stabilization. Starting with the Dawes Plan, named for the American Secretary of the Treasury and later Vice-President Charles Dawes, a series of agreements provided foreign loans to aid in German economic development and to help Germany meet her obligations. The most onerous effect of Germany's financial burden had been rampant inflation. As Charles Maier has pointed out, the severity of Germany's economic problems resulted in part from the demands of the treaty and other international causes and in part from government policy and the resistance of industrialists and labor unions to make any sacrifices to help the government meet its obligations.[7] Stresemann hoped that he could convince many factions who played a role in German policy to act in the national interest. He pushed the English, the French and the Americans to give him concrete concessions and support so he could add positive prospects of improvement to his calls for sacrifice and a commitment to the national interest.

Stresemann gained Germany's admission to the League of Nations and convinced the French to end the occupation of the Ruhr and to begin the evacuation of the Rhineland. Germany became a party to a series of international agreements signed at Locarno, Switzerland which created an atmosphere of optimism that a period of sustained peace was at hand. The euphoria of the "Age Of Locarno" was best illustrated by the ubiquitous pictures of Stresemann addressing the League of Nations, a source of pride for many Germans. Pride was in short supply during the Weimar years. As Arnold Brecht reported, "German democracy lacked the richness of symbols in which other democracies rejoice."[8] There were no heroes, no martyrs, and, for most of the history of the Republic, there were no days of commemoration. New symbols can be created as Mussolini was to demonstrate in Italy and Hitler and the Nazis were to show in Germany. However, the Weimar leaders, who had been instrumental in destroying the monarchy, depriving the German people of the flag many of them cherished and disassociating the symbols of the Protestant Church from the state, were not sufficiently sensitive to the power of symbols. Their attempt in 1928 to create a "Constitution Day" commemorative event was too little too late.

In spite of Stresemann's great accomplishments as one of the most reasonable leaders of the Republic, he is open to some serious criticism. Henry Turner has described his role in the illegal rearmament of Germany. Convinced, as were almost all German leaders, of the fundamentally unjust limitations on the German military imposed by the Versailles Treaty, Stresemann played a role in evading those treaty terms while working towards a fulfillment policy in other areas.[9] These evasions were carried out by developing and building weapons on foreign soil and camouflaging budgetary items to finance this rearmament. An unfortunate consequence of these evasions was that many government leaders adopted a defensive attitude towards the press or zealous radical politicians who tried to push the government to reveal its policies to the public. They also led to associations between reasonable supporters of the Republic and reactionary military leaders. The need to keep treaty violations secret may have resulted in the obstruction of justice by members of government in Feme and labor battalion cases and in the arrest and prosecution of investigative reporters such as Carl von Ossietsky.[10]

Stresemann's decision during the presidential election of 1925 to announce his support for General Paul von Hindenburg, the candidate of the conservative nationalist forces, had profound practical and symbolic consequences. Had Stresemann really preferred Hindenburg, his action would have seriously called into question the extent of his support for the Republic. However, evidence indicates that he preferred Wilhelm Marx, the candidate of the strongest pro-Weimar forces.[11] Worried about losing the support of the more conservative elements of his own party, he felt compelled to support Hindenburg publicly while hoping and expecting that Marx would win. Unfortunately, his hopes and expectations were ill-founded.

The presidential election of 1925 was a major defeat for the reasonable supporters of the Republic. It called into question how far Germany had come as a country with a citizenry with republican values and underscored the problems the Republic faced even during its most stable and prosperous period. It was the first true popular election of the President. The National Assembly that wrote the Weimar Constitution had initially chosen Friedrich Ebert President, and the Reichstag had extended his term in 1922.

Stresemann had commented that, in spite of his working-class background, the working people had not loved Ebert while the educated classes spoke of him with respect.[12] He was, on one level, a logical choice to be President almost in the Hegelian sense that he personified a further step on the road to greater freedom. Ebert was the political leader who symbolized the elections of 1912 in which the Social Democrats received one out of every three votes cast. He was the embodiment of the *Burgfrieden* during the early years of the war when Social Democrats gained a role in policy-making for the first time. He was known as a patriot who had lost two sons on the battlefield, and he was also the choice of Prince Max von Baden who was the last imperial Chancellor. He was a progressive and represented the possibility of a new democratic Germany.

When he became President, Ebert announced that he would be President of all the people, and he meant it. "I want to be and will act as the representative of the entire German people not as the leader of one political party."[13] At times, when he acted in what he thought was the national interest, he antagonized his old Social Democratic and union comrades. In spite of the bitterly critical caricatures of the satirist George Grosz, Ebert was *anständig* (morally upright). Yet he was no hero, and his reception at public gatherings, even those of Social Democratic workers, was cool and polite but unenthusiastic.

In spite of the lack of public enthusiasm for Ebert, there was little doubt that he would have been elected President in 1925, if he had not died unexpectedly. Social Democrats would have voted for him out of party discipline. Many middle-class Germans would have supported him because they had become accustomed to him in power and thought of him as a competent chief executive. They appreciated his accomplishments as an individual and ceased to see him as a Social Democrat. The best indication of his likely victory was that, until his death, none of the opposition parties was working hard to field an opponent.

Ebert's death created a real campaign for the presidency and a test for the new democracy. According to the Weimar Constitution, a majority of the votes cast was necessary for a candidate to win the election for President on the first ballot. Since there were many parties and multiple candidates, the vote was fragmented. Several of the parties on the political right were able to agree on a common candidate while the center left and the extreme right ran their own candidates. The results of this election were Jarres (DNVP, DVP, *Wirtschafliche Vereinigung*) 10,787,870, Braun (SPD) 7,836,676, Held (Bayr.V.P.) 990,036, Hellpach (Dem) 1,582,414, Ludendorff (*Völkisch*) 210,968, Marx (Ztr.) 3,988,659, Thälmann (KPD) 1,885,778.

The jockeying for coalitions began on the second ballot. The major pro-republican coalition partners, the SPD, *Zentrum* and the DDP, met to decide on a common candidate. Otto Braun had much to recommend him. The Minister-President of Prussia had received nearly eight million votes, and he was the best speaker and politician among the candidates. He also headed a Prussian coalition government which included Centrists, Democrats and even members of the People's Party. However, the leaders of the Center and Democratic Parties worried that many of their supporters would not vote for a Socialist and rejected the choice of Braun. The Social Democrats gave way in the interest of harmony. This decision was probably a mistake since Braun would have been a more effective candidate. While the SPD demonstrated its willingness to compromise and its ability to go beyond the working class, it also showed lack of conviction and strength. Clearly they could have played the Ebert card more strongly by arguing that most Centrists and Democrats would have voted for Ebert, a Socialist from a working-class background and by stressing Braun's ability to work with members of many parties as Ebert had done. The middle-class centrist parties evidenced their class prejudice and more narrow focus by backing Wilhelm Marx who became the left-center coalition candidate. A Catholic and a colorless speaker, he lost Protestant votes, could not carry the heavily-Catholic but more conservative Bavarian People's Party and inspired no one.

The coalition who had supported Jarres realized that he had already achieved his maximum vote and that, if they wished to win, they needed a candidate with wider appeal. They decided on General Hindenburg. The Communists continued to run their own candidate. When the votes were counted, the results were Hindenburg 14,655,766, Marx 13,751,615, Thälmann 1,931,151. Since the Constitution mandated that only a plurality was required on the second ballot, Hindenburg was elected.

Historians have argued that, if the Communists had supported Marx as some within the Communist International wished, Hindenburg could have been defeated. However, when the history of relations between the Communists and the Social Democrats is considered and given the unreconciled nature of the Communist Party, Communist support for a bourgeois candidate with Socialist backing seems almost inconceivable. Even had the Communists made this amazing move, the results cannot have been predicted by simple addition. While it is true that Communist voters were very disciplined, there would have been some defections in this case. It is impossible to know how many Catholic and other centrist voters might have been lost to Marx if he had Communist backing. A more promising strategy which might have made a difference would have been for the Communists to have released their voters with no official directions. Had they then let it be known that they preferred a vote for Marx without an official endorsement, Marx might have gained enough votes to win. However, that strategy would have required a larger view of events than the German Communist leadership could generate.

The winner was thus General Hindenburg, a national hero, but he had been a hero of the Empire not of the Republic. Hindenburg's success testifies to the aura of heroes. The reasons why certain individuals become and remain heroes appears to defy all logic. It is true that Hindenburg came from an old-line aristocratic family, and had reached the highest military rank. He was also identified with great early military victories on the eastern front.

However, he was in charge of the army and the state when Germany was defeated, and he played a major role in that defeat. Hindenburg was a prominent voice in convincing the Kaiser to abdicate and to flee to the Netherlands, although he always considered himself a monarchist. He lied consistently about the reasons for German surrender and played a role in developing the "stab in the back" legend. He posed as a symbol of moral uprightness, but he was not *anständig*. While presenting himself as an unpolitical man, he harbored personal political ambition and narrow partisan interests.[14] He claimed, as had Ebert, that he spoke for all the people, but he truly represented only a very limited part of the political spectrum. He regularly sacrificed national interest for the interest of the landed aristocrats and others in his circle. While he would technically support the Constitution, he was at best unenthusiastic about the Republic and its values. Through his choice of Chancellors and his willingness to use presidential emergency powers, he would contribute to the subversion of the Republic.

As an added note of irony, the man who was sent to convince General Hindenburg to run for President, although it is questionable whether he needed much convincing, was Admiral Tirpitz. The Admiral had maintained his image as hero although he contributed to a naval policy which was a precipitating factor in the war. His over-emphasis on the importance of naval power had the effect, in a time of limited funds available for armaments, of weakening the army. He favored a policy of unlimited submarine warfare provoking the United States into battle. His fleet fought little and with little effect, and his role in the decision for one last great battle contributed to a naval revolt. In addition, he was a major organizer of the Fatherland Party in 1917 which, in its platform of wide-ranging military expansion and racist anti-Semitism, presaged much that the Nazis would deliver. Thus, the election of General Hindenburg, "pushed" to run by Admiral Tirpitz, was a giant step backwards from the realization of a broadly based democracy. As Horst Möller has written, "The course of his (Hindenburg's) life was so symbolic of the past, while Ebert's was so symbolic for the new, for today for tomorrow. What a paradox that Ebert came before Hindenburg and not after him."[15]

Stresemann's decision to support Hindenburg publicly can be seen in the same light as David Lloyd George's accedence to the terms of the Versailles Treaty against his better judgment. It suggests the difficulties of trying to be statesman and party leader at the same time. As Foreign Minister, Stresemann had to cope with the President's narrow focus in dealing with the western powers. Wringing his hands at the problems of trying to explain foreign policy to Hindenburg, Stresemann persevered.

In 1928, at the Second Reparations Conference, he negotiated the Young Plan which gained reparations concessions for Germany. The plan, named for the American Owen D. Young, earned Young *Time Magazine*'s nod as the Man of the Year in 1929 and launched Stresemann on his last great political battle. The Second Reparations Conference was convened to reassess Germany's financial burden; it was attended by the Allied powers and Germany. The resulting reductions in reparations were not all that Stresemann had hoped for, but they were consistent with his fulfillment policy which traded German compliance for Allied consideration. However, the voices of opposition rejected the payment of any reparations just as they rejected any culpability for the war itself. Conservative and radical right parties united to try to defeat Germany's acceptance of the plan. The Conservatives and the Nazis, led by Hugenberg and Hitler, joined forces to generate a popular petition for a plebiscite as provided for in the Weimar Constitution. Unfortunately for them, the majority of the electorate saw the benefit of the Young Plan and approved it. While the opponents failed in their specific objective, they developed a unity which far exceeded that of the forces who rallied, often with little passion and enthusiasm, to support Stresemann's policies.

Stresemann's supporters in the business community did recognize that the Young Plan, like the Dawes Plan four years before it, made sense for Germany. Both agreements did not solve the reparations problems, but they made them more manageable. Their passage also spoke to the international financial and business communities about the reasonableness of Germans and encouraged the increased flow of investment and loans. I. G. Farben, created by the combination of five major chemical and dye companies, was the world's largest chemical conglomerate. Its leaders, Carl Bosch and Carl Duisberg, were primarily concerned with stability in the interest of a favorable business climate at home and abroad. They were major supporters of Stresemann because they believed that his policies encouraged improved relations between Germany and England, France and the United States and kept the peace between business and labor at home. "They made Farben the foremost corporate supporter of the man and the group that came to embody them best, Gustav Stresemann and the German People's Party (DVP)."[16] Stresemann's death in 1929 was a great blow to Farben and the Republic but spared him from some desperate battles which were just over the horizon.

The period of stability for the Republic was very short, while the development of democratic institutions and practices takes considerable time. Grooming democratic citizens was a complex process as well. Germany had to be re-schooled which required an educational system more in tune with the values that define citizens in a Republic. There had been attempts to reform education in the years before World War I such as Alfred Lichtwark's use of art to promote individual creative thinking in Hamburg and George Kirschensteiner's theory of the active involvement of the student in Munich.[17] However, these were small-scale uncoordinated efforts. The Weimar Constitution and legislation by the various states were more ambitious in their attempts to change the nature of the educational system. Two contemporary observers called the new Constitution, "the Magna Carta of the new German Schools."[18] Article 146 of the Constitution declared:

> The system of public schools shall be organically developed. The intermediate and secondary schools shall be built up on the basis of common elementary schools. This system shall be determined by the needs of all kinds of vocations, and for the reception of a child into a particular school, his abilities and inclinations shall be the deciding factor, not the economic and social status or the religious confession of his parents.

Under the Empire, students were tested at age nine and moved into one of three tracks. The most prestigious was the classical Gymnasium which stressed Greek and Latin, history and literature and was the path to the *Abitur* examination which led to the universities, the professions and many government positions. The second was the *Realschule* which stressed the sciences and modern languages and could lead to technical colleges and business jobs. The third track continued students in the *Volkschule*, and led to apprenticeships for trades. There were additional options for female students who could attend the Lyceen, Oberlyceen, and Mädchen Gymnasium. In the pre-war years, a few experiments promoted longer common elementary programs, allowed later switches, and enabled *Realschule* students to take the *Abitur* exam to attend universities. Female students were also allowed to gain admission to universities. Many middle-class parents who were eager to increase the likelihood that their children would be admitted to universities sent them to private preschools (*Vorschule*) in order to give them a head start on their quest.

While these experiments with overall reform were quite limited in the pre-war period, education reformers hoped that the Republic would make these changes on a large scale. The writers of the Constitution, in order to level the playing field, outlawed the preschools in Article 147. Regulation of university and technical college education was placed in the hands of the central government, while secondary and primary education was left up to state officials. Progressive education appeared to have the greatest scope for reform in Prussia where the state instituted modest changes. They narrowed the gap somewhat between the education of males and females, enabling more young women to attend universities. They raised the age of testing from nine to ten and increased the possibility of transfer from one track to another. Yet, little progress was made towards the creation of longer periods of common schooling, and the dominance of the Gymnasiums remained. The conflicts which developed between the more secular-minded Social Democrats and the representatives of the Catholic Center Party over the role of religion and religious bodies in the schools were obstacles to all school reform.

Education reformers advocated the need for civic education for the German public. They hoped that the elementary and secondary schools would provide their young boy and girl students with effective critical education necessary for democracy. However, as one observer commented, "All school reforms stand or fall with the teacher."[19] Most Weimar teachers were not democratic, and the problem intensified the further up the grade ladder one went. Secondary school teachers were more undemocratic than elementary level teachers and more under the influence of reactionary university professors. The Gymnasiums were seen as

Lernschule, where rigid rote methods of teaching geared to specific examinations were sometimes modified by an attempt to impart *Bildung*, translated by the Brockhaus Dictionary of the 1920s as "cultivation of the soul." Neither approach did much to create critical citizens with an understanding of politics or democratic processes.

Some progress was made in the area of adult education, and college level courses were given at evening continuation schools. The most successful of these institutions was loosely attached to the University of Frankfurt. Its courses were often taught by distinguished scholars who had not attained university positions because of their political affiliations or because they were Jews. A number of these scholars, such as Franz Neumann and Herbert Marcuse, lectured to classes of workers as part of their commitment to raise the consciousness of these workers and make them a political force for economic and social change. While the workers were a deferential group of students, it is not likely that they understood much of the course material which may have been designed to address the problems of the working class but was presented in the language of Kant, Hegel and Marx.

Pro-republican newspapers failed to influence the electrorate significantly. The problem of creating a sophisticated and critical electorate from a population with little political education and practice at decision-making was formidable. Just navigating through the newspapers of the day and understanding the differences in intent and technique among them was a substantial chore for the general reading public. Germany's finest newspapers, those with world-wide reputations such as the *Frankfurter Zeitung* of the Sonnemann family, the *Vossische Zeitung* of the Ullsteins, and the *Berliner Tageblatt* of the Mosses, were intellectually demanding publications that tried to maintain editorial neutrality and present balanced reporting and commentary. The Ullstein organization, through its many papers, reached about one million people a day. However it did not use its papers to promote republican values or to support the Republic strongly.[20] On the other hand, the Social Democratic and Communist newspapers on the left and the Nationalist and Nazi newspapers on the right made no attempt at neutrality and balance. While the Social Democratic press was pro-republican, it was drowned out by the shriller voices of the extremist press. Thus, most Germans had to choose between newspapers which had a subtle political message, no clear message at all, and extreme anti-Republican rhetoric.

With the schools not being geared to create critically thinking citizens and with the newspapers not doing what they might have to clarify issues, citizenship development did not progress very quickly. This was especially unfortunate during the peaceful middle period of the Republic. It was under these conditions, when people were not continually beset by crisis and when the shrill voices of the extremists generated less resonance, that real progress towards the creation of Republicans could have been made.

While Walther Rathenau and Gustav Stresemann steered Germany towards a reasonable course in foreign affairs and while Otto Braun and Carl Severing developed reasonable and successful policies on the Prussian state level, no dynamic leaders on the national level commanded the broad popular appeal needed to rally support for the Republic. A magnetic Republican leader would have been a significant force for the creation of more Republicans. With little inspiration from political leaders and little encouragement for democracy from the pulpit or the teacher's desk, the political education of many Germans made little progress. Left-wing intellectuals who were among the most creative element in the society were also not inclined to strengthen and support the Republic. The charismatic leader that was lacking among the Republicans was in Germany at the time, but he led the Nazi movement pledged to destroy the Republic.

Notes

1 David Felix, *Walter Rathenau and the Weimar Republic: The Politics of Reparations*, Baltimore, 1971.

2 Harry Kessler, *In the Twenties, the Diaries of Harry Kessler*, trans. Charles Kessler, New York, 1971, p. 71.

3 Louis L. Snyder, *The Weimar Republic*, Princeton, New Jersey, 1966, p. 152.

4 Robert A. Pois, *Friedrich Meinecke and German Politics in the Twentieth Century*, Berkeley, Cal., 1972, p. 25.

5 Winston Churchill, *Memoirs of the Second World War*, (one volume abridgement), Boston, 1987, p. 210.

6 Kessler, *In the Twenties*, p.186.

7 Charles Maier, *Recasting Bourgeois Europe: Stabilization in France,*

Germany and Italy in the Decade after World War I, Princeton, New Jersey, 1975.

8 Arnold Brecht, *The Political Education of Arnold Brecht: an autobiography, 1884–1970*, Princeton, New Jersey, 1970, pp. 215–16.

9 Henry Ashby Turner, *Stresemann and the Politics of the Weimar Republic*, Princeton, New Jersey, 1963.

10 Istvan Deak, *Weimar Germany's Left-Wing Intellectuals, A Political History of the Weltbühne and its Circle*, Berkeley, Cal., 1968, p. 189.

11 Kessler, *In the Twenties*, p. 263–5.

12 Horst Möller, *Weimar: Die unvollendete Demokratie*, München, 1985, p. 59.

13 Cuno Horkenbach (ed.), *Das Deutsche Reich von 1918 bis Heute*, Vol. I, Berlin, 1930, p. 131.

14 Andreas Dorpalen, *Hindenburg And the Weimar Republic*, Princeton, New Jersey, 1964.

15 Möller, *Weimar*, p. 66.

16 Peter Hayes, *Industry and Ideology: I. G. Farben in the Nazi Era*, Cambridgeshire, 1987, p. 48.

17 Arthur Hearndon, *Education, in the Two Germanies*, Oxford, 1974, p. 22.

18 Thomas Alexander and Beryl Parker, *The New Education in the German Republic*, New York, 1929, p. 243.

19 *Ibid.*, p. 319.

20 Modris Eksteins, *The Limits of Reason, The German Democratic Press and the Collapse of Weimar Democracy*, Oxford, 1975.

10

The German economy and the Weimar Republic

Economic factors played a role in the failure of the Weimar Republic as they did in the ultimate success of the Nazis. They were not, however, the only factors nor necessarily the decisive ones. The actions of political leaders, industrialists, land owners and union leaders contributed equally to the intensity of conflict that characterized the period. Their failure to deal effectively with economic developments exacerbated the problems and was often more significant than the realities of the crises themselves. It is true that, for some Weimar Germans as for some people in all societies at all times, economic considerations were their primary motivating drives. In times of crisis, such as the inflationary period which reached its height in 1923 and the depression which began in 1929, many people devoted much attention to economic issues which influenced politics and society as well as the marketplace. However, economic motivation was only part of the mix of factors determining behavior during the Weimar years. While these difficulties challenged the structure and strength of the new state, they did not make the failure of the Republic inevitable. As Donald Kagan writes, "modern democracies, at least, have shown that the masses may be moved not always, certainly not solely, by vulgar material self-interest."[1] Thus, economic factors were part of a matrix of forces within which the Weimar Republic evolved.

The nation emerged from defeat in a long and costly war that had tested and then overwhelmed her industrial strength. Germany had entered the war as the greatest industrial power on the European continent. In the course of half a century, Germany had overtaken Britain, which had been the world's first great industrial power and which, at the mid-point of the nineteenth century, had dwarfed Germany as a producing nation. In 1910, Germany produced 13.1 million tons of pig iron and 13 million tons of crude steel as compared with Britain's 10.2 million tons of pig iron and 7.6 million tons of crude steel.[2] Germany had built railroads, a merchant marine and a machinery industry at a very rapid rate. Two separate industrial sectors had catapulted the nation into the status of a major industrial power: heavy industries such as iron, steel and coal which catered mainly to domestic markets; and newer industries such as the chemical and electrical industries which concentrated on foreign markets. German industrialization was shaped by the the active role of government in the process, the primary role of large financial institutions and the speed of growth and large size of the production units.

Germany had developed a large and active labor movement which was focused around three different trade union organizations: the largest unions, called the free unions, closely allied to the Social Democrats; the Christian trade unions founded by members of the Catholic Center Party; and the so-called Hirsch Dunker Unions patterned on the non-ideological approach of the British trade unions but most sympathetic to the middle of the road secular parties.[3] During the war and in the earliest crisis years, organizers from all three union groups, as well as some of the more radical members of the lower middle class, worked with some success to organize salaried employees. However, most salaried employees were motivated to avoid these unions by a strong sense of class identity and a fear of being proletarianized. Furthermore, their great inclination towards nationalism and anti-Semitism drew them towards the *Deutschnationale Handlesgehilfen Verband* (DHV), Germany's largest white-collar union.[4] It identified first with the Nationalists and later with the Nazis.

The economic burden shouldered by the new Republic was compounded by the method by which Germany had financed the war. Karl Helfferich, the Secretary of the Treasury, announced to the Reichstag in 1914 that Germany was going to finance the war exclusively through borrowing.[5] While this strategy was the most politically-expedient method of war financing, it was the least sound from the financial point of view. The most sound approach would have been through increased taxation which would not have led to a huge national debt or inflated currency. However, after a period of sustained prosperity from 1896 to 1913, the German economy had turned down, and many economists and government financial experts worried that 1913 was the beginning of a depression cycle. They believed that increased taxes were likely to fuel a continued depression.

Without political leadership from the Kaiser, the executive branch did not feel strong enough to call for increased taxes under these uncertain circumstances. Political party leaders, fearful of shattering *Burgfrieden*, the fragile alliance agreed to by all the parties, were disinclined to call for increased taxes from the legislature. Certainly Generals Hindenburg and Ludendorff, who were making most of the major decisions in the last years of the war but had neither a constitutional or popular mandate for their actions, were not going to call for increased taxes. After the first year of the war, the Reichstag did raise some taxes, but tax revenue paid for little of the war effort, less than the French and far less than the British.

One of the first financial steps the government took as it prepared for war was to change the nature of the German currency. In 1875, the recently unified Empire had standardized the currencies of its twenty-six component states by creating the German mark. The government had also switched from a silver standard of backing its money to a gold standard. According to the Bank Law of 1875, German money had to be backed at least one-third by gold and the rest by three-month discounted bills adequately guaranteed. In 1913, the German mark, the British shilling, the French franc and the Italian lira were all valued at between four and five to the American dollar.[6] When the war began, the German government moved to protect its gold supply and provide a way of paying for the war. As of August 14, 1914, the ability to redeem currency for gold was suspended. Germany had gone off the gold standard and a new system of loan banks were set up to issue currency. Whereas the earlier issuing banks had to back their currency with gold and collateralized paper, these new banks had no such restrictions and just printed money. During the war, Germany's national debt, which had been a modest 300 million marks on the eve of the war, rose to 51 billion 200 million marks by its end.[7] In 1913 there were 6.6 billion marks in circulation while by 1918 33.1 billion marks circulated.[8]

This program of war financing precipitated the monetary inflation which was to continue through 1923. Prices of all goods and services rose because they were not pegged to the quantity of goods in circulation as was done in World War II and since rationing was thwarted by a huge black market. Therefore, soon more and more marks were chasing fewer and fewer goods.[9] The cost of living rose nearly twelve times in Germany during the war while it rose by a factor of three in the United States, four in Britain and seven in France.[10] Wage increases did not match the increase in the cost of living for the working class, but the workers' plight was eased by the intercession of the military in labor-owner negotiations. The generals intervened in the interest of continued co-operation with the Social Democratic Party and the prevention of labor unrest and disturbances which could threaten war materials production.[11]

There was no such intervention on behalf of the middle classes and their standard of living suffered the greatest percentage of decline during the war years. The relatively positive treatment of trade union workers continued during late 1918 and early 1919 when employers feared radical revolution, anarchy and the socialization of industry.[12] They wanted to strengthen labor unions whose leaders, fearing their own loss of power and the collapse of their organizations as well as the whole economy, were taking moderate positions and opposing revolution. The mutual fears of employers and union leaders led to the Stinnes-Legien Agreement of November 15, 1918 and to an agreement on the eight-hour working day, a major long-standing union demand.[13]

Employers' fear of more radical change motivated the pro-business political parties to accept tax changes and financial reforms introduced by Matthias Erzberger, the Republic's first Minister of Finance. Erzberger created a progressive income tax placing the major burden on the wealthy and the corporations. He also sponsored an increased inheritance tax which was accepted.

However, the economic burden created by the Treaty of Versailles and the almost constant political crisis made continued reform and even effective implementation of new tax policies extremely difficult. The thirteen per cent of the territory that Germany lost as a result of the treaty had been rich in agricultural and mineral resources. Germany had also lost 74.5 per cent of its iron ore, 68.1 per cent of its zinc ore and 26 per cent of its coal production.[14] In addition to these and other losses, the nation had to make huge deliveries of ships, locomotives and railroad cars to the victorious powers. Thus, the Germany that coped with the sharply increased national debt, the inflated currency and huge cash reparations payments, initially estimated at 132 billion marks pre-war currency value, was considerably poorer than the Germany of 1914. German industrial production at the end of the war was, using the 1913 figures (=100%), almost halved (=57%) by 1918.[15] The government also faced the enormous task of reintegrating ten million returning soldiers into the economy.

While the initial willingness of industrialists and trade union leaders to compromise and be co-operative helped considerably to improve the German economic situation, as soon as it appeared that the danger of radical socialist revolution had passed, the co-operative attitudes disappeared and narrow short-range interest came to the fore. The government struggled to rebuild the economy and to meet the obligations of the Versailles Treaty in the face of diminishing co-operation from business and labor and the demands of coalitions of political parties. The pressure to inflate the currency further became greater and greater. Germany was unsuccessful in the early Weimar years in getting help in the international money markets or in encouraging foreign investment and had drawn down gold reserves which were important to international exchange. As tax revenue failed to meet budgetary requirements, more money was printed. However, as Charles Maier cautions:

> It is important to reiterate that the inflation was not rooted in balance of payments or reparations difficulties, troublesome though these could be. It represented a particular outcome of political struggles at home. The frantic resort to the printing press was a form of taxation imposed by the prevailing industrial forces upon the weaker elements and was lent a degree of public approval because of prevailing bewilderment about the cause of inflation and general acceptance of the right's thesis that ultimately the allies were to blame.[16]

This form of taxation, in contrast to more straight-forward forms, did not take money out of circulation but circulated more devalued currency, aiding the heavily mortgaged industrialists and heavily taxing those on fixed incomes such as pensioners, those living on savings and students with stipends. It also hurt white-collar workers on salaries who could only renegotiate their remuneration over time and with difficulty. This latter group included clerks, civil servants, secondary and elementary level teachers and university professors.

Industrialists used the situation to pay off large debts and ignored the devastating effects the inflation was having on many. Exporters benefited from the low cost of German goods abroad and the advantage of being paid in foreign currency. A contemporary observer described other material benefits which accrued as a result of the policy of inflation in the years before 1923 when the situation reached the hyper-inflationary stage: "The returns from the sale of money abroad much more than balanced the losses on international trade in merchandise and capital items, and domestic production seems, on the whole, to have been substantially greater than would presumably have been achieved under a stable monetary standard."[17] Germany also paid less in reparations during these years as a result of this inflation. Yet German industrial production was still far below its pre-war levels. It was only about 55 per cent in 1923 of what it had been in 1913.[18]

Whatever benefits may have accrued to public finance and production from the inflation, its negative effects far outweighed the positive. The enormously unequal economic impact and the ruin it brought to many contributed to undermining confidence in the Republic for broad segments of the population. Thus politically and psychologically, the inflation attacked the very fabric of the Weimar state dependent on public support and co-operation. Broad segments of the middle class lost their savings making their fear of proletarianization a reality.

The character Pinneberg in Hans Fallada's novel *Kleiner Mann, was nun?* (*Little Man, What Now?*) struggles to preserve what he feels is his dignity as a middle-class clerk in the face of inflation and the derision of his wife's working-class family.[19] While white collar workers had special benefits, higher earnings and greater prestige in the pre-war years, the effects of the war and the inflation had placed them at a disadvantage. Pinneberg tries to distinguish himself from his working-class in-laws: "It's not just a question of money. We think differently from most working men, our needs are different." His response, taken as unfounded arrogance by his in-laws, gets a hostile reply: "Yes. And why? Because you're paid by the month instead of the week. Because you work overtime without pay. Because you don't mind being paid under scale. Because you never go out on strike. Because you're always scabs."[20]

Fallada ironically describes Pinneberg's wife's family as being unhappy about the marriage because they think that her white collar husband has a decreasing standard of living, no security, no protection and no one to negotiate for him. Thus, a reversal had taken place, and a class of people who had emphasized their status and monetary advantageous as compared to the working class in the pre-war era felt humiliated, angry and bitter. They directed much of that hostility towards the new Weimar government. While significant numbers of white collar workers had initially voted for middle of the road pro-Weimar parties, they quickly abandoned this support and shifted to the right. Many would ultimately support the Nazis.

Some of the most vulnerable members of German society were particularly hard hit by the inflation. War widows, orphans and disabled veterans, who were supported on, at best, modest government benefits, found themselves unable to acquire the basic necessities. They had to appeal to private charities which had limited funds for aid. Trapped by their fixed income and physical limitations, their situation deteriorated as inflation increased.

Members of the working class counted on their leaders to protect them from the inflation, and for a while that trust was well founded. Union leaders worked quickly to renegotiate wages for their members to keep up with inflation. As long as they could do so, they did not worry about the effects on the society as a whole.

The rural segment of the economy fared unevenly during this period. Large land owners, like the industrialists, could pay off debts. Family farmers who grew food in areas such as Bavaria did well during the first years of the inflation. However, agricultural workers who were on low fixed wages and did not have unions to protect them fared badly.

The French and Belgian decision to occupy the Ruhr in January 1923 in response to a minor default on reparations payments brought the inflationary situation to its final crisis phase. The Weimar government decided to initiate a policy of passive resistance to the occupation and asked workers not to work and owners to close plants and factories. This policy brought political support, but it was an economic disaster for many. The primary casualty was state finances. Unemployment rose; production and tax revenue dropped. In order to maintain public support and political coalition unity, the government offered aid to idle striking workers and non-producing industrialists. Following the end of passive resistance, further compensation was offered to industrialists for their losses. The ruling coalition refused to raise tax rates to compensate for money spent and lost revenues. Once again, the government turned to the printing presses. By this time, whatever benefits might have resulted from inflation were dwarfed by a currency situation which was now out of control.

Thus in 1923, Germany entered a state of hyper-inflation which would so scar the German psyche that the mere mention of inflation in Germany more than seventy years later can topple ministers and raise public alarm. By November 1923, the German mark, which had traded at 4.2 to the American dollar in July 1914, was trading at 4.2 trillion marks to the dollar, although it was not really trading at all because no one wanted it. At this point, there were no longer any real winners in the inflation. Other nations refused to accept German marks. Inflation far exceeded the unions' capacity to renegotiate contracts. Even farmers with food to sell found the normally inelastic demand for their products shrinking. Malnourished elements of the population had no assets to trade for food and no currency that anyone would accept. All property invested at fixed money values such as government bonds, mortgage bonds and savings bank deposits became worthless. Many people had their life savings wiped out. In the worst days of the height of the inflation, workers who could still manage it demanded that they be paid twice a day and given an hour off after each payment so that they could spend the money before it further depreciated.

By the end of 1923, the inflation was for all purposes over because the mark had lost all exchange value. A new currency was needed, and the public had to be convinced that no further devaluation was possible. The government needed money to operate and some sort of balanced budget. International negotiations, which led to the end of the Ruhr resistance and a suspension of reparations payments, helped stabilize the situation. A new currency, the Rentenmark, was issued based on the collateral of agricultural and industrial debt. This insubstantial basis was enough to stabilize the currency as confidence increased with international support. The negotiation of the Dawes Plan provided a substantial gold fund, loans for economic recovery and reparations relief. However, by the time the Dawes Plan was negotiated, the currency had already been stabilized. The basis of this stability was not the borrowed gold, but a balanced budget, a restricted quantity of currency and restored confidence in the soundness of the currency within Germany and abroad.

Following a difficult debate in the Reichstag, the Dawes Plan was passed. The French evacuated the Ruhr and the German economy rapidly improved. Although the recovery was not uniform, for example it did not extend to the agricultural sector and never cured unemployment, the period from 1924 to 1929 represented a positive change for many Germans. By 1927, Germany, though reduced in size and resources, was producing at pre-war rates. By 1929 Germany had become the world's second industrial power behind the United States. Real wages rose, and the standard of living for many increased dramatically. The gains that labor made during these years included binding compulsory arbitration of contract disputes, relatively high and industry-wide wage rates, increased unemployment insurance, many social welfare measures and large public works programs.[21]

The relative prosperity of this middle period was reflected in the Reichstag elections of 1928 when the pro-Weimar parties, particularly the Social Democrats, did well and the anti-Weimar parties lost ground. A less positive election result was that it gave electoral reinforcement to a decision that the Social Democratic Party had made in 1924. They had decided not to participate in ruling coalition governments on the national level and argued that, as an opposition party, they could defend the interest of their constituents without compromise. From 1924 to 1928, they implemented this strategy rather effectively, and this posture contributed to their electoral success in 1928. However, at the same time, they avoided responsibility for the overall running of the government and for the broader national interest. Their uncompromising advocacy of a narrow interest position contributed to creating a wage scale and level of social programs that exacerbated Germany's later economic problems. They rejoined and dominated the government coalition from 1928 to 1930, but, when the going got tough in 1930, they fled from government responsibility as they had in 1924. In these later years, they could do little for their constituents and failed to work for the general interest of the Republic when they were badly needed. The positive effect on their fortunes that opposition status had given them from 1924 to 1928 was not repeated, and the lesson they learned in the middle period was ultimately an unfortunate one for German democracy.

In spite of stabilization and growing prosperity, the bitterness of those who were ruined by the inflation would never disappear, and they remained fierce opponents of the Republic. Salaried employees and owners of small businesses as well as craft workers had suffered greatly and never fully participated in the prosperity of the 1924–29 years. The Nazis and others on the political right blamed the inflation and the continuing economic difficulties of some groups on speculators who were part of a "Jewish plot" thus adding another reinforcement to anti-Semitism already strong among elements of the middle class.

However, there were segments of German industry that emerged from the inflation with their debts paid and having benefited from numerous bankruptcies to acquire additional holdings. The inflation had led to a further consolidation of already concentrated industry. Germany had industrialized without creating an anti-trust movement like that which had developed in the United States. There were no German equivalents to the Sherman Anti-Trust Act of 1890 or the Clayton Anti-Trust Act of 1914. Monopolistic combinations within industries developed, and even the most extreme forms of these monopolies, the cartels, had legal status. Following the inflation, a further cartelized German industry emerged and moved to rebuild, modernize and expand capacity with the help from American loans. The dominance of big monopolies who confronted large labor unions created the possibility of corporatism, an association of big business and big labor, which some advocated and others feared.[22]

The perspective of industrialists and their assessment of labor relations varied according to the nature of their businesses and generally comprised two fairly distinct blocs. One bloc was made up of the more modern export-oriented industries such as the chemical, electrical, auto-parts and finishing industries; and the second included the heavy domestic industries such as coal, iron and steel. Proponents of the "bloc theory" argue that the export bloc had always been more forward-looking, more inclined to deal with labor unions, less hostile to the Republic and more resistant to the forces of the right. They see the heavy industry bloc as more conservative, very hostile to both labor unions and the Republic and sympathetic to right-wing forces.[23]

While the fear of Socialist revolution at the inception of the Republic created a climate in which even the heavy industry leaders were willing to co-operate with the unions and the Weimar government, that moment passed. Once more confident of the future, heavy industry then adopted an anti-republican, anti-labor policy designed to undo the earlier gains made by the unions. These industrialists worked towards the destruction of the Republic. Many supported the Nationalist Party and the growing influence of Alfred Hugenberg who had been a Krupp executive, a lobbyist for heavy industry and a media mogul for the far-right conservatives.

The export industry leaders were generally a more constructive force, and while they held sway within the industrial community, particularly during the 1924–29 period, better labor and political relations reigned. With the onset of the depression, the balance of power shifted within industry, and the heavy industry bloc became dominant again. They intensified their efforts to reverse the gains that the labor unions had won and to make sure that the Social Democrats played no role in Germany's government.

While German industry did frequently function in bloc-like patterns, there were, of course, businesses in both blocs that did not follow these paradigms. Export industries such as chemical concerns were not very progressive when it came to domestic policy, although they might have supported Gustav Stresemann's foreign policy because they benefited from improved international exchange rates. They too went on the anti-labor offensive once they felt the danger of radical change had passed.[24] The leaders of heavy industry were a vital part of the anti-republican bloc and made life difficult for the Republic. However, as Henry Turner suggests, many of these leaders were also not enthusiastic about the prospects of a Nazi state.[25]

The agricultural sector of the economy frequently did not respond in a pattern consistent with industry, and its economic interests did not always determine the directions of its political support. While some food producers fared better during part of the inflation period than did other segments of the society, in general the twenties were a depressed period for German agriculture. Even when industrial production had returned to pre-war levels in 1929, agricultural production was only 74 per cent of what it had been in 1913. In 1928, when industrial prosperity was at its height, farmers were rioting in response to foreclosures and depressed circumstances.

The agricultural sector can be divided into three groups: estate owners, family farmers and rural labor. By the mid 1920s when the segment of the population engaged in agriculture had dropped to 25 per cent of the population, the estate owners, most of whom were Prussian aristocrats, continued to wield the political power they had traditionally held. The Junkers, those who came from the East Elbian provinces of Prussia and could trace their aristocratic lineage back for many generations, were the dominant members of this group. Their power had stemmed initially from their wealth and their tradition of state and military service at the highest levels. Their connections to Bismarck and the ruling Hohenzollern family during the pre-war period maintained their political power at a higher level than their economic power dictated.

During the early years of the Republic, the aristocrats kept a low profile. They had concluded that the Republican leaders were preferable to the Communists who might have collectivized agriculture. Land owners had much to be thankful for, since the new government did very little to attack the estate system because it was caught up with political disorder, reparations and currency problems, and industrial rebuilding. Many of the new political leaders had no sense of agriculture or rural problems. Otto Braun was placed in charge of Prussian agriculture as his first appointment in the new state government in 1919. He did not last long in that position or achieve much because he had no real grasp of the problems or possible solutions and had no basis of communication with landowners. While they avoided political involvement, members of the landed aristocracy did continue to occupy important positions in the unreformed sections of the society, particularly the army and the judiciary. As large-scale producers with substantial financial needs, they also had close contacts with financiers and industrialists, although their economic interests did not always coincide.

The estate owners considered themselves the leaders of the rural sector but pursued their own narrow interests which often did not coincide with those of family farmers and rural laborers. Ironically these independent farmers and laborers looked up to the aristocrats and, for periods of time, followed their lead even when it was against their own economic interest to do so. However, in the mid-twenties, rural laborers began to move away from the domination of the aristocrats, and some of them supported the pro-Weimar parties including the Social Democrats. In the later crisis period from 1929 to 1932, the Social Democrats abandoned the rural laborers in their effort to protect their urban worker constituency at all costs and lost the Republic a valuable pool of supporters. Family farmers also broke with estate owners in the later twenties but showed no support for the Republic. Believing that neither the aristocrats nor the Republicans were protecting their interests, many turned to the Nazi Party.

The estate owners, facing reduced support from the other rural constituencies, protected their own interests by using their influence with President Hindenburg and by moving towards a recreated *Sammlung* policy (pre-war industrialist/estate owner alliance) with the heavy industry bloc. Estate owners played a role in bringing down the governments of Brüning and von Schleicher, both of whom proposed land reform. They were most comfortable with the government of von Papen and his "cabinet of barons" which included many aristocrats.

The outbreak of the world-wide depression in 1929 had disastrous effects. German prosperity of the middle Weimar years had been built in part on foreign loans first facilitated by the Dawes Plan. These loans were called in as American banks weakened, and this process began a steep downturn in the German economy. The successful negotiations of labor unions during the 1920s had created high wages for German blue collar workers. The lobbying of the Social Democratic Party had created an extensive and expensive network of social welfare legislation. A comparison between the United States and Germany in this area is quite revealing. In 1920 the percentage of the GNP (Gross National Product) devoted to public expenditures was 4 per cent in the U.S. and 10 per cent in Germany, and in 1929 it was 16 per cent in the

U.S. and 30 per cent in Germany.[26] The unions and the Social Democratic Party resisted surrender of these gains even as the economy plummeted.

German industrialists viewed this decline as an opportunity to accelerate the campaign they had been waging since the danger of radical revolution had passed of reversing gains made by labor. The concentration on profit and advantage of much of the industrial sector had been single-minded. Even during the Ruhr crisis of 1923, the leaders of heavy industry supported the government's passive resistance program as long as they could use shutdowns to weaken labor. They then made a deal with the French to help themselves. They also pushed for substantial compensation for any losses they suffered, even though this compensation contributed substantially to governmental budget problems and inflation. In the period from 1929 to 1932, as the depression deepened, business leaders engaged in massive layoffs often beyond immediate financial need without any thought to the overall state of the economy.

Unemployment had been a ubiquitous fact of Weimar life. The prosperity of the middle years had occurred while unemployment still remained relatively high. In January 1928, 1,862,000 Germans were unemployed. By January 1930, as the effects of the depression spread, the number grew to 3,218,000. In January 1932, 6,042,000 Germans were unemployed. From 1930 to 1932, the Brüning government tried to deal with the crisis by cutting government expenses, laying off government employees and attempting to balance the budget.

The Social Democrats objected to Brüning's policies which contributed to the unemployment of their worker-supporters and the decline of the unions. They could play only a minor role in the crucial decisions being made, however, since they refused to participate in a ruling coalition or to use their power to bring down Brüning. Furthermore, their leverage as the largest party in the Reichstag was seriously reduced as the business of government was carried on increasingly by presidential decree. In 1930 ninety-eight bills were passed by the Reichstag, while there were five enacted by presidential decree. By 1932 five were enacted by the Reichstag and sixty-six by presidential decree. In the crisis period of 1932, only Chancellor von Schleicher proposed a more vigorous approach to dealing with the depression which included extensive public works projects. However, he antagonized the estate owners because of his land reform proposals, and they prevailed upon President Hindenburg to replace him before he could attempt to implement his program.

Every nation in the western world struggled with the effects of the depression. In Germany, the economic crisis put great strains on a society where the divisions and the level of hostility were unusually high. The general lack of reasonable people who could put aside their own short-term interests in the interest of the larger community and everybody's future prosperity exacerbated the problems. Labor leaders had negotiated wage scales out of line with productivity when they had the power to do so. Industrialists sacrificed the interests of the nation to their profits. When they had the power, they cut their work forces below levels justified by their earnings while also reducing wage and benefit levels below what productivity justified. The Social Democrats, who had been the most nationally-minded of the parties through the Stresemann years, abandoned the broad view during the economic downturn. The Nationalists, who had never had a broad view, narrowed theirs still further. The Catholic Center Party, under the new leadership of Monsignor Kaas, narrowed its focus and pulled away from strong support for the Republic. Small one-issue and one-interest-group parties proliferated as many German voters turned inwards.

The Nazi Party triumphed in the crisis because it was not a narrow, provincial, one-issue, economic party. It was a national movement that never made clear what its economic program was. It did, however, provide a scapegoat for all the economic ills of Germany – the Jews – and a leader who argued that the economic crisis could be solved by the strength of will and decisiveness of the man at the top. The Nazis recognized the psychological elements that played such a strong part in the depression alongside actual material and financial factors. The supporters of the Republic had not been reasonable in dealing with their own and the national interest. A democratic electorate with an inclusive sense of community and humane values had not been created. Thus, a force which rejected the call to be reasonable and preached a concept of racial community based on irrationalism would be called upon to deal with the crisis in the German economy.

Notes

1 Donald Kagan, *The Outbreak of the Peloponnesian War*, Ithaca, New York, 1978, p. 74.

2 Fritz Ringer (ed.), *The German Inflation of 1923*, New York, 1969, p. 53.

3 Lewis and Clark, *Labour Law*, pp. 19–20.

4 Mosse, *Crisis of German Ideology*, p. 258.

5 Adam Ferguson, *When Money Dies: the Nightmare of the Weimar Collapse*, London, 1975, p. 21.

6 *Ibid.*, pp. 21–2.

7 Rudolf Stucken, *Deutsche Geld-Und Kreditpolitik 1914–1963*, Tubingen, 1964, p. 24.

8 A. Samuelson, *Le Mark: Historie De La Monnaie Allemande*, Paris, 1975, p. 38.

9 Stucken, *Deutsche Geld.*, p. 28.

10 Ferguson, *When Money Dies*, p. 40.

11 Gerald Feldman, *Army, Industry and Labor in Germany 1914–1918*, Princeton, 1966, pp. 197–235.

12 G. Braunthal, *Socialist Labor and Politics in Weimar Germany*, Hamden, Conn., 1978, p. 25.

13 *Ibid.*

14 Ringer, *German Inflation*, p. 71.

15 Möller, *Weimar*, p. 138.

16 Maier, *Recasting Bourgeois Europe*, p. 358.

17 Frank D. Graham, *Exchange, Prices and Production in Hyper-Inflation: Germany, 1920–1923*, Princeton, 1930, p. 321.

18 David Abraham, *The Collapse Of the Weimar Republic: Political Economy and Crisis*, 2nd. ed., New York, 1986, p. 28.

19 Hans Fallada, *Little Man, What Now?*, trans. Eric Sutton, Chicago, Illinois, 1983.

20 *Ibid.*, p. 18.

21 Abraham, *The Collapse of the Weimar Republic*, p. 31.

22 Maier, *The Recasting of Bourgeois Europe.*

23 Kocka, *Facing Total War*, Abraham, *The Collapse of the Weimar Republic.*

24 Craig, D. Patton, "The Myth of Moderation: German Chemical Employer Response to Labour Conflict, 1914–1924," *Central European History*, Vol. 24, No.1, January 1994, pp.32–3.

25 Henry Turner, *German Big Business and The Rise of Hitler*, New York, 1985.

26 Abraham, *Collapse*, p. 5.

11

The women's movement

The women's movement in Germany was characterized by a tension between the commonalities of tradition and biology that united women and the differences in political, economic and religious perspectives that often divided them. When German women received the right to vote as part of the changes that took place in November 1918, the extension of suffrage was more a revolutionary act of the socialists than it was a response to any organized suffrage movement on the part of German women. The women's movement, which had gained momentum in Germany in the late nineteenth and early twentieth century, did not focus on suffrage as a major agenda item as had the English and American women's movements.

Yet many German women were interested in women's issues. The largest German women's organization, the League of German Women's Associations (BDF-Bund Deutscher Frauenvereine) founded in 1894, had a membership of approximately 300,000 by the outbreak of World War I and numbered about 900,000 in the 1920s. This organization was dominated by middle-class women. Marion Kaplan notes that the BDF emphasized maternal clichés and adhered to bourgeois responsibility:

> Its 'feminism' evolved from the widening of women's narrow sphere within a framework of traditional social values. The BDF accepted the conventional notion that there were fundamental differences between the sexes, which destined them to serve important but different functions. The League, too, believed woman's instinctual maternal nature, her self-sacrificing personality, mild-

ness, and patience, would complement man's energy and initiative in the public sphere.[1]

The League stressed duty and service and avoided the equal rights issue so central to Anglo-American feminism. The organization did not advocate political agitation and instead stressed petitions, publications, and education. Until 1908, German women had been forbidden to organize for political purposes on the national and most state levels. At that time, there was a change in the law of associations which made such organization possible. Many German women organized their lives and their "feminist" activities around their religions, and there were Protestant, Catholic and Jewish women's organizations. The JFB (Jüdischer Frauenverband, Jewish Women's Association) had the longest involvement with the BDF, being associated with it from 1907 until Hitler took power in 1933. The Protestant women's organization was a member of the BDF from 1908–18, while the Catholic women's organization never joined it at all. For many Catholic and Protestant women who adhered closely to the more traditional aspects of their religions, even the moderate feminism of the BDF seemed too radical. More Jewish women seemed comfortable with the goals of the BDF, although Jewish women who were members of orthodox Jewish communities had more of a struggle to define themselves within their own families and communities and found it difficult to support any feminist movement. The socialists had their own women's organization, but they tended to see women's issues as part of the problems of the capitalist system which would disappear with the demise of capitalism.

The BDF was heavily involved in patriotic work during World War I. It set up the National Women's Service (Nationaler Frauendienst) to looked after families of men at the front and helped women find work. Its members set up soup kitchens, staffed hospital wards and participated in knitting circles. The BDF maintained a nationalist stance throughout the Weimar period, while the JFB and socialist women's organizations co-operated with and later joined international peace organizations.

Perhaps the most contentious area of feminist concern was the debate over reproductive rights. Most German women in the period before World War I praised marriage, extolled motherhood and held sexuality to be inextricably linked with reproduction. Even the more progressive socialists refused to accept birth control or abortion. The war changed these attitudes for many. Greater freedom for women, the absence, death and disabling of so many husbands, fiancés, fathers and brothers, and a generally more chaotic and insecure society contributed to behavioral and value changes. After the war, socialists, more radical feminists, and communists openly supported birth control and abortion. The communists were the most vociferous using the slogan, "your body belongs to you".

Mainstream German feminism, however, as well as some leading socialist feminists remained aloof from or hostile to the pro-abortion forces. At the same time, bourgeois feminists were willing to support birth control because, compared to abortion, they viewed it as the lesser of two evils. As late as 1928, the answer to unwanted pregnancies was still, according to Agnes von Zahn-Harnack, President of the BDF, "the education of our people to a restrained sexuality."[2] The BDF's major efforts in the area of sexuality were directed against those factors which they considered to be the clearest indications of the decline of morality under the Weimar Republic: "Sexual liberterianism, pornography, abortion, venereal diseases, advertisement for contraceptives and double standards of sexual morality."[3]

The Jewish Women's Association was the most liberal of the middle-class women's groups on matters of reproduction and sexuality, but their positions on these issues were still quite conservative and conflicted. The JFB urged its members to raise larger families. It objected to the use of birth control by Jewish women on religious grounds and because of concern about the declining Jewish birthrate. Yet, the leaders were aware of the widespread use of birth control among Jews before and after World War I. Describing such family limitation as "a sickness of the Volk soul" (*Volkseele*) caused by economic and emotional need, the JFB reluctantly preferred it to abortion.

While they opposed criminal punishments for people who resorted to abortion, the JFB opposed attempts to legalize it for many years. Its spokespersons viewed the law against abortion in general as having "educational meaning for the German people," and insisted on seeing "respect for life" firmly anchored in the German legal code.[4] In 1920, the JFB led the attack against bills introduced by socialists to abolish or at least modify Paragraph 218 of the Criminal Code, which made abortion a criminal offense. However by 1925, they changed their position and supported efforts to modify the paragraph. Recognizing the social and economic issues which encouraged women to seek abortions, JFB leaders called for better care for pregnant women, infants, and children, housing reforms, tax incentives for large families, care for unwed mothers and illegitimate children, and job security for unwed pregnant women. The JFB opposed abortions carried out for eugenic reasons, an idea growing in popularity during the Weimar period but ingendering additional conflicted debate.

Eugenics was a movement throughout much of the western world, led by developments in the United States. The male eugenics establishment in Germany was impressed by forced sterilization legislation in some twenty American states where, by the mid-1930s, approximately twenty thousand Americans, mostly residents of state mental hospitals and juvenile detention centers, were forcibly sterilized. They promoted such measures for Germany with some success during the Weimar period. The word itself was coined in 1883 by Sir Francis Galton, a well-known English statistician and cousin of the famous biologist, Charles Darwin. Its major supporters were found among well-respected educators, prominent scientists, social workers, and politicians. They believed that the future health of the human race could be radically improved by preventing the "unfit" from reproducing and encouraging the "fit" to have larger families.

Their definition of "fit' and "unfit" varied, allowing so-called racial criteria to be mixed with inherited diseases, mental illness, physical deformity, criminal behavior, and chronic poverty as the basis for encouraged abortions or even forced sterilizations. Racist anti-Semites wanted Jewish reproduction limited or suppressed. Jewish women combined with Catholic women and some Protestant women to oppose eugenics-motivated sterilization and abortion on religious grounds. However, many middle-class secular women's groups who were part of the BDF were responsive to the appeals of the eugenics advocates, thus further complicating the abortion debate.

The Social Democrats were hard-pressed during the campaigns for repeal of the anti-abortion legislation. While ideologically they were in favor of repeal, taking a public position in its support created significant practical political problems for them. These problems resulted from the fact that, in order to rule, the Social Democrats were dependent upon coalitions with the Catholic Center Party which was inflexibly opposed to any changes in this area. For most of the life of the Republic, the outcome was tepid compromise and stalemate.

The abortion issue flared up strongly during the final period of the Weimar Republic when the Communist Party tried to exploit this issue to gain women supporters. It had always been a factor in the lives of poor women but, during periods of economic crisis like the worldwide depression from 1929 to 1932, abortion became a particularly acute issue for increasing numbers of women who had no resources and needed to work. Working-class women, who were struggling to keep jobs and take care of families, often saw additional pregnancies as unbearable. As Atina Grossmann describes the situation during this period, "Women sought to limit their offspring by all possible means, on pain of death, disease and jail sentence and not infrequently also by infanticide and suicide. It was estimated on average every German woman underwent an abortion at least twice in her lifetime; probably figures for the working class were considerably higher."[5]

On February 19, 1931, Doctors Else Kienle and Friedrich Wolf who had performed many abortions were arrested in Stuttgart under Article 218 of the Criminal Code. Even in its reformed version of 1926, this law stated that it was still a crime punishable by a jail sentence for women to have abortions and for doctors or anyone else to perform or assist with them. The Kienle and Wolf cases became national issues but did not rouse majority support for a change in the laws. The controversy put severe strains on alliances among women's groups and pro-Weimar political parties. The issue was strongly exploited by the National Socialist Party which adamantly opposed abortion for racially-pure German women while supporting eugenic abortions for those they judged to be inferior.

The debate over reproductive rights was equalled in contentiousness by the discussion of the issue of women in the workplace. While most of the women's organizations favored expanding economic opportunities for women, they usually also accepted the idea that women should strive to work in special spheres where their "natural qualities and virtues" came to the fore.[6] These occupations included social work, the healing professions, office and shop work and domestic service. Even within these perimeters, the leaders of the women's movement still emphasized motherhood. Helene Lange, the most prominent leader of the League of German Women, argued that, "Motherhood is the most important career, because it includes the profession of educator of future generations."[7] She also sounded a common theme when, in the name of selflessness, she demanded docility from women: "Women ought to contribute to the German state and culture rather than selfishly to demand equality."[8] Those leaders of the women's movement, like Hedwig Dohm, who saw things differently were in the minority. She said, "Woman ought to study, because she wants to study, because the unhindered choice of a vocation is a main factor of individual liberty, of individual happiness."[9]

The issues of study, work and wages for women often highlighted class distinctions among women and women's groups. Many middle-class women were primarily homemakers and were interested in recruiting well-trained young women for domestic service. These women had their own influential lobbying organization in the League of German Homemakers. This association functioned under the umbrella of the BDF for the first part of the Weimar period but then withdrew as it became increasingly conservative and less in sympathy with many of the BDF's goals. Members of the Homemaker's League worried that, if too many women aspired to and received training for high paying jobs, the pool of women for domestic service would decrease. Therefore, they were often at odds with socialist women's groups who pressed for greater opportunities for women at highly skilled jobs. They even found the moderate employment and wage goals of the BDF more and more out of line with their views.[10]

The complex and often contradictory positions taken by women's groups on feminist issues carried over into participation in the political process as a whole. The high-point of women's active voting participation during the new era was the election for the National Assembly in 1919 which also marked the climax of their electoral support for parties clearly committed to the Republic. In that first election in which women participated, they voted in large numbers, supported parties of the left and center and sent thirty-six women to the National Assembly of whom eighteen were Social Democrats. Even in this assembly which oversaw the writing of the Weimar Constitution and created the Republic, women representatives complained of being ignored instead of being consulted and reported feeling "impotent, disappointed and resigned."[11] This pattern of reactions continued for women representatives during the entire Weimar period. In the early years following the election to the National Assembly, the percentage of women voting declined and their support for pro-Weimar left and center parties declined as well. This abandonment produced particular consternation within the ranks of the parties on the left, who had been responsible for the extension of suffrage, were most supportive of a "feminist" agenda and put up the largest number of women political candidates.

Female voters revealed in their ballots that they were often motivated by factors other than feminism. Women reacted particularly strongly to the inflation, rising food prices and unemployment, issues which might have attracted them to the pro-Weimar parties. But they were keenly disappointed by the Social Democratic Party's support of the so-called double earner legislation which sought to eliminate from the job market women who were married to employed husbands. The Social Democrats did not support maintaining those women in the work force who had been enlisted for war work if there were returning veterans who needed jobs.

Large numbers of women both entered the work force and changed their level of employment during World War I, often however with only fifty per cent of the pay of male workers. These women also often lost rights and protections concerning hours and safety conditions that had existed before the war. After the war, with millions of returning men and poor economic conditions, pressure built up to force women, particularly married women, out of the work force. For many unmarried women, work was necessary for survival, and statistics suggested that many of these women would never marry. For many married women, the economic needs of a family mandated work. The ideal of the super-woman who combined work and family was a vision often propagated by women's organizations which turned into an unrealistic burden.

Many women found their new conditions and demands untenable and became alienated from the Republic and its supporting political parties which they blamed for their plight. Thus as the twenties progressed, more and more women supported conservative and eventually radical rightist parties which rejected "the new woman" in favor of the traditional mother and head of family who did not work outside the home. Women evidenced little concern about the relative absence of conservative women candidates on the ballots and responded to the appeal of these parties to "participate in politics in order to preserve and enhance their status within their traditional roles."[12]

The BDF reflected this antipathy to the new government. It was not sympathetic to the parliamentary system and was actively hostile to the idea of party politics. Many of its aims were at cross purposes to the diversity and compromise of republicanism. "All these various aims can be summed up in the idea of the organic national community, the so called *Volksgemeinschaft*, the idea that German women and men were united by racial ties stronger than any ideological divisions, and that the aim of politics should be to strengthen these ties and eliminate the divisive influences of party conflicts."[13] These views indicated that, far from welcoming the Weimar Republic, the BDF, in common with most other middle-class organizations, had little understanding of the parliamentary system and rejected party politics as divisive and unpatriotic. As Gertrud Baümer declared "... the aim of the BDF was to unite women of all parties in exerting a 'motherly' influence over society."[14] Thus, the major women's group did not work to help women organize politically and even served as a deterrent in this area.

Another of the substantial obstacles facing women in their effort to organize and become active politically was their lack of political education and experience. The bans prohibiting women from organizing politically were only lifted gradually between 1908 and 1914. Neither schools nor families encouraged women to become informed about political issues or engage in political discussion and debate.[15] Even the socialists, who had forty years of experience in organizing the female proletariat, had concentrated on immediate economic issues and had not prepared women for sustained political activity. Unfortunately for the women's movement and for the Social Democratic Party, by the beginning of the Republic, the party had lost many of its most gifted women to old age, political violence or competing radical groups. As Werner Thönnessen observes:

> The women who led the Social Democratic women's movement from 1919 to 1939 differed fundamentally from the older generation of fighters for the cause of socialist revolution and women's liberation. They failed to distinguish themselves through outstanding achievements in the theoretical field (Luxemburg), the sharpness of their words, basic organizational work or impassioned educational campaigns to spread the revolutionary idea (Zetkin, Zietz, Baader).[16]

The political party that received the most consistent support from women was the Catholic Center Party. This party, which took traditional positions on women's issues, attracted women who had a strong religious commitment and who saw Catholicism as a more basic part of their identity than gender. The relationship of most German women to the Communist Party was most ambiguous. The Communist Party had a platform that embodied more feminist issues than any other party. It was committed to women's free access to all jobs at equal pay. It favored sex education, abortion and the availability of contraceptive information and devices. The Communist Party also nominated more women to run as candidates in local and national elections and was the only party that had women in major leadership positions. Yet, it got little electoral support from women. One reason for this failure was its ineffectiveness in communicating its message and its platform planks to women. Even its female leaders resisted making appeals specifically to women. They argued that capitalism was fundamentally responsible for women's exploitation, and, once communism was established, there would be no need for feminism. Many German women also found the Communist Party planks too radical and too anti-religious for them.

Many women believed that the promises the pro-Weimar parties had made to them and even the specific provisions of the Constitution were more illusion than real progress. The constitutional claims of equality for women, which were embodied in provisions 109, 119 and 128, were difficult to incorporate quickly into the civil and criminal codes. Article 109 stated that, "in principle men and women have the same civil rights." Article 119 declared:

> Marriage as the corner stone of family life and the preservation and increase of the nation is placed under the special protection of the Constitution. It is based on the equal rights of both sexes. It is the duty of the State and the Communes to foster the purity, health and social advancement of the family. Families with numerous children have a claim to proportionate assistance. Motherhood has a claim to the protection and care of the state.

Article 128 declared that "All provisions discriminating against women are abolished." This generalized principle, theoretically encouraging, seemed inconsistent with the, at least, short-term reality that most women encountered. Although the Civil Code of 1896, which was still in place when the Weimar Republic was created, guaranteed women free access to the job market, a husband also had the right to decide whether or not his wife could work. Civil Code reform dragged on during the twenties, and most judges were not willing to make decisions based on the new Constitution and the spirit of the new Republic, at least until the Civil Code itself had been changed.

The growing antipathy of many women towards the Republic is most glaringly evident in their evolving interest in National Socialism. For most of the 1920s, the Nazi movement was the territory of young males. However, by the later twenties, women were supporting the movement in increasing numbers. At first glance, it is surprising that women would support a movement that had as its main plank defining the proper functions for women the slogan "Kinder, Küche, Kirche" ("Children, Kitchen and Church"). The Nazi Party did have a women's component which functioned totally independently. However, it was more a result of the lack of political significance that the Nazis gave to women than of their respect for women's organizational ability. Thus, the Nazi Women's Auxiliary did not mean that the Nazis saw a political role for women or approved of the women's movement. As Gisela Bock notes "The NSDAP ... never allowed a woman to represent it and was the only party to demand the dismissal of women from parliament. Unlike the other parties, it also attacked the women's movement for its liberalism, pacifism, internationalism and the Marxist and Jewish influence within it."[17]

Yet, in spite of the Nazi view of women and the women's movement, increasing numbers of women began to withdraw support from pro-Republican parties. This reorientation towards right-wing conservative and radical parties reflected disillusionment for women who were not finding job and educational opportunities readily available. They often faced boring and routine work at lower salaries than their male counterparts. Many women had to assume a double burden (*doppelbelastig*) of the working woman and the mother with home and children to care for. For many of these women, their current situation did not look like progress, and the appeal of a protected, more limited home and family environment was great.

The life that most women led also contrasted sharply with the new film image coming from Hollywood or the UFA film studios in Germany. This image, which Detlev Peukert has called the "Myth of the Vamp," depicted a woman who was slender, self-assured, almost arrogant, with short hair, make-up, stylish clothing and a cigarette dangling from her lips.[18] This romanticized construct stood in stark contrast to the rational mother who might also work in the helping professions and had not the time, energy or inclination to be a vamp. Young women with office jobs or younger women in school might try to imitate the model, but most lacked the income and faced the opposition of teachers, employers and family. They were also made to understand that men did not marry vamps. For those already married and with children and perhaps a job as well, the difference between the life of the mythic vamp and their lives was one more reason for discontent.

While the vamp was an image rich in sexual content, there were other divergent desexualized images of women that played a significant role during the Weimar period. Observers of the period have noted that men's fantasies in the Weimar years were often based on two radically different images of women neither of which bore much relation to reality. On the one hand, there was the "White Woman", the mother and the nurse; and on the other hand, there was the "Gun Woman", a nightmarish vision of the female communist revolutionary leader. The saintly mother-figure was often contrasted with the woman of violence personified by Rosa Luxemburg.[19]

These dislocated images of women resonated in a society where family structures had deteriorated. The most poignant situation was the plight of mothers whose husbands had died in the war. Their level of government support was low and decent jobs were hard to find. These women struggled to be both mother and father while also working. Many other women were deserted by their husbands as changing patterns of behavior and the availability of a surplus of unmarried women led to marriage breakdowns. The growth of more fatherless families and the greater instability of the society contributed to a rise in juvenile crime which had not been a serious problem in Germany before World War I.[20]

The issue of prostitution also occupied women's groups and had a political component. While prostitution had always existed in German society, the number of prostitutes had increased as a result of the war and the economic crisis which followed it. There was also a greater willingness to address the issue rather than pretending it did not exist. Women's groups responded on three levels. They carried on campaigns to prevent young women from being recruited into prostitution by providing vulnerable young girls with job training, housing, and counseling. As part of this effort, they often became involved in international campaigns to combat white slavery, a practice where young girls were recruited, particularly among the poor of eastern Europe, with false promises of jobs and husbands and sent to Germany and other wealthier countries where they were met by men who pressured them to become prostitutes. Women's groups from many nations worked to support efforts to stop this trade, and local groups had volunteers at train stations and boat docks to meet young girls and offer them shelter and help. Bertha Pappenheim, who was a major figure in the JFB and BDF, was in the forefront of these efforts.[21]

A second thrust in the battle against prostitution was aimed at the red light districts which communities had allowed to develop. In these areas, prostitution, which was legal under Section 361, sub-paragraph 6 of the Criminal Code if permitted by a municipality and regulated by the police, was allowed to flourish. While public health problems were reduced by these measures, most women's groups believed that prostitution was demeaning to women and threatened the moral fabric of society. With the help of religious leaders, they were often able to have local laws changed and the districts disbanded. As part of this effort, they opposed the practice whereby young women who were not living with their families and were suspected of prostitution could be detained by the police and made to undergo painful and dangerous treatments. The death of a young woman from this treatment and the telling of her story in a book by her mother led to the so-called Bremen Morality Scandal in 1926 and to reforms of the system.[22]

The third level of attack in the anti-prostitution offensive was aimed at young men. Women's groups urged them to conform to the same moral standards they expected of their future brides and end the hypocrisy of the double standard of morality. While the women who participated in the anti-prostitution campaign had few illusions about eradicating it, their efforts to remove state sanction and tacit acceptance of the practice and to raise public consciousness of its victimization and dangers were successful.

Popular literature, published in journals such as the *Berliner Illustrirte Zeitung*, offers insight into the various ways in which women and their aspirations and options were perceived by the general public. This periodical was widely circulated and had a high proportion of women among its readers. One of its major features was that it printed popular novels in installments over a number of months. The images projected in these novels changed as their social context changed over time. One important watershed for the image of women was the war. In pre-war serialized novels such as *Das Eisen in Feuer* by Clara Viebig (1912) and *Seine Englishe Frau* by Rudolf Stratz (1914), the heroine is beautiful, gracious and worthy of respect. She is first and foremost wife and mother. She conforms to the conduct of her husband's family, and she acquires personal satisfaction by contributing to the happiness and well-being of others. Before marriage her loyalty to her parents, but above all to her father, goes without question. The heroine has no personal aspirations which may conflict with those of her family or friends. The single woman is destined to a life of loneliness and a feeling of uselessness. Since a woman is not encouraged to develop personal or professional goals, the single woman does not live her own life in any way; she accompanies the lives of others. The female protagonist may be intelligent, but she must never flaunt her intellectual superiority. She is modest and shy, dignified and conscious of her appeal. She is allowed a fighting spirit only in the cause of her family; she is helpless and pitiful if she has no relatives.

The portrayal of women in the popular serialized novels of the Weimar period became more complex and more layered than the pre-war paradigm. These novels take on the feel of the modern soap opera. They allow more scope for a woman's independence, but this freedom was always purchased with suffering and ambiguity. Vicki Baum, one of the most successful of the novelists whose work was serialized in the BIZ, frequently incorporated this trope in her narratives. Between 1926 and 1930, four of her novels were serialized: *Feme, stud. chem. Helene Willfür, Menschen im Hotel,* later dramatized as Grand Hotel, and *Zwischenfall in Lohwinkel.* A brief synopsis of one of her novels, *stud. chem. Helene Willfür,* provides considerable insight into how women were perceived in the Weimar period.

Helene Willfür, who has recently lost her father, must find work in the university laboratory in order to reach her goal to get a doctorate in chemistry. Her friend, Rainer, is studying medicine against his own will in order to keep peace with his father whose medical practice he will inherit. He gains Helene's sympathy but not her admiration because he is not willing to take responsibility for his own actions. The person she admires most is Professor Ambrosius who does not approve of a woman working for an advanced degree but is impressed by her determination and drive. He has an unfortunate marriage, and his wife deceives him. The professor attempts suicide, does not die but is blinded as a result of the attempt. Helene gives birth to Rainer's child and is forced as an unwed mother to abandon her studies before she finishes her doctorate. She refuses to give up and transfers to another university where her personal life is not known to finish her degree. She gets a job working in a scientific laboratory with the help of the recommendation of Professor Ambrosius with whom she then loses contact. After six years in the laboratory, she develops a marketable formula for a health tonic from which she derives a significant sum of money and a well-paying job with the firm manufacturing the tonic. A chance meeting with Professor Ambrosius leads to the establishment of a relationship and eventual marriage.

Helene is a different kind of woman from the heroine of the pre-war period. She is an independent individual with ambitions and values of her own. She suffers because she breaks some of society's rules and conventions, but she perseveres and overcomes all adversity. Ultimately, though with great sacrifice and considerable pain, she combines education, career, motherhood and marriage in an unconventional way. At the end of the novel, she is a chemist, mother and wife, an impossible heroine for the pre-war period but a model for the Weimar woman. However, as admirable as Helene is, she embodied a model to which very few women could conform.

Many Weimar women struggled to deal with the expectations of the super-woman and the realities of the "double burden". They encountered the resentment of men who had never really accepted the new woman and her place in the economy. They coped with the real cutbacks in government aid for mothers and families in the face of the depression. Under these circumstances, the romanticized nostalgic appeal of a conservative and reactionary view of the role of women began to look more and more appealing. As Renate Bridenthal and Claudia Koonz argue, the growing conservatism of German women during the course of the Weimar Republic must be seen "… in the context of the fraudulence of their supposed emancipation."[23] Contributing to women's disillusionment was the growing practice of political parties during the twenties and early thirties to offer women fewer party offices, to cut budgets for women's groups and publications and to send fewer women representatives to the Reichstag.

The Nazis promised women that which seemingly they had once had and gave their women's groups total autonomy during their rise to power. Thus, they began, in the last years of the Republic, to attract more and more women supporters. The Nazis openly claimed that they supported separate spheres for men and women which, while unequal, were both essential for the creation of a vibrant German state. The leaders of other political parties had never gone beyond the theory of separate but equal spheres for men and women and had done little to insure that the conditions would actually be equal.

Nazi women, who had not played a vital part in building the movement and whose numbers were very small in proportion to male participation in the party, would show great devotion and loyalty to the movement and would match the men in their intensity. Many of these women were willing to march with Nazi men in the streets and lend their womanly qualities of "stability, virtue and motherliness" to the movement. These women preferred the appeal of "Kinder, Küche, Kirche" and rejected the new woman as one who "voted, used contraceptives, obtained abortions and earned wages." They rejected the Republic which they concluded, on the one hand, had pushed women out of the better jobs of the war era and into low paying, arduous and boring jobs while, on the other hand, making motherhood and child-bearing more difficult and burdensome. For this burden, the government offered only the reward of Mothers Day with its flowers and possible one-day reprieve from drudgery. Women began to ignore the irony that supporting the Nazis was giving licence to a primitive and violent movement at odds with all human, nurturing and caring values.

Notes

1 Marion Kaplan, "Sisterhood Under Siege; Feminism and Anti-Semitism in Germany 1904–1938," in Renate Bridenthal, Atina Grossmann and Marion Kaplan, (eds), *When Biology Became Destiny, Women in Weimar and Nazi Germany*, New York, 1964, p. 181.

2 *Ibid.*, p. 183.

3 Richard J. Evans, *The Feminist Movement in Germany 1894–1933*, London, 1976, p. 237.

4 Kaplan, "Sisterhood under Siege", p. 183.

5 Atina Grossmann, "Abortion and Economic Crisis; the 1931 Campaign Against Paragraph 218," in Bridenthal, *When Biology Became Destiny*, p. 70.

6 Evans, *The Feminist Movement*, p. 237.

7 Marion Kaplan, *The Jewish Movement in Germany: the Campaigns of the Jüdischer Frauenbund, 1904–1938*, Westport, Connecticut, 1979, p. 64.

8 *Ibid.*

9 *Ibid.*, p. 65.

10 Renate Bridenthal, "Professional Housewives: Stepsisters of the Women's Movement", in Bridenthal, ed., *When Biology Became Destiny*.

11 Werner Thönnessen, "The Emancipation of Women" in *The Rise and Decline of the Women's Movement in German Social Democracy 1863–1933*, Frankfurt am Main, 1969, p. 86.

12 Renate Bridenthal and Claudia Koonz, "Beyond Kinder, Küche,

Kirche: Weimar Women in Politics and Work," in Bridenthal, *When Biology Became Destiny*, p. 44.

13 Evans, *The Feminist Movement*, p. 237.

14 *Ibid.*

15 James C. Albisetti, *Schooling German Girls and Women: Secondary and Higher Education in the Nineteenth Century*, Princeton, New Jersey, 1988.

16 Thönnessen, "The Emancipation of Women", p. 87.

17 Gisela Bock, "Racism and Sexism in Nazi Germany," in Bridenthal, *When Biology Became Destiny*, p. 160

18 Detlev J. K. Peukert, *Die Weimarer Republik, Krisenjahre der Klassischen Moderne*, Frankfurt am Main, 1987, pp. 104–5.

19 *Ibid.*, p. 111.

20 *Ibid.*, p. 97.

21 Kaplan, *The Jewish Feminist Movement*, pp. 110–25.

22 Elisabeth Meyer-Renschhausen, "The Bremen Morality Scandal" in Bridenthal, *When Biology Became Destiny*, p. 87.

23 Bridenthal and Koonz, "Beyond Kinder, Küche, Kirche," p. 34.

12

The situation of the Jews

The "Jewish question," as Germans euphemistically termed their anti-Semitism, is in many ways a key to understanding the Weimar Republic. Framing the discussion about Jews as a "question" inherently marginalized this group and signals that the problem actually resided in the German Christian community. Yet "the question" drew attention to the Jews for better or worse. The part that Jews played in the Republic and the way that Weimar's enemies identified Jews with it make this small group disproportionately significant. Jews represented less than one per cent of the German population, about 570,000 out of a population of sixty million. There were also about 100,000 Jews from eastern Europe who arrived in Germany during the Weimar period. Many of these Jews had been sent from Poland and Lithuania by the German army for war work, while others were refugees of pogroms in Ukraine and Poland.[1]

German Jews were overwhelmingly middle-class. Many were merchants with small businesses, cattle dealers in rural villages and self-employed professionals such as doctors and lawyers. Although individual Jews had been strikingly successful, Jews did not control the major industries nor did they possess the greatest fortunes in Germany. While anti-Semites frequently invoked the stereotype of the Jewish banker, Jews had only controlled private banks which were on the decline by the 1920s. In the large banks that controlled German finance and played such an important role in German industry, Jews were only occasionally prominent in management positions rather than as large bloc stock owners. As the popular Jewish author, Lion Feuchtwanger, commented in his novel *Success*, "In particular, exact statistics were produced of the wealth owned by the leading Jewish financial houses, statistics based on a feeling, not on scientific deduction or on a study of books and taxation records."[2] The Jewish population was more urban than rural and was particularly concentrated in a few of the largest cities with the largest group residing in Berlin.

German Jews were an acculturated group, committed to the German language and culture. They were well-educated and dedicated to being an integrated part of the population. Richard Bendix, whose father was one of the few Jewish judges in Germany, described this sense of identity:

> I cannot in truth speak of efforts to assimilate ... We did not live at all as aliens who wanted to become natives, but rather as natives who did not understand and objected strongly [when] they were looked on and treated as aliens. We in no way felt we were assimilated 'Jews,' but Germans like other Germans ... All other assets, to continue the image were German! We lived in German art and science as our own: German politics was and determined our fate. Our whole life was deeply rooted in German life and had no other foundation.[3]

During the Weimar period many Jews asserted themselves as artists, writers, theater directors, and independent scholars. As Walter Laqueur has written:

> Without the Jews there would have been no 'Weimar Culture' – to that extent the anti-Semites, who detested that culture, were justified ... They were prominent among Expressionist poets, among the novelists of the 1920s, among the theatrical producers, and for a while among the leading figures in the cinema ... Many leading theater critics were Jews, and they dominated light entertainment.[4]

Many of these cultural figures identified themselves as German as did Richard Bendix's father. Jacob Wasserman, a popular author declared in his autobiography, "I am a German, and I am a Jew, one as intensely and as completely as the other, inextricably bound together."[5] The Zionist movement was small in Germany. It was dedicated to convincing Jews to leave Europe and settle in the land that was British-controlled Palestine at the time and had been part of biblical Israel. German Jews believed that Germany was their homeland, and they were generally uninterested in moving elsewhere. Although most German Jews wanted to be both Germans and Jews, a small number did convert to Christianity and a larger number intermarried.

The truly accepted "Jewish-German" was a dream of many of Germany's Jewish citizens but one which receded rather than approached during the Weimar years. A sensitive Jew like Albert Einstein could see the situation more clearly when he returned from years in Switzerland: "When I came to Germany, I discovered for the first time I was a Jew, and I owe this discovery more to Gentiles than Jews. I saw worthy Jews basely caricatured and the sight made my heart bleed. I saw how schools, comic papers, and innumerable other forces of the Gentile majority undermined the confidence of even the best of my fellow Jews."[6] Walther Rathenau who emerged during the early Weimar years as the most important Jewish political figure in the Republic and who came from a wealthy family and had university training, said, "Every Jew no matter how wealthy or well educated comes to the realization that he will always live as a second class citizen."[7]

The Jews had been a persecuted group during much of the sixteen hundred years that they had lived on German soil. Over the centuries, Jews had been expelled from almost every part of German territory, often after attacks on their property and persons only to be invited back after a number of years.[8] Periods of large-scale violence accompanied the Crusades of the late eleventh and twelfth centuries and the Black Death of the fourteenth century. Large numbers of Jews left German territory during the plague years and settled in Poland changing the demography of Jewish development in Europe.

Anti-Judaism, which stressed the Jewish role in the crucifixion of Jesus, can be traced back to the Gospels. These basic components of the Christian Scriptures were written by communities of early Christians who were in the process of defining their own identity. The earliest Christians had been Jews and the earliest Christian communities had been made up of Jewish-Chrisitians. At the time of the writing of the Gospels, Jews and Christians had been in competition for souls and bodies. The Christians also wanted to appease their Roman rulers and disassociate themselves from the politically rebellious Jews. Thus, as the theologian Rosemary Reuter indicates, the theological roots of hatred of the

Jews were planted.[9] Christianity, which saw itself as the Second Israel, could only truly feel vindicated when, as the theologian and historian Franklin Littell states, the supersecessionist prophesies were fulfilled and Judaism disappeared.[10] The writings of the early church fathers, such as John Chrysostum, reinforced the Gospel image of the Jews and inspired much of western Christianity's anti-Jewish hatred.

Further religious reinforcement of hostility towards Jews came from Martin Luther. Luther was the initiator of the sixteenth- century Protestant Reformation, which played a major role in the evolution of German religious thought and practice. His translation of the Christian Scriptures from Latin to German contributed mightily to the development of the modern German language. Luther initially showed sympathy for the Jews whom he hoped to convert but became bitterly hostile when they failed to heed his call. "First their synagogues or churches should be set on fire, and whatever does not burn up should be covered or spread over with dirt so that no one may ever be able to see a cinder or stone of it. Secondly their homes should likewise be broken down and destroyed."[11] Luther then called for the Jews to be harried out of the land. Thus, German churchmen, both Protestant and Catholic, preached a message that was strongly anti-Jewish and focused on the crime of deicide. The Jews were the crucifiers of Jesus who remained a hard-hearted reprobate people in the heart of Christian Europe. Powerful strains from the Easter liturgy and revered music such as Bach's *St. Matthew Passion* contributed to the image.

The stubborn refusal of Jews to convert blended with economic resentment which was derived from the roles Jews had been forced to play in Christian Europe. For centuries, Jews were not allowed to own land or engage in crafts. Dealing in money, which until the Renaissance was forbidden to Christians, was one of the few areas open to Jewish endeavor. Although they fulfilled vital economic functions and were joined in these activities by Christians once the restrictions were lifted, Jews were accused of usury in the marketplace as they were accused in the pulpit of killing Christ.

In the nineteenth century, two significant ingredients were added to the mix: modern nationalism and racial biology. Nationalism which developed in response to the French Revolution stressed a unity based on language, culture, history and, for some nationalists, religion. While German Jews were committed to the German language, culture and history, the religious difference, added to centuries of prejudice and stereotyping, tended to exclude the Jews from many of the new national group identities developing in Europe. Racial biology was a new concept of group identity based on the belief in hereditary characteristics and differences in the blood which determined the characters and abilities of people. Race became a popular methodology for categorizing people who may have differed in skin color or may have just belonged to different national groups.

According to the new biological characterizations, Jews were a separate race whose goals and morality were alien to Germans and who were permanently conditioned by their biology. As Peter Gay states, "The new racial anti-Semitism transformed the slander against the Jew as Christ-killer into the slander of the Jew as exploiter and subverter; a poisonous mixture of pseudo-science and sheer assertion that secured substantial support late in the nineteenth century, it proved particularly hard to combat."[12]

In spite of the difficulties, the effort of an overwhelming number of German Jews to acculturate within German society appeared in many ways to be successful. Jews became a vital part of German culture. As Marion Kaplan indicates, Jewish middle-class women believed that making their families German was one of their central life missions. They carried out this mission through home furnishings, collections of classic German writings, piano lessons and reserved "proper" public behavior.[13] However, some commentators have concluded that this effort was ultimately doomed to failure. Gershom Scholem, a German Jew, came to believe that German Christians were not receptive to a dialogue with Jews and did not want them as part of German society:

> For it was precisely this desire on the part of Jews to be absorbed by the Germans, that the haters understood as a destructive maneuver against the life of the German people – a thesis repeated indefatigably by the metaphysicians of anti-Semitism – between 1830 and 1930; here the Jews are considered, to quote one of these philosophers, as 'the dark power of negation which kills what it touches. Whoever yields to it falls into the hands of death.'[14]

Anti-Semitism, a new word, whose origin is usually attributed to Wilhelm Marr, a scholar who in 1878 wrote a book entitled *The Battle of the Germans Against the Jews,* became the rallying call for anti-Jewish campaigns. In the 1880s and 1890s, a specific political movement which called itself "the anti-Semitic movement" competed in national elections. The party polled at a maximum about 300,000 votes and soon disappeared. Historians have debated the significance of this movement with some seeing its relatively modest vote and quick disappearance as signs of its insignificance.[15] Other historians such as Hans-Ulrich Wehler have made a stronger argument for the seminal nature of the movement tracing its disappearance to the co-opting of the issue of anti-Semitism by the much more established and mainline Conservative Party.[16] The significant "non-affiliated" lobbying organizations such as the Pan-German League which supported a militarily aggressive expansionist Germany also absorbed anti-Semitic ideas into their intellectual arsenal.[17]

At the same time, the socialist movement, the most popular secular and anti-religious movement in Germany, also exhibited strong anti-Jewish currents. These developed from the same secular roots as the racial variant of hostility towards Jews. Robert Wistrich surveys sources of anti-Semitism in Enlightenment and socialist thought:

> Modern racial anti-Semitism in Germany, like Marxism itself, grew out of this secular anti-Judaism expressed in the writings of such radicals as Bruno Bauer, Ludwig Feuerbach, Friedrich Daumer, Friedrich Wilhelm Ghillany, Richard Wagner and Wilhelm Marr. The young Hegelians themselves built on the post-Christian (and anti-Christian) tradition of eighteenth-century French Enlightenment 'philosophes' such as Voltaire and d'Holbach whose rationalist attack on the Old Testament held Jewry responsible for the 'barbarism', fanaticism and intolerant obscurantism which the Catholic Church had inflicted on the world.[18]

Thus ironically, Jews were seen by Christian clergy as a threat to the very existence of Christianity, while secular critics accused Jews of being responsible for all that was wrong with Christianity. At the same time, these secular critics accused Jews of being the ultimate money lenders and capitalists. For many German socialists, including some who had come from Jewish roots themselves, Judaism and capitalism became synonymous. Karl Marx frequently used popular anti-Jewish epithets when commenting on rival socialists such as Ferdinand Lassalle who happened to be Jewish.

Popular anti-Semitism grew within the working class as many workers also made the association of Jews and capitalism. Only when the socialists became convinced that racial anti-Semitism was a strong weapon in the hands of their enemies on the right did they begin efforts to oppose it and to educate their rank and file about its distortions and dangers. Simultaneously, however, many Germans who felt that godless socialism threatened their society and its values pointed at Jewish socialist leaders and concluded that socialism and Judaism were synonymous. The fact that a number of prominent members of the Spartacist revolutionary movement in Berlin and Bavaria were Jews, such as Rosa Luxemburg and Kurt Eisner, strengthened this attitude, although only a small number of Jews were sympathetic to the radical left.[19] Thus long before the rise of Nazism, Germans built on a long history of hostility to Jews and defined them as both molders and destroyers of Christianity and as both enemies and promoters of capitalism.

Jehuda Reinharz points out that, while anti-Semitic misinformation, lies, stereotypes and hatreds multiplied:

> no significant replies were made to anti-Semitism by large segments of the German Jewish community until the 1890s when two organizations were created: the Centralverein deutscher Staatsbuerger judischen Glaubens [Central Association of German Citizens of the Jewish Religion] ... and the Zionistische Vereinigung für Deutschland [Zionist Association for Germany] ...[20]

The *Central Verein*, which was the larger and more influential of these organizations, constantly stressed the commitment of German Jews first to Germanness (*Deutschtum*) and second to Jewishness (*Judentum*).[21] German Jews took the criticism of the anti-Semites to heart and did not analyze the accuracy of the stereotype because victims often incorporate the prejudices of their oppressors as part of their own self-image. Ismar Schorsch has described a typical appeal to German Jewish organizations from the Alliance Israélite Universelle (International Jewish Alliance): "He [All Jews] must avoid every display of arrogance, superiority, aggressiveness and ostentation. If possible, he should take up a craft; if not he should support efforts to see that others do. All business is to be conducted honestly and conscientiously regardless of the customer's religion."[22] This international Jewish organization, based in France, accepted elements of the late nineteenth-century stereotype of Jews. Its leaders hoped that, if they could steer young Jews, particularly poorer ones, away from business or the professions and into crafts or farming, they could diffuse some of the hostility directed at Jews. Their efforts showed limited understanding of anti-Semitism and anti-Semites but reflected their earnest desire to appease their enemies and ease their fears.

World War I made demands on all Germans, including Jews. The record of Jewish participation in the German armed forces was quite impressive. Of the approximately 570,000 Jews who were German citizens, 96,000 joined the armed forces with 40,000 of those in combat and 12,000 killed. On a percentage basis, Jewish participation in the war effort was higher than that of non-Jewish Germans. However, the anti-Semites refused to accept the numbers published by the army itself and put out propaganda accusing the Jews of avoiding military service, particularly combat, and demonstrating cowardice under fire. They accused the Jews of staying home and making large profits while true Germans were at the front bleeding and dying. As a result of long-standing prejudices and stereotypes, many Germans chose to believe the anti-Semitic propaganda rather than the hard evidence which contradicted it. Ernst Toller, a well-known revolutionary and playwright in the 1920s, described the situation of one fiercely patriotic Jew named Friedrich in a dialogue with fellow soldiers:

FRIEDRICH But how could you live without a country? I'd go mad with all this horror if I couldn't grit my teeth and say 'It's all for my country.'
SECOND SOLDIER You're a funny one to talk like that.
FRIEDRICH Why any funnier than you?
FIRST SOLDIER And you a foreigner. Ha, ha!
FRIEDRICH I'm not a foreigner. I'm one of you.
SECOND SOLDIER If you fought with us a thousand times you'd still be a foreigner.[23]

In the period following the end of the war, Jews from the new nations of central and eastern Europe moved into Germany. The Germany they entered was suffering from economic and political turmoil and struggling to find a new identity. Immigrants had never been particularly welcome in Germany, but, in the twenties, hostility towards newcomers intensified, and Jewish immigrants were even more resented. Eastern European Jews had already been what Jack Wertheimer calls *Unwelcome Strangers* in the more peaceful pre-World War I period.[24] Acculturated, educated and reasonably prosperous German Jews, themselves, greeted their eastern brethren with mixed emotions. They were sympathetic to their plight and willing to help, but worried about the effect of these unacculturated Jews on Germans, particularly anti-Semites. Included among the eastern European Jews were Hebrew writers, scholars and publishers fleeing from Russia. These Jews, unlike their German co-religionists, remained more firmly attached to their Jewish cultural heritage and the language of the Bible. Thus, ironically in the 1920s, while anti-Semitism grew stronger, Germany simultaneously became a center for Hebrew culture.[25]

Other refugees also drifting into Germany from Eastern Europe brought sustenance and new materials for German anti-Semites. Alfred Rosenberg, an engineer and aspiring journalist and philosopher from Riga, Latvia who was born into a family with German ethnic roots, was a prime representative of this migration. Rosenberg brought with him a copy of an anti-Semitic text used by the Czarist secret police. He translated this work into German and introduced it to the Nazi movement. This tract, *The Protocols of the Elders of Zion*, would become the most infamous piece of anti-Semitic propaganda. An invention of eighteenth-century French Jesuits, it was used in their fight against the secular masonic movement. Agents of the Russian secret police adopted it, substituting Jews for masons, to rouse the Russian populace to fury against the Jews and divert their anger and frustration from the government and landlord class that oppressed them.[26] The document purported to be a meeting of wealthy and prominent Jews who were engaged in a conspiracy to dominate the world. In a Germany where large numbers of people did not understand the reasons for their defeat in the war or the causes of their economic difficulties, conspiracy theory was very popular. Long-standing anti-Semitism made it likely that a Jewish conspiracy would be believable to many people.

The economic and social circumstances of Jews in Weimar Germany contributed to their visibility and vulnerability. As Albert Lindemann has pointed out, the growth of late nineteenth-century anti-Semitism was in part the reaction to the rise of the Jews.[27] The lifting of legal restrictions on Jews and the greater educational opportunities available allowed many in western Europe to rise quickly to middle-class status in business and some of the professions. A small group became very wealthy and prominent. These Jews owned department stores, were managers of large commercial banks or owners of small investment banks. However, most Jews in Weimar Germany were middle class. About sixty-one per cent were included in those engaged in trade and commerce.[28] Many owned small retail businesses. Many were small-scale wholesalers particularly in women's ready to wear clothing. Jews were strongly represented in the medical and legal professions, although they had limited access to the judiciary. About eleven per cent of the doctors and sixteen per cent of the lawyers in Weimar Germany were Jews.[29] They were also very visible in the press, the theater and other branches of the arts.

The entry to most professions was through education, and many Jews aspired to become students at universities and technical colleges. However, beginning in the period before World War I, German states established quotas for Jewish students at their universities. These restrictions were aimed primarily at eastern European Jews who were not German citizens. The acquisition of German citizenship for anyone who could not demonstrate ethnic German roots was a complicated, difficult and long procedure. The Germans had not developed a concept of citizenship like that of the French which was a product of the Enlightenment and the French Revolution or like that of the Americans which was based on the immigrant experience. Thus, state-sponsored educational opportunities for German Jews were restricted, and the opportunities for Jewish immigrants were restricted even more.

Faculty positions at German universities remained difficult for Jews to achieve throughout the Weimar period. Therefore, many of the most prominent Jewish scholars worked through independent research institutes because they could not obtain university positions. The most famous of these institutions was the Frankfurt School which included among its members the psychologists

Theodor Adorno and Eric Fromm, the political theorists Hannah Arendt, Franz Neumann and Herbert Marcuse, the sociologist Max Horkheimer and the literary critic Walter Benjamin.[30] Other scholars worked at institutions such as the famous library and research center set up by the Warburg family.[31]

Their commercial, professional and intellectual activity brought many Jews into contact with other Germans who often resented their apparent success. Yet, contrary to the propaganda assertions of the radical and conservative right that Jews were getting richer while most Germans were growing poorer during the first half of the 1920s, most Jews were getting poorer as well. These years were particularly bad for merchants with small businesses and white collar workers; categories into which many Jews fell. Like other Germans who had worked their way up to the middle class, Jews experienced the fear of proletarianization, of falling into the working class. This fear was quite common among all members of the German lower middle class. Many Jews faced financial ruin, and the inability of some to cope with loss of income and status was reflected in a high suicide rate. A general lack of confidence in the economic future was one cause of a declining birth rate among Jews during this period. Ruth Gay has pointed out, "Whereas at the beginning of the century Jews in Prussia had produced 35 children per thousand annually ...; it would be only 11 in 1927. This was even lower than the French birth rate, notoriously among the lowest in Europe which stood at 19 per thousand in 1924"[32]

While the Nazis were the most effective users of anti-Semitism for political purposes, most Weimar political parties invoked anti-Semitic rhetoric as part of their political appeal. The German Nationalists and the right wing of the People's Party constantly used anti-Semitic diatribes. Elements of the Catholic Center Party, which was a bulwark of the Weimar Republic, were not above resorting to anti-Semitism to gain support. On the left, the Social Democrats and Communist Parties were officially opposed to anti-Semitism. However, the Social Democrats had a tough job convincing all their leaders of this plank and getting the message to the rank and file. The Communist Party had its own version of anti-Semitism which it cloaked under its fierce anti-capitalist rhetoric.

Jews ultimately proved powerless to act politically to check anti-Semitism. They faced the problems of their numbers, their heritage, their lack of influence among the power brokers, their lack of firm allies, the indifference of much of the population and the irrational hatred of their enemies. As only about one per cent of the population, their numbers were insufficient to make them a factor as a voting bloc. Their ghetto heritage had taught Jews to fear public protest and calling attention to themselves. Jews had tried for centuries to exert influence quietly and diplomatically behind the scenes by appeals to prominent individuals who might be sympathetic. These tactics were much less appropriate in a mass democracy than in an aristocratic monarchy and tended to reinforce stereotypes of Jewish conspiracy and manipulation.

There was also, however, a tradition of active self-defense among a small minority of the Jewish community. These Jews urged aggressive action. Some Jewish student groups were willing to fight anti-Semites. The Vedrina Group from Breslau, for example, had a three-ring symbol with the Latin motto "nemo me impine lacessit," ("no one injures me with impunity").[33] Alfred Doblin, a Jewish writer whose novel, *Berlin Alexanderplatz*, was one of the most important of the 1920s, caught this spirit when one of his main characters says, "Hail and rain come out the air; no one can do anything about it, but against many other things you can defend yourself. So now don't cry as I used to: its fate! its fate! You can't respect that sort of thing as fate. You have to recognize it, seize it and destroy it."[34]

Whether Jews chose to be aggressive in their own defense or to work more quietly, their influence was minimal on those power brokers who did exert significant political influence, particularly directors of heavy industry, landed aristocrats and trade union leaders. Jews were not significantly represented among the constituencies of these men. They also had little clout with and little sympathy from those important popular opinion molders: the clergy and the teachers. Even in important areas such as the press where Jews were well-placed to exert influence, Jewish press lords like the Ullsteins and the Mosses bent over backwards to demonstrate their German nationalism and to distance themselves from causes seen as specifically Jewish. Therefore, Jewish organizations like the Central Verein could do little to stem the tide of growing anti-Semitism. Few Jews were themselves in high positions in government circles either in the civil service or in the legislative or executive branches. According to 1925 statistics, of the five hundred highest state officials, only fifteen were Jews or people of Jewish descent. Of the 608 Reichstag deputies at the time of one of the largest assemblies, only six were Jews or of Jewish descent, and two Jews sat in the Prussian Landtag. Only two Jews served in the twenty-two Reich cabinets.[35]

In many ways, Berlin was the heart of German Jewry and displayed both their achievements and their difficulties. Berlin included 173,000 Jews within its borders during the Weimar years, constituting 4.3 per cent of the city's population. About twenty-five per cent of those Jews were not German citizens. Most were from eastern Europe, particularly Poland, Russia and Galicia, which had been part of the Austrian Empire.[36] There were more synagogues in Berlin than in any other city in Europe, including twelve great community synagogues each with more than two thousand seats. Most of Berlin's synagogues were classified as liberal, and their services were directed at Jews who were modern in dress, strongly German culturally and politically moderate.

In spite of their moderate financial success, the Jews of Berlin were in no way immune from the economic downturns that affected German life. During the severe inflation of 1923, the Jewish community ran nineteen soup kitchens, seven shelters and an employment information and placement office for the destitute Jews of the city.[37] At the height of the depression in 1931, about 15,000 Berlin Jews were out of work, and about one-quarter of all Jews in the city were receiving supplementary aid from the organized Jewish community.[38] Clearly by the later years of the Weimar period, Jewish economic fortunes were on the decline. Changes in industry and in the sale of agricultural products marginalized many Jewish merchants and businessmen, and many Jews began to fall from the middle class. The number of Jews being trained in law and medicine at the University of Berlin declined as well. By the end of 1928, the Jewish population was itself declining as deaths outnumbered births by ten to seven, and intermarriage and conversion rates rose. Thus, in many ways, the prospects for German Jewry as projected by the Berlin experience were not positive in the late Weimar years.

At the same time, what Peter Gay calls a "Berlin Jewish spirit" infused a significant part of the cultural and intellectual life of the capital.[39] The contributions of Jews in the arts, the sciences, and the scholarly professions helped to make Weimar Germany the vibrant, creative place which it was. The Jewish community, declining in birth rate and economic strength, harassed and hounded by its enemies on the right and finding little help anywhere, tottered precariously as Hitler and the Nazis came to power. In many ways, it symbolized the plight of the Weimar Republic; Germany's humane democracy and its Jews would fall together.

Notes

1 H. G. Adler, *The Jews in Germany: from the Enlightenment to National Socialism*, Notre Dame, Indiana, 1960. p. 126.

2 Lion Feuchtwanger, *Success*, trans. Willa and Edwin Muir, New York, 1984 (1930), p. 197.

3 Richard Bendix, *From Berlin to Berkeley: German Jewish Identities*, New Brunswick, New Jersey, 1986, p. 81.

4 Walter Laqueur, *Weimar, a Cultural History 1918–1933*, New York, 1980, p. 73.

5 Quoted in Donald Niewyk, T*he Jews in Weimar Germany*, Baton Rouge, Louisiana, 1980, p. 100.

6 Quoted in Frederick V. Grunfeld, *Prophets Without Honour: a Background to Freud, Kafka, Einstein and their World*, London, 1979, p. 161.

7 Quoted in Harry Kessler, *Walther Rathenau: His Life and Work*, New York, 1930, p. 37.

8 Salo Baron, *A Social and Religious History of the Jews*, New York, 1960, Vol. 1–VIII.

9 Rosemary Reuter, *Faith and Fratricide: Theological Roots of Anti-Semitism*, New York, 1974.

10 Franklin Littell, *The Crucifixion of the Jews*, New York, 1975.

11 Quoted in Robert Wistrich, *Anti-Semitism: the Longest Hatred*, New York, 1991, pp. 39–40.

12 Peter Gay, Introduction in Ruth Gay, *The Jews of Germany: a Historical Portrait*, New Haven, 1992, p. xi.

13 Marion Kaplan, *The Making of the Jewish Middle Class: Women, Family and Identity in Imperial Germany*, New York, 1991, p. 63.

14 Gerschom Scholem, *From Berlin to Jerusalem: Memories of my Youth*, trans. Harry Zohn, New York, 1980, p. 90.

15 Peter G. J. Pulzer, *The Rise of Political Anti-Semitism in Germany and Austria*, New York, 1964.

16 Hans-Ulrich Wehler, *The German Empire 1871–1918*, trans. Kim

Traynor, Providence, Rhode Island, 1985.

17 Roger Chickering, *We Men Who Feel Most German; a Cultural Study of the Pan-German League 1886–1914*, Boston, Mass., 1984.

18 Robert Wistrich, "Socialism and Judeophobia – Anti-Semitism in Europe before 1914" *Leo Baeck Yearbook 1992*, XXXVII, London, 1992, p. 118.

19 "Germany" *Encyclopedia Judaica S. V.*, Jerusalem, 1971, p. 477.

20 Jehuda Reinharz, *Fatherland or Promised Land: the Dilemma of German Jews 1893–1914*, Ann Arbor, Michigan, 1975, pp. 1–2.

21 *Ibid.*, pp. 70–1.

22 Ismar Schorsch, *Jewish Reactions to German Anti-Semitism, 1870–1914*, New York, 1972, p. 47.

23 Ernst Toller, "Transfiguration," in *Seven Plays*, New York, 1936, p. 69.

24 Jack Wertheimer, *Unwelcome Strangers: East European Jews in Imperial Germany*, New York, 1987.

25 "Weimar Culture," *Encyclopedia Judaica*, p. 487.

26 Norman Rufu Cohn, *Warrant for Genocide; the Myth of the Jewish World Conspiracy and the Protocols of the Elders of Zion*, New York, 1967.

27 Albert S. Lindemann, *The Jew Accused: Three Anti-Semitic Affairs (Dreyfus, Beilis, Frank) 1894–1915*, Cambridgeshire, 1991.

28 Niewyk, *The Jews in Weimar Germany*, p. 13.

29 *Ibid.*

30 Martin Jay, *The Dialectical Imagination: a History of the Frankfurt School and the Institute of Social Research, 1923–1950*, Boston, 1973.

31 D. Wuttke, "Abby Warburgs Kulturwissenschaft," *Historische Zeitschrift*, 256, 1993, pp. 1–31.

32 Ruth Gay, *The Jews of Germany*, p. 202.

33 *Ibid.*, p. 212.

34 Quoted in Grunfeld, *Prophets Without Honor*, p. 278.

35 Richard Black, *If I Were A Jew*, New York, 1933, p. 14.

36 Monika Richarz, "Erfolg und Gefährdung in der Weimarer Republik" in *Juden in Berlin 1671–1945, Ein Lesebuch*, Berlin, 1988, p. 179.

37 Niewyk, *The Jews in Weimar*, p. 18.

38 Richarz, "Erfolg und Gefährdung", p. 180.

39 Peter Gay, *Freud, Jews and Other Germans: masters and victims in modernist culture*, New York, 1978.

13

National Socialism within the Republic

The failure of the Republic and the rise of the National Socialists are often linked together in a causal relationship. Frequently the Weimar Republic is only seen as an anti-room to Nazi Germany. Clearly it was far more than that. The Weimar Republic did not have to fail, but even when it did it, there were alternatives to the National Socialist state. The champions of these alternatives were thwarted, often by their own limitations as well as by circumstances beyond their control, and Adolf Hitler stepped in to fill the vacuum of leadership. The role that he and the Nazis played in the life and death of the Republic reveals much about its strengths and weaknesses.

Adolf Hitler became the most successful and popular political leader whom the Republic produced. When he was named Chancellor in January 1933, his party was the closest thing to a majority party that Germany had seen. Following three Chancellors who ruled without substantial popular support, two of whom had no popular political base at all, Hitler was closer to the original constitutional idea of a Chancellor. He was the least in need of a diverse coalition government, although, at first, he did represent a political fusion.

In significant ways, he was a representative Weimar figure. Like the saddler Friedrich Ebert and the printer Otto Braun, Adolf Hitler had none of the credentials which had traditionally been important for positions of prominence and prestige in German society. His family was insignificant. He had no academic degrees and had not even successfully finished secondary school. He owned no land and had no money. While he was a war veteran, he had never attained a higher rank than corporal. In fact, in class terms, he was on a lower level than Ebert or Braun. Although his father, an Austrian customs official, had been a member of the lower-middle class, Hitler, himself, belonged to the *lumpenproletariat* who had no fixed trade or profession and drifted from one precarious situation to another.

Hitler was born in Braunau am Im in Austria near the Bavarian border. He grew up in the Austrian Empire and attended the Kaiser Franz Oberrealschule in the city of Linz. He was a largely indifferent student and never received his high school diploma. His writing always showed signs of his lack of formal education, and his reading consisted mainly of popular periodicals and novels. Even when he later attained fame as an orator, his critics always commented on his lack of an educated vocabulary. However, none of these limitations detract from the fact that he was a man of extraordinary ability who, considering his humble origins and many disadvantages, would achieve incredible things. The staggering evil he did speaks to his want of humane values and moral principles not to his lack of intelligence or competence.

As a teenager, he moved to Vienna with dreams of being a visual artist or architect. He was twice rejected for admission to the Art Academy in Vienna. He lacked the requisite academic credentials without which he needed to demonstrate unusual artistic ability to gain admission. While his drawings were pleasant, they were those of an imitator. His hope of being a realist painter was beyond his draftsmanship and dexterity, and he detested the more modern painting styles which might have provided more scope for whatever artistic ability he possessed (although he totally lacked the required innovative imagination). Squandering the money he received from his father's government pension, from his mother and from his aunt, he ended his Vienna days living in shelters for homeless and down and out men.

At the same time, he discovered a political hero in Karl Lueger, the mayor of Vienna. Lueger had created a Christian Socialist political movement which combined a commitment to municipal socialism, including public power and transportation, with a campaign to attract owners of small businesses and craftspeople. Lueger's tactics relied upon attacks on bankers, financiers and owners of large businesses combined with a powerful demagogic dose of anti-Semitism. Hitler also read racist periodicals such as *Ostara* which described history as a continuing struggle between racially pure Aryan heroes and Jews who wanted to defile and corrupt the purity of the race. He saw hundreds of performances of Wagnerian operas drenched in romantic images of heroic violence and developed his speaking skills by haranguing other men at the homeless shelter where he lived.

In 1913, he fled across the German border to Munich in order to avoid service in the Austrian army; a year later he volunteered for the German army. His avoidance of military service in Austria was based on his contempt for the Austrian Empire as a backward, polyglot agglomeration in which the superior Germans were being swamped by inferior Slavs and Jews. He had admired Germany from afar as a much more homogeneous and racially-pure state that was dynamic and primed for territorial expansion and world power. His enlistment was the first concrete manifestation of his conviction. Although Hitler never attained even non-commissioned officer's rank in the German Army, such an achievement was highly unlikely for a non-German with no special qualifications in his favor. He did, however, distinguish himself as a courier and received two Iron Crosses, a first and a second class, the former being very rare among enlisted men.

Hitler was among the very few World War I veterans who loved their war experiences. He carried his enthusiasm into the post-war period and worked in Munich as an agitator for the military, speaking against left-wing parties and urging nationalism and counter-revolution. His activities led to membership in a small right-wing group called the German Workers Party which he soon dominated. This party changed its name to the National Socialist German Workers Party. The contraction of the first parts of the first two words created the term "Nazi" which became the popular name for the party and for its leader's guiding principles. The street corner orator who spoke in Munich in 1919 and the dictator of Germany who died in his bunker in Berlin in 1945 had the same goals and the same view of the world. Predicated on a paranoid sense that Germany was surrounded by enemies, Hitler's plan called for a Germany restored to "Great Power" status, able to expand militarily and attain the *Lebensraum* (living space) that the dynamic, creative German people required and deserved. To succeed he would need to solve the "Jewish problem" which threatened to destroy the German people.

The fledgling National Socialist Party initially attracted young men, many of whom were war veterans, who either had never had a place in the civilian economy and society or could not fit back into their former places. As a result of their war experiences, many of these men had become violent and took their bitterness and anger into the streets on behalf of their new political party. They were organized into auxiliary paramilitary units designed to provide a public show of strength and security for party speakers and to threaten and harass opponents. Their initial SA (*Sturmabteilung*) and subsequent SS (*Schutzstaffel*) units were duplicated by other political parties including the Communists and the Social Democrats. However, the Nazi paramilitary organizations were much closer to the heart of the party than were those of other groups.

Most of the early leaders of the Nazi Party, such as Heinrich Himmler and Alfred Rosenberg who would stay with Hitler until the end, also came from unimpressive backgrounds and lacked the standard prerequisites for success. An exception to this pattern was Hermann Göring, air ace and war hero with connections by marriage to the aristocracy. Göring would become the second most popular figure in the Nazi movement. Although atypical by background, his beliefs and behavior typified the violent profile of the Nazi. In recruiting men for the SA he used a poem, written by the Italian poet Gabrielle D'Annunzio, which appealed to the most primitive drives of the violent men of Weimar Germany.

> Do you wish to fight? To kill?
> To see streams of blood?
> Great heaps of gold?
> Herds of captive women?
> Slaves?[1]

As extreme as the poem seems, Hitler and Göring would give a generation of young men the opportunity to do these things within only six years of the end of the Republic. Young men were initially inspired to join the party by General Ludendorff who, with General Hindenburg, had wielded almost dictatorial political power during the war. By 1918, Ludendorff had evidenced support for the Fatherland Party, a radical nationalist and anti-Semitic group active briefly in 1917 and 1918. He was an outspoken propagator of the stab-in-the-back lie and associated with extreme political radicals and fringe mystics. As the Nazis gained notoriety, he supported their cause.

Other supporters whom the fledgling party attracted came from the lower middle class which had suffered the greatest loss of status and, comparatively, of income during World War I. These shopkeepers, craftsmen, clerks, teachers and lower-level civil servants were opposed to the new Republic which they identified with defeat, the factory, the vamp and the inflation. They hated anything they identified as modern and were bitter and alienated enough to opt for radical solutions.

In November 1923, Hitler and the Nazis attempted to take advantage of the bitterness and anger that had resulted from numerous crises and to seize control of Germany by a two-step process. They would first take over Bavaria. Then, in combination with those Bavarian leaders willing to co-operate, they would march on Berlin in imitation of Mussolini's and his Fascists' successful march on Rome.

Italian Fascism and National Socialism had much in common and, for a time in the twenties, the Nazis were referred to as Fascists, and Hitler was called the German Mussolini. Both Italian Fascism and National Socialism rejected representative legislative democracy in favor of a dictatorship based on a concept of identity between one leader and the people. The leader was to embody in his very person the hopes, aspirations and values of the true members of the community. Both Nazism and Fascism rejected reason and logic and substituted emotion and instinct as guides to decision-making and action. Both systems stressed the division of all people into friends and foes. The essence of politics for both was the identification of the foe and the willingness of the community of friends to kill the foe. Both movements rejected individualism in favor of the sacrifice of the individual to a greater whole. They also agreed on a Social Darwinist view of life dominated by struggle, where nations battled against one another for survival and where the strong survived while the weak fell by the wayside. Both Fascism and Nazism glorified war. Consistent with this adversarial ethos, strong gender separations were stressed. The goal for young males was to be soldiers, while young females were seen as future mothers.

In spite of many similarities, there were crucial differences between these two movements. For Hitler and the National Socialists, racism, primarily anti-Semitism, was vital to defining the community and the enemy. This factor never played the same role for Mussolini and the Italian Fascists. While both groups beat, tortured, and murdered political opponents, only the Nazis developed genocidal mass murder programs.

The Nazi Putsch failed in its first phase because the Bavarian officials who seemed willing to co-operate changed their minds, and, under pressure from General von Seeckt and his associates at central army headquarters, the military units in Bavaria and the police fired on the Nazi marchers. Seventeen people died in the attempt, and Hitler was arrested. He was charged with high treason and could have faced a firing squad or a long jail sentence and possible deportation. He was not a German citizen and had never renounced his Austrian citizenship.

Hitler's arrest and trial began with a jurisdictional dispute over whether he would be tried by the Bavarian state courts or by the special political courts of the central government. The Bavarian leaders demonstrated sympathy for the defendant and his cause by fighting hard to retain jurisdiction and resisting pressure to deport Hitler. They knew that he would be treated more harshly in Berlin. A deal was struck between the central government and Bavaria in which Bavaria would try Hitler in exchange for agreeing to dissolve special state tribunals created during the crisis of 1923 when martial law had been temporarily instituted. These courts were of questionable legality, and their continuation after the end of the crisis was a clear violation of the national Constitution.

The Bavarian authorities allowed Hitler to use the trial as a propaganda platform and evidenced their sympathies with a light sentence. Karl Bracher described how:

> Just as the abortive putschist managed to turn the courtroom into a platform for his sweeping indictment of the 'Jew Republic,' so the execution of his sentence also helped him in every possible way. Instead of being deported as an unwelcome alien, as was planned in the fall of 1924, Hitler was given what was almost a vacation in Landsberg Castle, in the company of forty of his jailed followers.[2]

Fortress imprisonment had always been considered the most honorable type of punishment.

While incarcerated, Hitler dictated the first volume of his political autobiography *Mein Kampf* to his loyal follower Rudolf Hess.[3] In this work, actually read by very few in the following years, he laid out in rough form his goals for his future program. Few significant historical figures have made their intentions so clear. Yet, his opponents in Germany and observers elsewhere failed to take him seriously. When his party began to make substantial electoral gains, observers like the editors of *The New York Times* had little trouble figuring out what goals he had set out, based on their reading of *Mein Kampf*. In representative articles such as "Conquest of Russia One Aim of Hitler" and "Anti-Semitic Fight Looms in Reichstag," they commented on his intention to conquer Russia and to deal with the Jews.[4] In the latter article, they wrote, "since they first set out in pursuit of votes in 1922, anti-Semitism has been one of their chief slogans."[5] Thus, *The Times* and others who chose to read the signs identified the two tracks which would eventually lead to Stalingrad and Auschwitz.[6]

When Hitler emerged from prison as the result of an amnesty in December 1924, his prospects and those of his movement seemed bleak. The party was disorganized, short of money and, in electoral terms, was on the decline. The first crisis stage of the Weimar period had passed, and stabilization was at hand. For the next five years, Hitler worked tirelessly and with great faith to build a mass political movement, but the masses seemed to be showing little interest. During this period, Hitler demonstrated his organizational ability and his great understanding of mass politics. He knew that a mass political movement requires a superstructure and a leadership cadre. He worked to build the former and recruit the latter. The Nazis organized in every city and town and in the rural areas. He appreciated the advantages of the new technology for political purposes and used the automobile, the airplane and the radio. He and his able lieutenant, Joseph Goebbels, developed their capacities to use mass propaganda techniques, and they honed their considerable oratorical skills.

Hitler understood that appealing to a mix of self-interest and idealism could be very effective in building a popular political movement. He recognized that German youth hungered for idealism while they concluded that most other political parties represented limited materialistic interests. As Conan Fischer claims, "This [stress on idealism] is not to argue that Nazi supporters wished their identities and interests to be subsumed within a homnogeneous mass, and the NSDAP's plethora of ancillary formations testified to the care it took to subscribe to its supporters particular interests and aspirations."[7] Thus at the same time, Hitler suggested, in the name of idealism and national interest, that his movement cared about the practical needs of peasants, craftsmen, shopkeepers, soldiers, mothers, unemployed workers and students as long as they were racially-pure Germans. However, as Fischer convincingly argues, Hitler always was aware that his movement was, "... more than just a diffuse aggregation of particular interest ..."[8] He promised that he would recapture the glorious German past in an even better future. He pledged to eliminate the indecision, the paralysis, the self- interest that characterized the government of the Republic. He was, in the term coined by Jeffrey Herf, a reactionary modernist.[9] Hitler combined a rejection of "modern culture", which he deemed decadent, and a rejection of the financial and commercial market system, which he branded as Jewish, with an admiration and support of technology, particularly that which was of military value. He accepted the need for heavy industry which was required for national greatness, but it had to be subordinated to the political needs of the people and the racial community. He also was a hater, a racist anti-Semite and an advocate of violence, beliefs he only occasionally thinly disguised.

When the world depression began in 1929, Hitler and his movement were ready. The vote for the National Socialists rose dramatically, and their seats in the Reichstag increased from 12 in 1928, to 107 in 1930, and to 230 in 1932. By 1932, the National Socialists were attracting more than thirty-seven per cent of the vote, a stunning achievement in a field where over thirty parties were on the ballot. On the state level, the party was also doing extremely well, achieving its first cabinet position in Thuringia and making dramatic gains in Prussia which, as has been indicated, was the bulwark of the Weimar Republic.

The success of the Nazis raises two key questions: Who were the Nazi voters? Who provided the financial support for the Nazis' push to power? Some of the Nazi voters came from the groups who had supported the party from the beginning: young men and members of the lower middle class, teachers and civil servants. The party had won the battle for the youth during the

Weimar period, and increasing numbers of university students were supporting it.

The rejection of the Republic by large numbers of university students and their professors and their embracing of the irrationalist Nazi movement was a great blow to German democracy. As the Nationalist Reinhold Wulle wrote in 1919, "Who has youth, has the future."[10] The universities which Weimar students entered created an atmosphere which molded their *Weltanschauung* and made their allegiances more comprehensible. Peter Gay explains that, "The universities in which Germans took such ostentatious pride, were nurseries of a woolly-minded militarist idealism and centers of resistance to the new in art or the social sciences; Jews, democrats, socialists, in a word outsiders, were kept from the sacred precincts of higher learning."[11]

University students responded to Ernst Jünger's glorification of the man of action and the battlefield.[12] They preferred the image of the transcending quality of steel and fire to the more sober message of the two most popular anti-war novels of the Weimar period, Remarque's *All Quiet on the Western Front,* and Arnold Zweig's *The Case of Sergeant Grishka.*[13] Many university professors lived the life of the mind yet cheered when Nazi orators like Hermann Göring attacked intellectuals and reasoned discourse and claimed to think with their blood. Some, such as the world-famous philosopher Martin Heidigger, found Nazi philosophy in tune with their fascination with death and rebirth.[14]

The Nazi party appealed to young people and intellectuals by promising transformation and practicing the politics of transcendence. They promised a new German person in addition to a new German society. While the pro-Weimar parties talked about making specific improvements in people's lives, the Nazis talked about totally new lives for people. They had a vision of the future, a mission. They called themselves a movement rather than a party. They had a charismatic leader and a semi-religious aura. Only the Communists talked in similar terms, and their message lacked the romance and violence of the Nazi call to arms.

In spite of the mythic nature of the Nazi appeal, Hitler was always careful not to attack Christianity directly. He stressed his Catholic upbringing and his belief in God. There were factions in the party who were fiercely anti-Christian, but Hitler always claimed that they were fringe groups which he could not control.

The Nazis promised a return to a society with Christian values and had many religious supporters including some among the clergy. The Nazi position on religion gave them an advantage in their struggle against the Communists. Yet, in the elaborate ceremonies, rallies, uniforms and oaths that the Nazis created, they may have been laying the groundwork for a future pagan Nazi religion to replace Christianity.

The Catholic Church worried about the degree of control the movement exerted over its followers and the level of obedience it demanded. It, therefore, barred its flock from membership in the party, particularly in its paramilitary organizations. In spite of the bans, many Catholics supported the Nazi movement; but, relative to their percentage of the population, there were fewer Catholic members of the movement than Protestants. However, when the Nazis took power, the Catholic Church dropped its opposition, and a covenant between Berlin and Rome paved the way for full participation by German Catholics in the Nazi regime.

Many of the new Nazi voters had previously voted for middle of the road bourgeois political parties. The collapse of the political center was a key feature in the last period of the Republic. Farmers, who had voted for regional parties such as the Bauernbund (BBB) in Bavaria and the equivalent in Schleswig-Holstein and Saxony, began to vote for the Nazis. They were attracted by the party's effective organizational efforts, able local leaders, and propaganda which built on the tradition of German cultural science and depicted the peasant as the truest representative of pure Germanness. An impressive aspect of the Nazis' growing success was their ability to attract members and voters who embraced modern technology, research and the factory as well as those who hearkened back to a pastoral agricultural and craft society. Engineers and doctors supported the party in substantial numbers, and many joined the elite paramilitary group, the SS.[15]

More surprisingly, the party was beginning to attract a significant number of women voters. The Nazis took an extremely conservative and traditional position on women's issues. Their slogan, "Kinder, Küche, Kirche," defined their view of women's proper role in the society. The party had consistently glorified motherhood and defended the traditional family. Hitler vowed that he would cleanse Germany of the pornography, obscenity, prostitution and overt displays of homosexuality that he blamed on the licence and decadence of Republican leaders. Conservative middle-class women found the ultra traditional message appealing. Many women who had initially embraced the Republic turned towards the Nazi movement out of disappointment and bitterness over what they saw as unfulfilled promises and abandoned goals.

Many Germans would later claim that they supported Hitler because of his economic program. However, very few Germans had any information about what his economic program actually was. He always claimed that economics was not very important to him. In generalized terms, he defined his economics as a means to help bring about restored German greatness. His approach shifted with the different constituencies he courted. For instance, the Nazis targeted specific economic groups as the effects of the depression intensified concentrating on farmers and workers particularly hard hit by the downturn in the economy. While they promised decisive leadership, the nature of their economic program was far from clear. As economic historians are still trying to define the nature of Hitler's economic program even today and cannot decide whether he was a Keynesian with a radical program or a conservative with a program no different from the bureaucratic/governmental response of the Brüning government in late 1931, it is unlikely that German voters had a clear idea of what that program would be.[16] Since Hitler took a pragmatic approach to economics, he was able to dismiss criticism that he had abandoned opposition to big business capitalism which had been basic to the Nazi program in its earliest days. By the early 1930s, he was reassuring bankers and industrialists that they would play a key role in the new National Socialist Germany. In this area as in many others, Hitler was able to use his hostility to the Jews to resolve contradictions.

There is no serious question of the genuineness of Hitler's hatred of Jews while there are many questions about its origins. However, there is also no question that he used anti-Semitism for political purposes as well. He argued, when asked if he were an enemy of capitalism, that he had no problem with genuine German capitalism but was only opposed to international Jewish-financed capitalism. When asked how he could be the leader of a movement which had Socialism in its name and yet railed against Communists and Social Democrats, he argued that he had no problem with genuine German Socialism but was opposed to international Jewish Bolshevism. Thus, he could be for and against many things at the same time.

The last group among whom the Nazis began to make significant gains were the blue collar workers. They had always been on the political left and had been resistant to early Nazi appeals. The city of Berlin, with its strong working-class Socialist and Communist organizations, proved a hard nut for the Nazis to crack. In 1928, they sent their best man, Joseph Goebbels, to head the organization in Berlin and compete for the loyalty of the working masses. He was helped by world-wide economic crisis and the political short-sightedness of the Social Democrats. As unemployment rose and the Weimar government of Heinrich Brüning followed a deflationary policy while the Social Democratics refused to topple his government, workers began to desert the trade unions and the Social Democratic Party. Some supported the Communists, and others began to find their way into the Nazi Party. The Nazi Party retained the support of the groups that had early on been its principle supporters: disaffected war veterans, young men, and members of the *Mittelstand*. The major gains in voters for the movement in the period from 1930 to 1933 came from elements who had supported middle of the road political parties and parties on the right. The most surprising category of new supporters came from the ranks of women. The National Socialists also made substantial gains among farmers. The Nazis benefited from the collapse of the parties of the middle and also benefited from the loss of votes by the Nationalist Party.

As the effects of the depresion intensified, the Nazis began to do better in attracting supporters from the working class. While it is true that many workers who advocted more radical action than the Social Democrats appeared willing to support turned towards the Communists, others began to vote Nazi. As Michael Kater indicates, many of these voters even shifted back and forth from the Communists to the Nazi Party.[17] However, the Nazi Party remained primarily a party of the *Mittelstand*, and the number of working-class members, while growing, stayed below their percentage of the population.

Ironically, it can be argued that Hitler and the Nazis were the only advocates of a system of popular representation and political party government during the last years of the Weimar Republic. From 1930 to 1933, Germany appeared to be moving towards presidential dictatorship. Brüning, von Papen and von Schleicher became Chancellor only because they had the confidence of President Hindenburg. They had no legislative majorities and ruled by the authority of presidential decrees. When Hindenburg ran for re-election in 1932, only Hitler and the Nazis mounted a significant challenge. The parties which had made up the Weimar coalitions were demoralized and feared that there were only three grim choices: Hitler and the Nazis, a Communist dictatorship, or the continued rule of Hindenburg. Thus, there were no real advocates of popular parliamentary government left in Germany.

The rule of reasonable men and women had come to an end at the national level and only continued at the state level, particularly in Prussia. It is not clear what these reasonable supporters of the Republic thought might come when the aged Hindenburg died. Their abdication of forceful efforts to restore true pro-Weimar government meant that the only challengers to this new presidential dictatorship were the Nazis and the Communists. It is conceivable that a type of permanent presidential dictatorship could have evolved if the army, the land owners, the clergy and the industrialists supported it and if the liberals and socialists refrained from challenging it. However, no such union developed because no leader with Hindenburg's prestige emerged.

The position of the industrialists during this crisis and the support they gave the Nazis evolved as circumstances and the Nazi program changed. Certainly the early program of the National Socialist Party, which attacked big business and finance, and the lower-class profile of its leadership did little to inspire industrialists to support the movement. For most of the years of struggle, only a few eccentric industrialists such as Fritz Thyssen and Emil Kirdorf contributed any money to the party.[18] Industrialists preferred the Nationalist and People's Parties but also contributed money to the Center and Democratic Parties. However, Henry Turner concludes that they were not terribly successful in gaining much payback for their contributions. "These efforts of big business to use its money to gain influence over the non-socialist parties and to secure representation of its interests in the parliaments of the Republic yielded disappointing results."[19] Most of the money the Nazis raised during the twenties came, not from industrialists or financiers, but from their rank and file members.

These supporters gave generously, often compounding their own difficult financial circumstances by doing so. They gave because they believed and they had no immediate expectation of monetary payback.

When the Nazis and the Communists made big gains in the election of 1930, industrialists had to worry about the radical left for the first time since the early days of the Republic. Several options were open to them. Some saw presidential dictatorship as the best hope of protecting capitalism and preventing Communism from gaining power. Some began to contribute money to the National Socialists as the lesser evil. Others hoped to preserve their influence by keeping avenues of communication open to all non-Communist forces that had a chance to achieve power. The possibility of recreating an agreement between the industrialists and the unions which had been so important during the early crisis of the Republic was not an option because the unions had lost a great deal of their power during the depression with its years of high unemployment. Thus, the alternative of corporatism that had been developing during the 1920s was destroyed by the depression and the re-emergence of the primacy of politics through the rise of the Nazi Party.[20]

Alfred Hugenberg's decision to join an alliance with Hitler in 1930 reflected his own growing ideological extremism and his belief that Hitler and the Nazis could provide help in his personal quest for power. His decision did not represent the position of many industrialists who had been members of the Nationalist Party and whose spokesman Hugenberg had been for many years. However, the path taken by Hugenberg and the Nationalists was a great aid to Hitler's ambitions.

Hugenberg, who had written an academic dissertation on the role of farmers in the settlement of northwest Germany, made his mark in business and communications. In 1909, Gustav Krupp appointed him the chairman of the ten-member Board of Directors of the huge family-owned heavy industry conglomerate based in Essen.[21] In 1914, Hugenberg left this position to create Ausland G.m.b.h., a holding company for the co-ordination of industrial investment in the media. With this base, he began to build a media empire designed to advance the interests of German industrialists, particularly those in the heavy domestic industry sector such as iron, steel and coal. During the war, he became a leading member of the Fatherland Party and was strongly in favor of territorial expansion and racist anti-Semitism. During the Weimar period, he worked primarily to enlarge his media empire and to gain control of the German Nationalist Party.

He was extremely successful. Modris Eksteins has calculated that, "A rough estimate would be that Hugenberg enjoyed some form of control or influence over close to one half of the German Press by 1930."[22] He owned only a part of this empire directly, but he was able to use economic pressure to influence a large segment of the small provincial newspapers in Germany. He manipulated this press power to advance his political message. He operated a wire service, the Telegraphy Union (TU), to which 1600 newspapers subscribed. While his wire service was smaller than the Wolff's Telegraph Bureau (WTB), it operated on a different premise. The WTB was basically impartial, while the TU was in Eksteins' words "unashamedly nationalist and conservative in political tendency."[23] In addition to his press and wire service operations, he directed Scherlhaus, a major publishing company, and controlled UFA, the most significant German film company.

When Hugenberg took control of the Nationalist Party in 1928, he was determined to destroy the Republic and to become the dominant force in the new Germany. In many ways, his view of Germany's future coincided with Hitler's expansionism and anti-Semitism. However, he judged the Nazi movement as lower-class and envisioned the new Germany ruled by a conservative elite. Hugenberg recognized Hitler's talents and believed that the Nazis could be used to channel mass unrest, gain electoral success, and contribute to the destruction of the Weimar government. As early as 1923, the Hugenberg press had identified Hitler as "an exceptionally popular speaker" and an "organizer of unaccustomed talent who was able to liberate innumerable workers from the bond of international socialism and convert them to the Nationalist cause."[24] By 1930, Hugenberg and Hitler had become allies first in the battle against the ratification of the Young Plan. Their supporters gathered signatures to put the question on the ballot and then campaigned to have the plan rejected. Although their efforts failed, they forged effective links between their two parties. The alliance, called the Harzburg Front, also grew to include the conservative anti-Weimar veterans organization, the Stahlhelm.

While Hugenberg believed he would gain much from this alliance, more immediate and more substantial gains accrued to Hitler and the Nazi movement. The Nazis gained access to media outlets which opened up millions of new supporters to their message. They also gained an element of respectability and, thus, the votes of those who had no problem with Nazi anti-republicanism or anti-Semitism but were only willing to support respectable racist anti-republicans – not rabble. The alliance with Hugenberg also allowed Hitler to approach industrialists and financiers more easily for money. However, by the early 1930s, the relationship between Hugenberg and some of his early industrialist backers had become strained. He appeared to some of them more intent on advancing his ideological views than promoting the interest of industry.

The last major obstacle to Hitler's move towards power came from a strange source, General von Schleicher, who had been named Chancellor by President Hindenburg in late 1932. Von Schleicher was a favorite of Hindenburg's from his days on the General Staff. In an effort to maintain his own political influence, von Schleicher moved to block Hitler from coming to power. He developed a two-fold strategy to thwart Hitler's ambitions. He would force the Nazis into frequent and expensive elections and, thus, would deplete their resources and alienate their less committed supporters. His first move in this direction was successful, and the Nazis, who had enjoyed dramatically increasing electoral support since 1930, suffered their first setback although they still remained the largest party in the Reichstag. The second aspect of von Schleicher's plan centered around the creation of a strange popular coalition movement. He would rally blue collar workers, rural agricultural workers, and those Nazis who anticipated actual socialist reform. He envisioned a deficit-spending public works program to put people back to work and a land reform program to appeal to agriculture workers and farmers with small holdings. He hoped to use presidential power and army support to buy him time to create this alliance and put his program into operation.

The prospects for success were not great, but von Schleicher did not have the opportunity to try. The large land owners in the Hindenburg circle were alarmed at the prospect of land reform and used the agency of Franz von Papen to influence the aged President to desert his long-time associate, von Schleicher. They convinced Hindenburg to name Hitler Chancellor. They argued that Hitler could be controlled and limited by making him choose von Papen as Vice-Chancellor and a cabinet which included Alfred Hugenberg and the Stahlhelm leader Franz Seldte.

Once again, as had been true since at least 1923, people underestimated Adolf Hitler. Von Papen thought he could use Hitler to consolidate his own power. Hugenberg had the same expectation. President Hindenburg considered Hitler to be a non-entity and was sure smarter men would control him. The Communists were convinced that he would fail and that a Communist revolution would follow. They would all be wrong and millions would die, in part because of these errors in judgment.

Notes

1 Quoted in Joachim Fest, *Faces of the Third Reich*, trans. Michael Bullock, New York, 1970, p. 71.

2 Karl Bracher, *The German Dictatorship: the Origins, Structure and Effects of National Socialism*, trans. Jean Steinberg, New York, 1970, p. 127.

3 Adolf Hitler, *Mein Kampf*, trans. Ralph Manheim, New York, 1971.

4 "Conquest of Russia One Aim of Hitler" *The New York Times*, September 29, 1930, p. 11; "Anti-Semitic Fight Looms in Reichstag," *The New York Times*, September 21, 1930, p. 3.

5 "Anti-Semitic Fight", p. 3.

6 As an example, Eberhard Jäckel, *Hitler in History*, Hanover, New Hampshire, 1984.

7 Conan Fischer, *The Rise of the Nazis*, Manchester, 1995, p. 127.

8 *Ibid.*, p. 125.

9 Jeffrey Herf, *Reactionary Modernism: Technology, Culture, and Politics in Weimar and the Third Reich*, Cambridgeshire, 1984.

10 Peter Stachura, *The German Youth Movement 1900–1945*, New York, 1981, p. 38.

11 Peter Gay, *Weimar Culture: the Outsider as Insider*, New York, 1970, p. 3.

12 Ernst Jünger, *In Stahlgewitten; aus dem Tagebuch eines Stossstuppführers*, Berlin, 1929.

13 Erich Maria Remarque, *All Quiet on the Western Front*, A. W. Wheen, New York, 1958; Arnold Zweig, *The Case of Sergeant Grishka*, trans. Eric Sutton, New York, 1928.

14 Bullivant, "Conservative Revolution," in Phelan, *Weimar Dilemma*, p. 56.

15 Herf, *Reactionary Modernism*; Robert J. Lifton, *Nazi Doctors: Medical Killing and the Psychology of Genocide*, New York, 1986.

16 Harold James, "Innovation and Conservatism in Economic Recovery: the Alleged 'Nazi Recovery' of the 1930s," in Thomas Childers and Jane Caplan, eds, *Reevaluating the Third Reich*, New York, 1993, pp. 114–39.

17 Michael Kater, *The Nazi Party: a Social Profile of Members and Leaders, 1991–1945*, Cambridge, Mass., 1983, p. 55.

18 Henry Ashby Turner Jr. *German Big Business and the Rise of Hitler*, New York, 1985, p. 89.

19 *Ibid.*, p. 27.

20 Charles Maier, *Recasting Bourgeois Europe: Stabilization in France, Germany and Italy in the Decade after World War I*, Princeton, New Jersey, 1975.

21 John A. Leopold, *Alfred Hugenberg: the Radical Nationalist Campaign against the Weimar Republic*, New Haven, 1977, p. 5.

22 Modris Ecksteins, *The Limits of Reason: the German Democratic Press and the Collapse of Weimar Democracy*, London, 1975, pp. 80–1.

23 *Ibid.*, p. 76.

24 Leopold, pp. 22–3.

Conclusion

The goal of this study was to recognize the challenges faced by those who shaped the Weimar Republic, to rejoice in their accomplishments and to learn from their failures.

The Weimar Republic's Constitution was written by liberals who were committed to democracy and republican government and hoped that a normative climate of peace, order and prosperity would characterize the history of the new nation. The impressive document they produced made provision for crisis but was based on the assumption that crisis would be the unusual exception which need not affect the essential character of the new nation. However the Republic was born in chaos, faced numerous crises, and spent close to half its life coping with these exceptional situations.

The new state developed as a compromise between an Empire that many wanted to preserve and a radical Bolshevized Germany that some wanted to create. It was a Republic without strong democratic traditions to support it and without a body of teachers, clergy and political leaders to confirm its values. Bismarckian and Wilhelmine German society had been characterized by a paternalistic and harsh family structure and by rigid and authoritarian schools. It was a society which was hostile towards the "other" or outsider and saw a polarized world of friends and enemies. Embittered by a long and costly war, an unexpected defeat, and peace terms regarded as universally unjust, the German people were a difficult population to govern under a new liberal participatory system. Women, younger men, socialists, Jews were suddenly either a part of the political process for the first time or appeared to have access to power for the first time. The changed position of Jews and women created fear and uncertainty among the more traditional groups within the society and spurred on the newly formed radical right.

Faced with left and right-wing uprisings, political terrorism, and runaway inflation, the Republic's first years were especially conflicted. Since its parliamentary system was based on the European rather than the English model, coalitions of parties with different constituencies, philosophies, and goals had to struggle to maintain legislative majorities. While coalition governments can be stable and successful, the substantial differences of class, religious affiliation, ideology and tradition which conditioned the behavior of the Weimar political parties made the stability and success of its coalitions more problematic and led to twenty-two cabinets in its fourteen-year history. Weimar coalition governments constantly confronted the reality of parties on both sides of the political spectrum who were fundamentally opposed to the existence of the Republic itself. Assailed by the widespread effects of the world depression beginning in 1929 just when stability and growth seemed to have been achieved, the Republic faced its final test. Ultimately it lacked the resources to overcome this challenge and was destroyed.

Nevertheless in spite of these problems, the Weimar Republic was the first real democratic state in German history. It allowed its citizens an unparalleled amount of personal freedom. All people could participate in politics in the voting booths, in the meeting halls and in the streets. Women became a part of the political process, and their organizations moved from the periphery to play more significant roles. The League of Jewish Women fought for the rights of women and Jews and against anti-Semitism and the oppression of women. Those who had been outsiders during the Empire, such as political leftists, Jews, and homosexuals, had more opportunities than ever before, politically, educationally, and economically. The state of Prussia took significant steps towards creating a major police force with a commitment to democratic government and individual rights. Institutions such as the Bauhaus attempted to redefine the position of the artist within society and made Germany the center of cutting-edge developments in the arts. Reasonable men and women from cultural leaders such as Walter Gropius to political leaders such as Otto Braun and Gustav Stresemann worked to make the Republic a success.

The lessons of Weimar begin with the realization that there are no invisible hands to resolve political and economic conflicts when all parties are only committed to their particular ends and will not make compromises and concessions for the greater good of the society. Uncompromising industrialists, labor leaders, socialists and conservatives allowed the National Socialists and the Communists, who spoke the language of idealism and community, to capture the political center stage and to drive out the parties of the reasonable. Leaders insensitive to the idealism of young people left the rhetoric of idealism to the radicals and lost the youth. Socialists and liberals who could not or would not speak in the language of traditional morality alienated churchmen and women and left the rhetorical moral highground to the radicals.

The Weimar experience proves that republican government has little chance of survival if democracy and an open accepting society are not valued by the teachers, clergy, judges and politicians within a society. A democratic constitution can only be successful when the normative condition is the overwhelmingly dominant situation and when the majority truly take its assumptions as given. A democratic minority is in an impossible position against an anti-democratic majority. Democratic societies must carefully weigh how much freedom of action they will allow to radical groups who are openly committed to the destruction of democratic institutions. The dilemma of the reasonable members of Weimar society continues to be a challenge to advocates of democracy today.

Selected documents

Document 1

"Spartacus Manifesto", cited in Louis Snyder (ed.), *Documents of German History*, (New Brunswick, New Jersey: Rutgers University Press, 1958), pp. 374–6. Originally quoted in *The New York Times*, November 29, 1918.

The Spartacist revolution was a landmark event which took place in early 1919 during the transition from the Wilhelmine Monarchy to the Republic. It contributed to shaping much of Weimar history. "The Spartacus Manifesto" outlines the thinking of many who felt that Germany was in need of a radical socialist revolution in 1919.

PROLETARIANS! MEN AND WOMEN OF LABOR! COMRADES!

The revolution has made its entry into Germany. The masses of the soldiers, who for four years were driven to the slaughterhouse for the sake of capitalistic profits, the masses of workers, who for four years were exploited, crushed, and starved, have revolted. That fearful tool of oppression – Prussian militarism, that scourge of humanity – lies broken on the ground. Its most noticeable representatives, and therewith the most noticeable of those guilty of this war, the Kaiser and the Crown Prince, have fled from the country. Workers' and Soldiers' Councils have been formed everywhere.

Proletarians of all countries, we do not say that in Germany all the power has really been lodged in the hands of the working people, that the complete triumph of the proletarian revolution has already been attained. There still sit in the government all those

Socialists who in August, 1914, abandoned our most precious possession, the International, who for four years betrayed the German working class and at the same time the International.

But, proletarians of all countries, now the German proletarian himself is speaking to you. We believe we have the right to appeal before your forum in his name. From the first day of this war we endeavored to do our international duty by fighting that criminal government with all our power, and branding it as the one really guilty of the war.

Now, at this moment, we are justified before history, before the International, and before the German proletariat. The masses agree with us enthusiastically; constantly widening circles of the proletariat share the knowledge that the hour has struck for a settlement with capitalist class rule.

But this great task cannot be accomplished by the German proletariat alone; it can fight and triumph only by appealing to the solidarity of the proletarians of the whole world.

Comrades of the belligerent countries, we are aware of your situation. We know very well that your governments, now since they have won the victory, are dazzling the eyes of many strata of the people with the external brilliancy of this triumph. We know that they thus succeed through the success of the murdering in making its causes and aims forgotten …

The imperialism of all countries knows no "understanding"; it knows only one right – capital's profits; it knows only one language – the sword; it knows only one method – violence. And if it is now talking in all countries, in yours as well as ours, about the "League of Nations," "disarmament," "rights of small nations," "self-determination of the peoples," it is merely using the customary lying phrases of the rulers for the purpose of lulling to sleep the watchfulness of the proletariat.

Proletarians of all countries! This must be the last war! We owe that to the twelve million murdered victims; we owe that to our children; we owe that to humanity.

Europe has been ruined through the infamous international murder. Twelve million bodies cover the gruesome scenes of the imperialistic crime. The flower of youth and the best men of the peoples have been mowed down. Uncounted productive forces have been annihilated. Humanity is almost ready to bleed to death from the blood-letting. Victors and vanquished stand at the edge of the abyss. Humanity is threatened with the most dreadful famine, a stoppage of the entire mechanism of production, plagues, and degeneration.

The great criminals of this fearful anarchy, of this chaos let loose – the ruling classes – are not able to control their own creation. The beast of capital that conjured up the hell of the world war is not capable of banishing it again, of restoring real order, of insuring bread and work, peace and civilization, justice and liberty, to tortured humanity.

What is being prepared by the ruling classes as peace and justice is only a new work of brutal force from which the hydra of oppression, hatred, and fresh bloody wars raises its thousand heads.

Socialism alone is in a position to complete the great work of permanent peace, to heal the thousand wounds from which humanity is bleeding, to transform the plains of Europe, trampled down by the apocyphal horsemen of war, into blossoming gardens, to conjure up ten productive forces for every one destroyed, to awaken all the physical and moral energies of humanity, and to replace hatred and dissension with fraternal solidarity, harmony, and respect for every human being …

Proletarians of all countries, when we now summon you to a common struggle, it is not done for the sake of the German capitalists who, under the label of "German nation," are trying to escape the consequences of their own crimes; it is being done for our sake as well as yours. Remember that your victorious capitalists stand ready to suppress in blood our revolution, which they fear as their own. You yourselves have not become any freer through the "victory," you have only become still more enslaved. If your ruling classes succeed in throttling the proletarian revolution in Germany, as well as in Russia, then they will turn against you with redoubled violence. Your capitalists hope that victory over us and over revolutionary Russia will give them the power to scourge you with a whip of scorpions and to erect the thousand-year empire of exploitation upon the grave of socialism.

Therefore the proletariat of Germany is looking toward you in this hour. Germany is pregnant with the social revolution, but socialism can be realized only by the proletariat of the world.

And therefore we call to you: "Arise for the struggle! Arise for action! The time for empty manifestoes, platonic resolutions, and high-sounding words has gone by! The hour of action has struck for the International!" We ask you to elect Workers' and Soldiers' Councils everywhere that will seize political power and, together with us, will restore peace.

Not Lloyd George and Poincaré, not Sonnino, Wilson, and Erzberger or Scheidemann; these must not be allowed to make peace. Peace is to be concluded under the waving banner of the socialist world revolution.

Proletarians of all countries! We call upon you to complete the work of socialist liberation, to give a human aspect to the disfigured world, and to make true those words with which we often greeted each other in the old days and which we sang as we parted: "And the International shall be the human race."

Document 2

Franz Schoenberner, "Description of Aspects of Fighting during the Spartacist Uprising," in Franz Schoenberner, *Confessions of a European Intellectual* (New York, Macmillan Co., 1946), pp. 107–8.

The editor of the popular critical humor magazine *Simplizissimus* describes the fighting during the uprising, commenting on the differences between German and Russian revolutionaries and stressing what he felt to be the fundamental behavior pattern of Germans even in extraordinary times.

A lot of comical and heartbreaking stories circulated as illustrations of this fact. In Berlin during the street fighting around the Schloss, the masses hurrying for cover under machine-gun fire dutifully avoided taking the short cut over the lawn. At the risk of being killed in the detour, they scurried around the little gates which symbolized a sort of eleventh commandment: "*Das Betreten des Rasens ist verboten*," a phrase meaning much more and proving much more effective than the simple English Formula "Keep off."

It was true that the sailors occupying the Imperial Palace in Berlin had carefully spread layers of newspaper – probably of revolutionary newspaper the *Red Flag* – under the machine guns they mounted at the windows in order not to scratch the wonderful inlaid floor. Determined fighters, they were willing to shed their blood for the revolution, but if possible without causing damage save to their own lives.

On the top of the famous Brandenburger Tor, dominating the street Unter den Linden, were machine guns whose fire made traffic through the Friedrichstrasse impossible. There was a terrible jam, and so, by mutual agreement between the White and Red street fighters, at regular intervals, marked by flag signals, the civil war was stopped briefly every half-hour so that the traffic through the Friedrichstrasse could proceed as usual.

In the first days of the revolution in Berlin the main telegraph office had been occupied by the elite of the Red troops, some sailors from Kiel. They were armed to the teeth, their pockets loaded with hand grenades, and were resolved to defend this important nerve center to the last man. The operators had decided to stay at their posts. Everything worked well. The only difficulty was the question of food. There were, of course, some cases with so-called iron rations stored in the building for such an eventuality. But according to regulations these cases could not be opened without a written order of the government. With growling stomachs, the wild revolutionaries sitting beside their machine guns pondered this difficult problem. They finally decided to send a deputation to the Reichstag, the seat of Ebert's provisional government. Braving the hail of bullets in the streets, the deputation finally arrived in the Reichstag. They could not get through to Ebert, but they waylaid Wolfgang Heine, a well-known lawyer and socialist parliamentarian, who had assumed the office of Minister of Justice. When in the midst of the turmoil he finally understood what they wanted, he told them of course they should go ahead and open the cases.

But returning, by miracle without injury, these three men were seriously reprimanded by their comrades. Where was the written order of the government? It couldn't be helped; another deputation must go to the Reichstag. Again they pushed through to Wolfgang Heine, who, baffled by this rigid sense of legality, decided to save the situation personally.

In a government car he hurried to the telegraph office and, introducing himself as the new Minister of Justice, he gave the solemn assurance that the cases could and should be opened. But, though almost fainting from hunger, the soldiers of the revolution were not so easily convinced. Anyone could claim to be a minister and, by the way, it was not the Minister of Justice who was competent in this matter, but the Postal Minister or the head of the government himself. And the order must be given in writing. In vain Heine exhausted his forensic eloquence against an adamant legalistic attitude; finally, crestfallen, accompanied by the delegates, he returned to the Reichstag. Somehow he managed to have a formal order typed on official paper, and to find Ebert himself. "You must sign that," he told him, "or our men in the main telegraph office will die from hunger sitting on the cases of iron rations."

Document 3

Arnold Brecht, "Gustav Noske, the Social Democrats and the Spartacist Revolution," in Arnold Brecht, *The Political Education of Arnold Brecht: an Autobiography 1884–1970*, (Princeton, New

Jersey, Princeton University Press, 1970), pp. 142–5.

Arnold Brecht was a civil servant, first under the Wilhelmine Monarchy and then during the Weimar years when he served first the national government and then the state government of Prussia. Brecht became a strong supporter of the Republic and of the Social Democrats who played such an important role in it. In this passage he comments on the plight of the Social Democratic leaders during the Spartacist uprising and particularly on the role of Gustav Noske who directed the crushing of the uprising.

> Convinced Communists who believed the only possible deliverance for the world lay in an authoritarian Socialist system, ready to reduce the influence of the bourgeoisie by all possible means, acted only logically when they condemned and resisted the policy of Ebert, Scheidemann, and Noske. But anyone who rejects Bolshevism and approves of the transition to general elections ought not to indulge in superficial mockery of the "pitiful revolutionaries" who had not even proved able to create a revolutionary army. He ought rather to explain how that might have been done under the circumstances described. A military army of Spartacists would have inevitably led to the establishment of a Communist system in Germany; and it was this that Ebert and Scheidemann wanted to avoid. They were convinced opponents of such a system, in the interest of both the working classes and their own ideals of freedom, self-determination, justice, and culture. By far the larger section of the working classes were behind them in this and certainly have no reason to maintain that they were betrayed by them. A moderate revolution is far more difficult to carry through than one which is radical, extremist, and determined to apply any means.
>
> I have been speaking so far only of the three months from the beginning of the German Revolution to the elections for the National Assembly. After the convening of the National Assembly, no cabinet was able to create purely Socialist troops, because the Socialists were not in the majority. The problem was then how to create a truly democratic army through co-operation between the pro-democratic bourgeois parties and the Social Democrats. Even their combined forces held a parliamentary majority for only a short time. After the elections of June, 1920 up to the end of the First Republic in 1933 there was in a German parliament neither a Socialist majority, nor even a majority of the pro-democratic parties. Is it to be expected that a nation which has no pro-democratic majority will make strenuous efforts to create a pro-democratic

army or to replace anti-democratic army leaders with pro-democratic ones? Can one reproach cabinets, in which opponents of democracy hold seats or which, if composed only of democrats, have only a minority behind them, for not having taken decisive steps to democratize the army? Ought one not in this situation to direct the reproaches at those sections of the German population who cast their votes for anti-democratic parties rather than at the failure of the cabinets?

But more might have been done, and ought to have been done, in order to avert brutality in the civil war and to punish those responsible. Noske did not want brutality. But he was not far-sighted enough to prevent it and after it had happened to expose and punish the guilty persons. His faults here were the reverse of his admirable courage and manly resolve. These qualities had won him the affection and loyalty of the workers and sailors in Kiel. He hoped to win over the people in Berlin in the same way. When, to his horror, many acts of violence were committed, he was victim to a temptation which many leaders have felt, from Caesar to Napoleon, to cover up for his own men in order not to lose their loyalty, or at least, not make too careful inquiries.

The maiden-speech which Noske had delivered in the Reichstag as a young deputy twelve years previously (on April 25, 1907) was characteristic of him. "Abolition of the army," he said at that time, "has never been advocated by the Social Democrats. Rather, we Social Democrats are the ones who have mocked at and opposed bourgeois fantasies regarding disarmament, and have pointed out that the economic antagonisms that exist at present between the various nations are still so strong that no single nation can so much as think of disarming ... In the resolution, which was cited by the War Minister, the point is aversion to militarism. But, gentlemen, aversion to militarism is by no means the same as aversion to defense (*Wehrhaftigkeit*); militarism and resolve to defend one's country are two totally different things. What we oppose in militarism is unnecessary drill, maltreatment, the isolation of the officers as a separate caste, the army's being interpreted as a means of power to maintain superiority of the wealthier classes over the poorer ones ... I declare once again: our wish is that Germany be as valiant (*wehrhaft*) as possible; our wish is that the entire German nation has an interest in those military establishments which are necessary for the defense of our fatherland. But this can be achieved only when outdated establishments are no longer held fast ..."

During the critical weeks before and after the acceptance of the Treaty of Versailles, Noske might easily have become military dictator in Germany. But he was a convinced Social Democrat. He did not want to become a military dictator, although he knew that he had the capacity and that the atmosphere was favorable for him. The man had steady nerves. A mass meeting had declared that if Noske were to appear, they would make *Hackepeter* (mincemeat) out of him. Noske decided to go. I accompanied him in the car. He conversed with me quite calmly. Then, stepping before the meeting and received with a great uproar, he forced the crowd to listen to him, and by his objective, manly manner of speaking pacified the gathering.

It was not actually necessary that the connection between German democracy and remnants of the old army should lead to the collapse of democracy. If Germany had been given a peace treaty which was less challenging to all the national concepts of honor; if the honest democratic governments of Ebert, Scheidemann, Fehrenbach, Wirth, Marx, Stresemann, Hermann Müller, etc., had received support comparable to that offered the Adenauer government after the Second World War – then it would by no means have been impossible to keep control over the military. That all this was to be denied the German governments, Ebert and Noske could not know during the first months after the revolution. They acted in accordance with honest democratic beliefs and the upright desire to put Germany and the German nation back on their feet after a dreadful defeat; they did this to the best of their knowledge and belief. That was my impression at the time, and it still is. Those were dreadful months.

Document 4

"The Military Provisions of the Versailles Treaty," cited in Louis Snyder, *Documents of German History*, pp. 378–80. Original source, Great Britain, *Parliamentary Papers*, 1919.

The Versailles Treaty was viewed by almost all Germans as a humiliating and incredibly harsh peace treaty with terms that a major nation could not long endure. The military provisions were among the most galling to rank and file Germans and to almost all political leaders including those who supported the Republic.

SECTION I: MILITARY CLAUSES

CHAPTER I: EFFECTIVES AND CADRES OF THE GERMAN ARMY

Art. 159. The German military forces shall be demobilized and reduced as prescribed hereinafter.

Art. 160.

(1) By a date which must not be later than March 31, 1920, the German Army must not comprise more than seven divisions of infantry and three divisions of cavalry.

After that date the total number of effectives in the Army of the States constituting Germany must not exceed one hundred thousand men, including officers and establishments of depots. The Army shall be devoted exclusively to the maintenance of order within the territory and to the control of the frontiers.

The total effective strength of officers, including the personnel of staffs, whatever their composition, must not exceed four thousand.

(2) Divisions and Army Corps headquarters staffs shall be organized in accordance with Table No. 1 annexed to this Section.

The number and strengths of the units of infantry, artillery, engineers, technical services and troops laid down in the aforesaid Table, constitute maxima which must not be exceeded.

The following units may each have their own depot:

An Infantry regiment;
A Cavalry regiment;
A regiment of Field Artillery;
A battalion of Pioneers.

(3) The divisions must not be grouped under more than two army corps headquarters staffs.

The maintenance or formation of force differently grouped or of other organizations for the command of troops or for preparation for war is forbidden.

The Great German General Staff and all similar organisations shall be dissolved and may not be reconstituted in any form …

CHAPTER II: ARMAMENT, MUNITIONS AND MATERIAL

Art. 168. The manufacture of arms, munitions, or any war material, shall only be carried out in factories or works the location of which shall be communicated to and approved by the Governments of the Principal Allied and Associated Powers, and the number of which they retain the right to restrict.

Within three months from the coming into force of the present Treaty, all other establishments for the manufacture, preparation, storage or design of arms, munitions, or any war material whatever shall be closed down. The same applies to all arsenals except those used as depots for the authorised stocks of munitions. Within the same period the personnel of these arsenals will be dismissed …

Art. 170. Importation into Germany of arms, munitions and war material of every kind shall be strictly prohibited.

The same applies to the manufacture for, and export to, foreign countries of arms, munitions and war material of every kind.

Art. 171. The use of asphyxiating, poisonous or other gases and all analogous liquids, materials or devices being prohibited, their manufacture and importation are strictly forbidden in Germany.

The same applies to materials specially intended for the manufacture, storage and use of the said products or devices.

The manufacture and the importation into Germany of armoured cars, tanks and all similar constructions suitable for use in war are also prohibited.

Document 5

"German Chancellors 1919–1933," Bundesarchiv, Koblenz.

The Weimar Republic was characterized by governments that frequently changed, hence the numerous Chancellors, Cabinets and Foreign Ministers during its brief period of existence.

German Chancellors from 1919 to 1933

Term	*Chancellor*	*Party*
February 13–June 2, 1919	Philip Scheidemann	Social Democrat
June 21, 1919–March 26, 1920	Gustav Bauer	Social Democrat
March 28–June 8, 1920	Herman Müller	Social Democrat
June 25, 1920–May 4, 1921	Konstantin Fehrenbach	Centrist
May 10–October 22, 1921 October 26, 1921–November 14, 1922	Joseph Wirth	Centrist
November 22, 1922–August 12, 1923	Wilhelm Cuno	(no party)
August 13–October 3, 1923 October 6–November 23, 1923	Gustav Stresemann	German People's Party

November 30, 1923–May 26, 1924 June 3–December 15, 1924	Wilhelm Marx	Centrist
January 15–December 5, 1925 January 20–May 12, 1926	Hans Luther	(no party)
May 17–December 17, 1926 January 29, 1927–June 12, 1928	Wilhelm Marx	Centrist
June 28, 1928–March 27, 1930	Hermann Müller	Social Democrat
March 31, 1930–October 9, 1931 October 9, 1931–May 30, 1932	Heinrich Brüning	Centrist
May 31–December 1, 1932	Franz von Papen	(no party)
December 2, 1932–January 28, 1933	Kurt von Schleicher	(no party)
January 30, 1933–April 29, 1945	Adolf Hitler	National Socialist German Workers' Party (German dictator from March 24, 1933 [Enabling Act] to April 29, 1945)

Document 6

"Weimar Constitution, Selections," in Frederick Watkins, *The Use of Emergency Powers under the Weimar Constitution*, (Cambridge, Mass., Harvard University Press, 1938), pp. 180, 182, 184, 190, 194, 204.

"The Weimar Constitution," The Weimar Constitution, seen as a model document by many contemporaries, attempted to create a federal republic which tried to combine aspects of presidential and parliamentary systems with a commitment to social justice. Articles 20–22 describe the nature of the Reichstag and the new voting system and those eligible to vote. Articles 6, 7, and 12 indicate the federal nature of the Republic and articles 13–15 indicate the dominance of the central power. Articles 46–49 delineate the powers of the president. Article 48 outlines the critical emergency powers of the President. Article 73 adds the concept of a referendum to the constitution. Articles 119–123 make marriage, motherhood and child welfare into keystones of the new republic.

Art. 6. The Reich shall have exclusive legislative competence for:

1. foreign affairs (*Beziehungen zum Ausland*)
2. colonial matters
3. questions relating to nationality, freedom of travel and residence (*Freizügigkeit*), immigration, emigration and extradition
4. the organization of defense forces
5. coinage
6. customs, as well as the unity of customs and trading areas and freedom of commerce.
7. post and telegraph, including the telephone.

Art. 7. The Reich shall have legislative competence for:

1. civil law
2. penal law
3. judicial procedure, including the execution of penalties and legal aid between authorities (*Amtshilfe*)
4. matters relating to passports and police supervision of aliens (*Fremdenpolizei*)
5. poor relief and the care of vagrants
6. matters relating to the press, associations and assemblies
7. policies relating to population, (*Bevölkerungspolitik*), maternity relief, welfare of infants, children and youth
8. public health, veterinary matters and the protection of plants against disease and pests
9. labor laws, insurance, and the protection of laborers and employees, and employment bureaus
10. the establishment of Reich organs of vocational representation (*Berufliche Vertretung*)
11. provision for war veterans and the surviving dependents of deceased soldiers
12. laws relating to expropriation
13. the socialization of natural resources and economic undertakings, and also the production, manufacture, distribution and price regulation of economic wares for the benefit of the general economy (*Gemeinwirtschaft*)
14. trade and commerce, weights and measures, the issue of paper money, banks and banking and the stock exchanges (*Börsenwesen*)

Art. 12. So long as and insofar as the Reich refrains from exercising the right of legislation, the Lands shall retain the right of legislation. This does not apply to matters for which the Reich has exclusive competence of legislation.

The government of the Reich has the right of veto in regard to Lands laws relating to matters within the scope of Article 7, Number 13, insofar as the general welfare of the Reich is thereby affected.

Art. 13. Reich law takes precedence over Lands law.

Where there are doubts or differences of opinion as to whether a legal provision of a Land is compatible with Reich law, the competent Reich or central authorities of a Land may, in accordance with particulars prescribed by the Reich law, appeal for decision to a Supreme Court of the Reich.

Art. 14. The laws enacted by the Lands shall be executed by the authorities of the States, unless the laws of the Reich determine otherwise.

Art. 15. The government of the Reich exercises supervision in such matters as are within the legislative competence of the Reich.

Insofar as the laws of the Reich are to be executed by the authorities of the Lands, the government of the Reich may issue general instructions. The government is empowered to send commissioners to the central authorities of the Lands and with their permission, to the lower state authorities, to supervise the execution of the laws of the Reich.

It is the duty of the government of the Lands, at the request of the government of the Reich, to rectify defects which have become manifest in the execution of Reich laws. Where differences of opinion arise both the government of the Reich and the government of the Land may appeal for decision to the Constitutional Court.

THE REICHSTAG

Art. 20. The Reichstag is composed of the delegates of the German people.

Art. 21. The delegates represent the whole people. They are subject only to their own conscience and are not bound by instructions.

Art. 22. The delegates are elected by universal, equal, direct and secret ballot by men and women over twenty years of age according to the principles of proportional representation. The election day must be a Sunday, or a public holiday.

The Reich Election Law will regulate details.

Art. 46. The Reich President appoints and dismisses the public officials of the Reich and officers of the defense forces, unless otherwise provided by law. He may allow the right of appointment and dismissal to be exercised by other authorities.

Art. 47. The Reich President has supreme command (*Oberbefehl*) over all the defense forces of the Reich.

Art. 48. If a Land fails to fulfill the duties incumbent upon it according to the Constitution or the laws of the Reich, the Reich President can force it to do so with the help of the armed forces.

The Reich President may, if the public safety and order in the German Reich are considerably disturbed or endangered, take such measures as are necessary to restore public safety and order. If necessary he may intervene with the help of the armed forces. For this purpose he may temporarily suspend, either partially or wholly, the Fundamental Rights established in Articles 114, 115, 117, 118, 123, 124 and 153.

The Reich President shall inform the Reichstag without delay of all measures taken under Paragraph 1 or Paragraph 2 of this Article. On demand by the Reichstag the measures shall be repealed.

In case of imminent danger the government of any Land may take preliminary measures of the nature described in Paragraph 2 for its own territory. The measures are to be revoked upon the demand of the Reich President or the Reichstag.

Details will be regulated by a Reich law.

Art. 49. The Reich President exercises the right of pardon for the Reich.

Reich amnesties require a Reich law.

Art. 73. A law enacted by the Reichstag shall be made the subject of a referendum, if the Reich President so determines within a month.

A law, the proclamation of which has been postponed on the application of at least one-third of the members of the Reichstag shall be subjected to a referendum, if one-twentieth of the persons qualified to vote so submit.

A referendum shall further be instituted if one-tenth of the persons qualified to vote initiate by petition the introduction of a bill. An elaborated bill must underlie such people's initiative. The bill shall be submitted to the Reichstag by the government together with a statement of its own point of view. No referendum shall take place if the petitional bill is passed unaltered by the Reichstag.

In regard to the budget, taxation laws and laws relating to pay and salaries, only the Reich President may inaugurate a referendum.

A Reich law shall regulate the procedure for referendum and initiative.

THE GENERAL WELFARE (*GEMEINSCHAFTSLEBEN*)

Art. 119. Marriage as the cornerstone of family life and the preservation and increase of the nation is placed under the special protection of the Constitution. It is based on the equal rights of both sexes.

It is the duty of the State and the Communes to foster the purity, health, and social advancement of the family. Families with numerous children have a claim to proportionate assistance.

Motherhood has a claim to the protection and care of the State.

Art. 120. To provide their children with a thorough physical, spiritual, and social education is the supreme duty and natural right of parents, whose activities shall be supervised by the State.

Art. 121. The same conditions shall be created by law for the physical, spiritual and social development of illegitimate as for legitimate children.

Art. 122. Youth shall be protected against exploitation and also against neglect of their moral, mental or physical well-being. The States and Communes shall make the necessary arrangements.

Compulsory measures for their welfare may only be ordered on the basis of law.

Art. 123. All Germans have the right to assemble peacefully and unarmed without giving notice and without special permission.

A Reich law may make previous notification obligatory for assemblies in the open air, and may prohibit them in the case of immediate danger to the public safety.

Document 7

"Weimar Constitution, Selections," cited in Louis Snyder, *Documents of German History*, pp. 390–2.

Articles 109–137 of the Weimar Constitution provided Germans with their basic rights. Articles 151–165 provided for the protection of property and the rights of working people.

THE INDIVIDUAL

Art. 109. All Germans are equal before the law. Men and women have the same fundamental civil rights and duties. Public legal privileges or disadvantages of birth or of rank are abolished. Titles of nobility ... may be bestowed no longer ... Orders and decorations shall not be conferred by the state. No German shall accept titles or orders from a foreign government.

Art. 110. Citizenship of the Reich and the states is acquired in accordance with the provisions of a Reich law ...

Art. 111. All Germans shall enjoy liberty of travel and residence throughout the whole Reich ...

Art. 112. Every German is permitted to emigrate to a foreign country ...

Art. 114. Personal liberty is inviolable. Curtailment or deprivation of personal liberty by a public authority is permissible only by authority of law.

Persons who have been deprived of their liberty must be informed at the latest on the following day by whose authority and for what reasons they have been held. They shall receive the opportunity without delay of submitting objections to their deprivation of liberty.

Art. 115. The house of every German is his sanctuary and is inviolable. Exceptions are permitted only by authority of law ...

Art. 117. The secrecy of letters and all postal, telegraph, and telephone communications is inviolable. Exceptions are inadmissible except by national law.

Art. 118. Every German has the right, within the limits of the general laws, to express his opinion freely by word, in writing, in print, in picture form, or in any other way ... Censorship is forbidden ...

THE GENERAL WELFARE

Art. 123. All Germans have the right to assembly peacefully and unarmed without giving notice and without special permission ...

Art. 124. All Germans have the right to form associations and societies for purposes not contrary to the criminal law ...

Art. 126. Every German has the right to petition ...

RELIGION AND RELIGIOUS SOCIETIES

Art. 135. All inhabitants of the Reich enjoy full religious freedom and freedom of conscience. The free exercise of religion is guaranteed by the Constitution and is under public protection ...

Art. 137. There is no state church ...

ECONOMIC LIFE

Art. 151. The regulation of economic life must be compatible with the principles of justice, with the aim of attaining humane conditions of existence for all. Within these limits the economic liberty of the individual is assured ...

Art. 152. Freedom of contract prevails ... in accordance with the laws ...

Art. 153. The right of private property is guaranteed by the Constitution … Expropriation of property may take place … by due process of law …

Art. 159. Freedom of association for the preservation and promotion of labor and economic conditions is guaranteed to everyone and to all vocations. All agreements and measures attempting to restrict or restrain this freedom are unlawful …

Art. 161. The Reich shall organize a comprehensive system of [social] insurance …

Art 165. Workers and employees are called upon to co-operate, on an equal footing, with employers in the regulation of wages and of the conditions of labor, as well as in the general development of the productive forces …

Document 8

"Bavaria to fight Defense Measures," *The New York Times*, July 9, 1922, p. 3.

This article recognizes the conflict between the state government of Bavaria and the central government which was a continuing Weimar theme.

BERLIN, July 8. – The Bavarian Prime Minister, Count Lerchenfeld, in an interview with the Munich papers warns the German Reichstag not to impose upon the Bavarian people such "unconstitutional laws" as the Bill for the protection of the Republic. He hopes, however, that it may still be possible to overcome objectionable parts of the Bill, "because the Bavarian people would be driven to despair. Your law cannot change wrong into right. Thus I speak in grave anxiety over the Federal situation."

Lerchenfeld's objections are mainly directed against that part of the Bill in question which threatens any officer or official with immediate dismissal … He believes it would bring about a catastrophe in Bavaria if the jurisdiction of her own courts were curtailed or superseded by orders from Berlin in certain political cases.

Nevertheless, Lerchenfeld had to admit to an interviewer that the present Bavarian laws were insufficient for suppression of revolutionary movements.

"The Bavarian Government itself has been the object of such attacks repeatedly," he admitted, "especially by the anti-Semitic and extreme Nationalist Parties. Certain Bavarian newspapers nearly daily advise the removal of our Government by violence, but the Bavarian Government has always been able to protect itself without Federal interference."

Lerchenfeld seems to have forgotten that it was Noske and the northern regiments who liberated Munich from the bloody rule of the Sparticists.

Document 9

"The German Republic's Trail of Blood," *The Literary Digest*, July 8, 1922.

This article discusses the phenomenon of the Feme murders whilst highlighting the assassination of Walther Rathenau.

THE ASSASSINATION OF DR WALTHER RATHENAU is the 378th political murder in Germany since the formation of the Republic, and some press dispatches point out that in 353 cases the guilty persons either escaped or were acquitted by reactionary courts. Most of the murderers have eluded capture, we are told, because the Monarchists have a well-organized network throughout Prussia, Bavaria and Hungary, through which murderous fugitives land in safe places. "Who is next?" is the question on everybody's lips in Berlin, it is said, while those who fear for the future of the Republic are hoping that the Government will be ruthless in carrying out the protective measures deemed necessary to safeguard Germany and peace in Europe. Besides suppressing Monarchist propaganda and forbidding meetings against the Treaty of Versailles, planned by the former Kaiser's adherents, we are told that the Cabinet means to reorganize radically the judiciary system of the country in order to clean out the reactionary elements. The police courts will be particularly effected, while the army also is to be reorganized in order to rid it of the pest of Monarchism.

Berlin dispatches tell us of a demonstration in favor of the Republic in the Lustgarten which was attended by 200,000 persons, and meanwhile the chairmen of the Majority Socialist and the Independent Socialist parties, together with some trade unions, have demanded of Chancellor Wirth dissolution of the Reichstag, and new elections with the following program: "First, a democratic republic; second, transformation of the Reichwehr and safety police into trustworthy Republican forces; third, dissolution of all reactionary organizations." Chancellor Wirth in his speech in the Reichstag severely denounced the machinations of the Pan-Germans, who, he said, have created an atmosphere of murder in the country, and he is quoted further:

"A state of political bestiality prevails. I need only mention poor Frau Erzberger, whose husband was murdered and who is constantly receiving letters announcing the intention to defile her husband's grave. Is it surprizing, then, that I also received letters yesterday, headed 'on the day of Rathenau's execution,' and declaring: 'You men of fulfillment mania have not listened to the voices of those who have tried to dissuade you from a bad policy. Let hard fate, therefore, take its course, so that the fatherland may prosper.'

"That is a system of political murder, and we must all work against this atmosphere.

"I was a spectator at the Lustgarten demonstration; its proceedings were orderly, calm and disciplined. But, gentlemen of the Right, do not deceive yourselves. Below this discipline and calm there lies a volcano, the eruption of which, should it occur, would teach you a severe lesson ...

"The Allied Governments, during the past year, have inflicted on the German Government almost continual humiliations. I recall Upper Silesia, the sufferings of the Saar population and the sorrows of the Rhineland. It is impossible for a nation of sixty millions to live under the rule of commissions, and it is impossible to keep democratic Germany alive under such conditions."

Document 10

"Description of Rathenau's Funeral," by friend Harry Kessler, in *In The Twenties: The Diaries of Harry Kessler*, (New York, Holt, Rinehardt, Winston, 1971), pp. 185–6.

Tuesday, 27 June 1922

Rathenau's funeral. From noon on all work stopped as a token of mourning and protest against political murder.

The funeral ceremony was held in the Chamber of the Reichstag. The coffin lay in state, mounted behind the speaker's rostrum and under a large black canopy suspended from the ceiling. The Chamber was hung with black and transformed into a sea of flowers and plants. Enormous palms flanked the coffin at its four corners. The speaker's rostrum was shrouded in black and buried, as was the Government Bench, beneath magnificent wreaths with ribbons in the Republican colours, black-red-gold. The galleries, draped with crepe, were decorated with banks of blue and pink hydrangeas. Long crepe veils hung from the ceiling's arc-lights, which were turned on. The galleries, like the Chamber itself, were packed. There was not one empty seat, not even among the Nationalists. The focal point was the coffin, draped with a huge flag in the national colours. At its foot there lay two immense wreaths, of red and white flowers, to right and left of the colours.

At noon the Chancellor led Rathenau's mother into the Imperial box. She sat down in the seat whose back was still embellished with a crowned W. The old lady was evidently in full control of herself, but her complexion was as pale as wax and the face behind the veil might have been carved from stone. These features, all colour drained from them through grief, touched me most. She stared motionlessly at the coffin. Kreuter, who visited her yesterday, says that she is the embodiment of retribution. Her sole desire is to take time to write to Helfferich, condemning him as the murderer of her son, and then die.

Wirth, having escorted her to her place, left the box. A moment later he was to be seen below in the procession led by Ebert. The orchestra, out of sight in the vestibule behind the coffin, played the *Egmont* overture. Ebert stepped in front of the coffin and spoke, very softly, almost inaudible from emotion, but well. After him came Bell, representing the Reichstag, his tone clearly articulated, his words moving. Lastly, and mediocre, a Pastor Korell, on behalf of the Democrats. Then the musicians played the Siegfried Funeral March from *Gotterdämmerung*. This undoubtedly brought the ceremony inside the Chamber to its highest pitch of emotion. In the circumstances the effect was overwhelming. Many of those around me wept. The historic significance of this death echoed from the music in the hearts of those present.

The coffin was carried through the lobby to the entrance stairway. At the foot of the steps stood a Reichswehr company, in field-grey uniform, steel-helmeted. The drums rolled and the resonant tones of a funeral march rose muffled into the air, strangely like distant thunder. The coffin, wrapped in the national colours, was laid on the hearse which was swathed in red roses. Slowly, to the accompaniment of drum-beats, the cortège set off. In spite of the rain, or perhaps because of this grey gossamer appropriate to the muffled roll of the drums, the impression made upon the spectators was almost even more intense than it had been in the Chamber. Lassalle's dream of passing through the Brandenburger Tor as President of a Republic of Germany was today fulfilled by the Jew Rathenau because of his martyrdom in the service of the German people.

Document 11

"Secret Orders and Murder in Germany," *The Literary Digest*, May 5, 1923.

TWO HUNDRED BODIES, mostly of men who stood forth as champions of the democratic idea, are buried along the road that crosses Germany from despotism to the new and still struggling Republic. They were travellers along the highway, they paid the penalty for their faith by meeting death from ambush, and the bands of killers who sent them to their death, says a recent investigator of conditions in Germany, "it will threaten Liberalism throughout Central Europe." The German murder-bands, known under a variety of names, and many of them with a multitude of autonomous ramifications, are casting a "lengthening shadow over Germany," testifies Charles Merz, writing in the May issue of *Our World* (New York). They are, he says, "growing every day in power – vast, inscrutable, and cautious." "How does this sinister power work?" he asks, "What will it mean to the peace of Europe?" His reply runs:

Five men sit around a table in the *Freude Garten*, in Munich or Berlin. Never more than five. Waiters hurry past them, wiping with white aprons their foaming steins of beer. Across the room some noisy family is celebrating a birthday with laughter and much thumping on the table. A violin is playing Wagner. It is a typical German *biergarten*, sluggish, crowded, warm – everybody willing to drink the health of everybody else. But these five have a special toast. They drink to a death tomorrow.

"Konsul," the most sinister of all the German secret societies, is organized in Groups of Five. One man knows the other four with whom he meets and works. He knows the organizer who first enlisted him, and who has long since vanished from the scene. Beyond that he knows nothing. He does not even know the members of another Group of Five. The trial of the men who came near killing Maximilian Harden showed that the director of the plot did not know from whom the money came for his "expenses." It reached him by general delivery mail.

Always, orders for these Groups of Five arrive mysteriously. Some central bureau pulls the strings. And "Konsul" keeps its secrets. The actual culprits may be caught, in any case of murder; but this loose form of organization shields the men who set the machinery in motion. That is what happened in the case of Walther Rathenau. And, undoubtedly, it will happen again tomorrow. For "Konsul" has not run its course in Germany.

Document 12

"Einstein has temporarily fled from Germany because of threats that he will be killed," *The New York Times*, August 6, 1922.

Professor Albert Einstein, originator of the theory of relativity, has fled from Germany temporarily because he was threatened with assassination by a group that caused the murder of Dr Walter Rathenau, German Foreign Minister, according to a letter from Professor Einstein cancelling an engagement to address a meeting here.

Efforts to induce the noted scientist to return, in view of the Government's success in coping with the situation, are said to have so far proved unavailing.

Receipt of the letter was announced by the President of the German Physicists' Association, before which Dr Einstein was to discuss his relativity theory at the organization's 100th anniversary meeting. It was received soon after Dr Rathenau's assassination, and stated that Dr Einstein had learned that he was also listed to be killed and had, therefore, decided to go abroad.

It appears that Dr Einstein's friends and admirers had been more concerned in keeping the scientist safe in this manner than he was himself, and were doing their utmost to prevent, or at least postpone, his return. Dr Einstein is not accompanying the expedition to Christmas Island, contrary to previously announced plans.

Considerable comment was caused in Geneva early last week by the absence of Dr Einstein from the meeting of the members of the Intellectual Committee of the League of Nations to begin the work of organization. He had been designated to represent Germany, but did not appear. It was said he was unable to leave his work at the University of Berlin.

Dispatches from Germany soon after the Rathenau murder quoted police authorities there as accusing the notorious "Consul" organization of having marked twelve leading politicians, editors and financiers of Jewish extraction for assassination, including Dr Rathenau, Theodor Wolff, editor of the *Berliner Tageblatt*, and Max Warburg, the Hamburg banker.

Document 13

"Gustav Stresemann speaks to the League of Nations on Germany's admission to League," September 10, 1926, cited in Louis Snyder, *Documents of German History*, pp. 404, 405, 408.

Original source: The League of Nations Official Journal, Special Supplement No. 44, p. 51, No. 22.

Mr President: Ladies and Gentlemen.

The President of this High Assembly and the President of the Council of the League of Nations have been good enough to accord Germany a joyful welcome on her entry into the League. In addressing you from this platform I feel it my first duty to express Germany's thanks to these two gentlemen and to the Assembly. Allow me at the same time to express our gratitude to the Swiss Government, which is now extending its traditional and generous hospitality to Germany as a member of the League of Nations.

More than six years have passed since the League was founded. A long period of development was thus necessary before the general political situation rendered it possible for Germany to enter the League, and even in the present year great difficulties have had to be overcome before Germany's decision could be supplemented by the unanimous decision of the League. Far be it from me to revive matters which belong to the past. It is rather the task of the present generation to look to the present and to the future. I would only say this, that, although an event such as Germany's entry into the League is the outcome of a long preliminary process of development, yet that very fact constitutes perhaps a surer guarantee of its permanence and of its fruitful results …

The co-operation of the peoples in the League of Nations must and will lead to just solutions for the moral questions which arise in the conscience of the peoples. The most durable foundation of peace is a policy inspired by mutual understanding and mutual respect between nation and nation.

Even before her entry into the League, Germany endeavoured to promote this friendly co-operation. The action which she took and which led to the Pact of Locarno is a proof of this, and as further evidence there are the arbitration treaties which she has concluded with almost all her neighbours. The German Government is resolved to persevere unswervingly in this line of policy and is glad to see that these ideas, which at first met with lively opposition in Germany, are now becoming more and more deeply rooted in the conscience of the German people. Thus the German Government may well speak for the great majority of the German race when it declares that it will wholeheartedly devote itself to the duties devolving upon the League of Nations.

During the past six years the League has already taken in hand a substantial portion of these tasks, and has done most valuable work. The German delegation does not possess the experience which the members here assembled have acquired. We believe, however, that, as regards the new work which lies before us, the subjects dealt with first should be those in which the individual nations can do most by combining in joint institutions. Among other institutions which the League has created, we have in mind the World Court, which is the outcome of efforts made to establish an international legal order ...

Germany's relations to the League are not, however, confined exclusively to the possibilities of co-operation in general aims and issues. In many respects the League is the heir and executor of the Treaties of 1919. Out of these Treaties there have arisen in the past, I may say frankly, many differences between the League and Germany. I hope that our co-operation within the League will make it easier in future to discuss these questions. In this respect mutual confidence will, from a political point of view, be found a greater creative force than anything else. It would, indeed, be incompatible with the ideals of the League to group its members according to whether they are viewed with sympathy or with antipathy by other Members.

In this connection I reject most emphatically the idea that the attitude hitherto adopted by Germany in matters concerning the League of Nations has been dictated by such sympathies or antipathies.

Germany desires to co-operate on the basis of mutual confidence with all nations represented in the League or upon the Council.

Document 14

"Locarno Agitated by Rumors of Plot to Kill Stresemann," *The New York Times*, October 5, 1925, p. 1.

LOCARNO, Switzerland, Oct. 4. – On the eve of the Locarno Conference the preparations have been marred by a persistent rumor that German Nationalists have planned to assassinate Dr Stresemann rather than permit him to conclude with the Allies a compact for the security of Europe laid within the terms of the Treaty of Versailles.

Discovery of the plot by the Berlin police is responsible, it is understood, for the strange action of Dr Stresemann and Dr Luther in leaving the special German delegation train at Bellinzona and motoring to Locarno after dark last night.

The Swiss police were extremely vigilant and tried to force even the newspapermen to leave the railway station before the arrival of the train. It also has been remarked that every train carrying passengers for Locarno has for the past two days been patrolled by Swiss detectives.

The situation was aptly expressed by a Swiss newspaperman, who declared last night that the Swiss Federal Council had gone into a session of prayers for the safety of the various delegates and their assistants.

The German delegation officially knows nothing of the alleged plot, but information from other sources indicates that it is a fact.

Document 15

"The Catechism of Hate," *The New York Times*, January 19, 1925, p. 16.

The German Attitude to France Recalls That of Carthage to Rome.

To the Editor of The New York Times:

A dispatch from Paris tells us that a "Catechism of Hate" has been published and distributed in the Rhineland territory by a German Nationalist organization. Here are some of its precepts:

"Thou shalt hate France eternally.

"Thou shalt break the bonds and chains with which the hereditary foe would bind thy country.

"Thou shalt fill thy heart with disgust and contempt for all French manners and customs.

"Thou shalt nurture in the soul of thy children the sentiment and the desire for a bloody revenge.

"Thou shalt feed the burning flame of revenge.

"Thou shalt await with faith the great day that will bring thee peace and revenge."

Many readers will be reminded of the oath of Hannibal, who, when he was a boy, was led to the altar by his father and required to swear eternal enmity to Rome. It would be well – for Germans, especially, – to remember not only the oath, but the disastrous sequel of the story, which may be said to have been written under the famous legend "Carthage must be destroyed!" How the Cathaginians exhibited their wonderful enterprise and valor in the Punic wars, and yet how Scipio carried the war into Africa, and in the end the City of Carthage was utterly destroyed and the site was plowed over and sown with salt, and the remnant of the inhabitants were sold into slavery.

From Germany's attitude since the great war that was so disastrous to her, and from the discovery of her secret preparations, the inference appears to be plain that she contemplates repeating the sorrowful experiment. In that event, it may be regarded as a certainty that the great powers will come to the aid of France even more readily than in 1914 – and this time not unprepared, nor will there be any euphemistic armistice to soften the blow of a surrender, nor any lack of promptness and severity in collecting reparations.

It behoves the Germans to remember the fate of Carthage; the war may be carried across the Rhine next time. And yet, as has been remarked, there is an unaccountable perversity in the working of the German mind. The best educated German woman that I ever have met – widow of a famous American – exclaimed at the beginning of the World War, "We could forgive France – but England, never!" Think of it!

ROSSITER JOHNSON
New York, January 13, 1925

Document 16

"Dollar Quotations for the Mark," Fritz Ringer (ed.), *The German Inflation of 1923* (New York: Oxford University Press, 1969), p. 79.

Dollar Quotations for the Mark; Selected Dates, 1914 and 1919–23 (monthly averages)

July, 1914	4.2
January, 1919	8.9
July, 1919	14.0
January, 1920	64.8
July, 1920	39.5
January, 1921	64.9
July, 1921	76.7
January, 1922	191.8
July, 1922	493.2
January, 1923	17,972.0
July, 1923	353,412.0
August, 1923	4,620,455.0
September, 1923	98,860,000.0
October, 1923	25,260,208,000.0
November 15, 1923	4,200,000,000,000.0

Jan. 1919 figure computed from Swiss quotations. Source: *Statistisches Jahrbuch für das Deutsche Reich*, 1921–22 to 1924–25.

Document 17

"Deutsche Bank to Weimar Republic Bondholders," *This Week in Germany*, German Information Center, New York.

Americans who bought dollar-de-nominated bonds from the Weimar Republic and their heirs are finally getting the return on their investment, 57 years after Nazi Germany suspended interest payments. In advertisements placed recently in major newspapers in the United States, Deutsche Bank Securities Corporation asked owners of bond titles from the German federal debt administration to turn in their so-called 'coupons' at the New York branch of Deutsche Bank's securities wing in exchange for new bonds of the Federal Republic of Germany. A spokesperson for Deutsche Bank Securities confirmed that the new bonds will mature in 2010 – 86 years after the original bonds were to expire. They will also pay 3 per cent interest, but only for the years since German unification in 1990.

American financier Charles G. Dawes and the company of Owen D. Young introduced $210 million of the bonds to the U.S. during the 1920s, as part of an international plan to help Germany pay reparations after the First World War. Interest payments were suspended in 1937. Under the terms of the London Debt Agreement of 1953, Germany had to compensate the bondholders for the interest payments, but only after unification occurred. Following the fusion of the two Germanys in 1990, the issue that was long in abeyance again became contentious, and interest began to accumulate anew on the old obligations, bringing the debt to about $70 million.

Document 18

"Women's Peace Parley forced to suspend by German Nationalist riot at Innsbruck," *The New York Times*, July 15, 1925.

VIENNA, July 14. – Today a meeting of the Women's International Congress for the Protection of Racial Minorities, also known as the International League for Peace and Freedom, at Innsbruck, was prohibited by the Provincial Government as a result of the rioting which broke out in the first session last night.

The opening session was invaded by several hundred German nationalist students, who by hooting and shouting prevented French, Czech and English women from speaking. An American woman, a Mrs. Lewis, though repeatedly interrupted, was allowed to finish.

Denouncing the excesses, a detachment of the Social Democratic

Workers' Guard entered the gallery and tried to eject the Nationalist disturbers and protect the women. This led (to) further disorders, which were quelled by the intervention of the police. The authorities then forbade today's meeting on the ground that it might lead to serious disturbances.

The Nationalist students complained that the League was taking up the defense of all national minorities under foreign rule except the Germans. They also excoriated certain German women members of the League who, in collaboration with French women, published a pamphlet accusing the Imperial German Government of responsibility for the World War.

Document 19

"The Twenty-five Points of the German Workers' Party, 1920," cited in Louis Snyder, *Documents of German History*, pp. 393–6. Originally published in Raymond E. Murphy, ed., *National Socialism*, US Department of State, Publication 1864 (Washington, 1943), pp. 222–5.

The program of the German Workers' Party is limited as to period. The leaders have no intention, once the aims announced in it have been achieved, of setting up fresh ones, merely in order to increase the discontent of the masses artificially, and so ensure the continued existence of the party.

1. We demand the union of all Germans to form a Great Germany on the basis of the right of self-determination enjoyed by nations.

2. We demand equality of rights for the German people in its dealings with other nations, and abolition of the peace treaties of Versailles and Saint-Germain.

3. We demand land and territory (colonies) for the nourishment of our people and for settling our excess population.

4. None but members of the nation may be citizens of the state. None but those of German blood, whatever their creed, may be members of the nation. No Jew, therefore, may be a member of the nation.

5. Anyone who is not a citizen of the state may live in Germany only as a guest and must be regarded as being subject to foreign laws.

6. The right of voting on the leadership and legislation is to be enjoyed by the state alone. We demand therefore that all official appointments, of whatever kind, whether in the Reich, in the coun-

try, or in the smaller localities, shall be granted to citizens of the state alone. We oppose the corrupting custom of Parliament of filling posts merely with a view to party considerations, and without reference to character or capacity.

7. We demand that the state shall make it its first duty to promote the industry and livelihood of citizens of the state. If it is not possible to nourish the entire population of the state, foreign nationals (non-citizens of the state) must be excluded from the Reich.

8. All non-German immigration must be prevented …

9. All citizens of the state shall be equal as regards rights and duties.

10. It must be the first duty of each citizen of the state to work with his mind or with his body. The activities of the individual may not clash with the interests of the whole, but must proceed within the frame of the community and be for the general good.

We demand therefore:

11. Abolition of incomes unearned by work.

12. In view of the enormous sacrifice of life and property demanded of a nation by every war, personal enrichment due to a war must be regarded as a crime against the nation. We demand therefore ruthless confiscation of all war gains.

13. We demand nationalization of all businesses (trusts) …

14. We demand that the profits from wholesale trade shall be shared.

15. We demand extensive development of provision for old age.

16. We demand creation and maintenance of a healthy middle class, immediate communalization of wholesale businesses premises, and their lease at a cheap rate to small traders, and that extreme consideration shall be shown to all small purveyors to the state, district authorities, and smaller localities.

17. We demand land reform suitable to our national requirements …

18. We demand ruthless prosecution of those whose activities are injurious to the common interest. Sordid criminals against the nation, userers, profiteers, etc., must be punished with death, whatever their creed or race.

19. We demand that the Roman Law, which serves the materialistic world order, shall be replaced by a legal system for all Germany.

20. With the aim of opening to every capable and industrious German the possibility of higher education and of thus obtaining

advancement, the state must consider a thorough reconstruction of our national system of education …

21. The state must see to raising the standard of health in the nation by protecting mothers and infants, prohibiting child labor, increasing bodily efficiency by obligatory gymnastics and sports laid down by law, and by extensive support of clubs engaged in the bodily development of the young.

22. We demand abolition of a paid army and formation of a national army.

23. We demand legal warfare against conscious political lying and its dissemination in the press. In order to facilitate creation of a German national press we demand:

a) that all editors of newspapers and their assistants, employing the German language, must be members of the nation;

b) that special permission from the state shall be necessary before non-German newspapers may appear. These are not necessarily printed in the German language;

c) that non-Germans shall be prohibited by law from participation financially in or influencing German newspapers …

It must be forbidden to publish papers which do not conduce to the national welfare. We demand legal prosecution of all tendencies in art and literature of a kind likely to disintegrate our life as a nation, and the suppression of institutions which militate against the requirements above-mentioned.

24. We demand liberty for all religious denominations in the state, so far as they are not a danger to it and do not militate against the moral feelings of the German race.

The party, as such, stands for positive Christianity, but does not bind itself in the matter of creed to any particular confession. It combats the Jewish-materialist spirit within us and without us …

25. That all the foregoing may be realized we demand the creation of a strong central power of the state. Unquestioned authority of the politically centralized Parliament over the entire Reich and its organizations; and formation of chambers for classes and occupations for the purpose of carrying out the general laws promulgated by the Reich in the various states of the confederation.

The leaders of the party swear to go straight forward – if necessary to sacrifice their lives – in securing fulfillment of the foregoing points.

Document 20

"Forty are Wounded in German Clashes," *The New York Times*, December 8, 1930, p. 6.

BERLIN, Dec. 7 (AP). – More than forty persons were seriously injured, one probably fatally, in the usual Sunday political clashes in Berlin and other German cities today.

At Bernau, near Berlin, Communists stoned a parade of Fascists and then hurled stones at police who stepped in to quell the riot. Twenty policemen and Fascists were taken to the hospital.

At Dortmund one Fascist was reported to be dying as a result of injuries in a Communist–Fascist fight.

A Fascist attempt to break up a parade of the Republican Reichsbanner at Hamelin, near Hanover, resulted in ten being seriously injured and many slightly.

A dozen were reported wounded in riots here.

Twelve Fascists were seriously wounded by bullets at Bonn, in the Rhineland, and as a precaution against further trouble the police prohibited a Fascist torchlight procession scheduled for tonight.

The Berlin theatre showing the German version of the motion picture "All Quiet on the Western Front," where Fascists recently broke up a performance by shouting and releasing white mice, was the scene of another demonstration tonight, although no trouble occurred inside. Crowds of Fascists collected in the square opposite the building and shouted, "Germany, awake!" until they were dispersed by the police.

Document 21

"Fascists Make Big Gains in Germany, Communists also Increase Strength as Moderates Drop in Reich Election," *The New York Times*, September 15, 1930, p. 1.

The standing of the leading fourteen parties at the time of the dissolution of the Reichstag is shown in the first column of figures. Indicated results from yesterday's election, based on the votes counted early this morning, according to returns received from the Berlin bureau of *The New York Times* and from *The Associated Press*, are shown in the second column of figures.

	Old House	*New House*
German Nationalists	78	41
Revalorization party	2	No report
National Socialists or Fascists	12	107
Christian National Peasants	9	9
Conservatives	0	5
Economic party	23	23
Hanoverians	4	No report
German Peasants	8	9
German People's party	45	26
Bavarian People's party	17	18
Catholic Centre, or Centrists	61	69
Democrats (now German State party)	25	22
Socialists	152	143
Communists	54	76

The official final totals in the election were given as: Socialists 8,572,016, Fascists 6,401,210, Communists 4,587,708, Centrists 4,128,929, Nationalists 2,458,497, People's 1,576,149, Economic party 1,360,585, States 1,322,608, Bavarians 1,058,556; total vote cast, 34,943,460.

Bibliographical Essay

This brief essay provides the reader with suggestions for more specialized reading in each of the major areas that the book explores. These selected works provide particularly useful information or provocative interpretations of developments. The works presented here are in English which in many cases is the original language of the work and in other cases is the result of translation. These works highlight the vitality and significance of the Weimar Republic as an independent area of study as well as a staging ground for the rise of Hitler and the Nazis.

Imperial Germany and World War I

Two classic and important studies of the Kaiserzeit and World War I period are Hans-Ulrich Wehler, *The German Empire 1871–1914*, trans. Kim Traynor, Oxford, 1985, and Jürgin Kocka, *Facing Total War: German Society 1914–1918*, trans. Barbara Weinberger, Leamington Spa, 1984. These works by prominent German historians present the *Sonderweg* (separate path) theory of German development. Geoff Eley and David Blackbourn challenge this theory in *The Peculiarities of German History: Bourgeois Society and Politics in the Nineteenth Century*, New York, 1984. Roger Chickering's, *We Men Who Feel Most German: a Cultural Study of the Pan-German League 1886–1914*, Boston, Mass., 1984, provides insight into the period by studying the patriotic organizations as well as the general atmosphere. Andrew Bellon's *Mercedes in War and Peace*, New York, 1993, is a useful case study in understanding corporate policy and labor during the pre-war, as well as the later Weimar and Nazi periods.

The Weimar constitution and the peace settlement

Louise Holborn, Gwendolen Carter, and John Herz's comparative study of German constitutions, *German Constitutional Documents since 1871*, New York, 1970, provides a useful resource for looking at the relationship of the Weimar Constitution to the Imperial German Constitution that preceded it and the Federal German Constitution that followed it. Alan Sharpe's, *The Versailles Settlement: Peacemaking in Paris*, New York, 1991, presents a provocative recent reinterpretation of the negotiation and nature of the Versailles Treaty.

Weimar Prussia

Dietrich Orlow's , *Weimar Prussia, 1918–1925: the Unlikely Rock of Democracy*, Pittsburgh, Pennsylvania, 1986, is a significant study of Prussia as the bulwark of the Weimar Republic. Daniel Borg's, *The Old-Prussian Church and the Weimar Republic*, Hanover, New Hampshire, 1984, is a useful discussion of the role of the largest Protestant church group in Prussia during the Weimar years.

Weimar Bavaria

Ian Kershaw's, *Popular Opinion and Political Dissent in the Third Reich*, Oxford, 1983, provides a good description of Bavarian history during the Weimar years. Geoffrey Pridham, *Hitler's Rise to Power: the Nazi Movement in Bavaria 1923–1933*, New York, 1973, describes Bavaria during the period when Nazism rose from a small movement within the state to become the major national movement which took power in Germany. Lion Feuchtwanger, *Success*, trans. Willa and Edwin Muir, New York, 1930, is a long but very readable Weimar novel which captures the mood and major developments in Bavaria in the early Weimar period through the eyes of a sensitive writer.

Weimar women

When Biology Became Destiny: Women in Weimar and Nazi Germany edited by Renate Bridenthal, Atina Grossman, and Marion Kaplan, New York, 1984, is a collection of essays by leading women's historians which describe the women's movement and the major issues for women in both the Weimar and Nazi periods. Marion Kaplan's *The Jewish Feminist Movement in Germany: the Campaigns of the Jüdischer Frauenbund, 1904–1938*, Westport, Connecticut, 1979, describes the struggle of the organization that confronted women's problems as well as anti-Semitism. Detlev Peukert's *The Weimar Republic: Crisis Years for Classical Modernity*, New York, 1994, provides a good analysis of the various images of women and the role these images played in the Weimar era.

The Jews under the Weimar Republic

Ruth Gay's *The Jews of Germany: A Historical Portrait*, New Haven, Connecticut, 1992, is a comprehensive presentation of the entire course of the history of Jews in Germany. Donald Niewyk's *The Jews of Weimar*, Baton Rouge, Louisiana, 1980, is a focused analysis of the nature of the Jewish community, the status of Jews, and the role of the "Jewish question" during the Weimar period. Jehuda Reinharz's *Fatherland or Promised Land*, Ann Arbor, Michigan, 1975, is a study that highlights the tug of war that German Jews faced between the strong desire to be Germans and the appeal of the Zionist objective.

The economy

Charles Maier's *Recasting Bourgeois Europe: Stablization in France, Germany, and Italy in the Decade after World War I*, Princeton, New Jersey, 1975, is an important comparative study of the major economic and political developments in Germany, Italy and France in the post-World War I period. David Abraham's *The Collapse of the Weimar Republic*, 2nd ed., New York, 1986, provides useful tools of analysis and characterizations of economic groups and their relation to politics during the Weimar era. Henry Turner, *German Big Business and the Rise of Hitler*, New York, 1985, is the major study of the role of the leaders of the Weimar business community. Adam Ferguson's *When Money Dies*, London, 1975, is a significant study of the inflation of the early 1920s. An interesting new study of the impact of American business techniques on Germany is Mary Nolan's *Visions of Modernity: American Business and the Modernization of Germany*, New York, 1994.

The police

Paul Bookbinder, "The Weimar Police Experiment," in *Police Studies* is a discussion of the new and important Prussian police force created by the Social Democratic leaders of Prussia. Hsi-Huey Liang, *The Berlin Police Force in the Weimar Republic*, Berkeley, California, 1970, is a significant study of the police in the Prussian and national capital, Berlin, during the Weimar Republic. George Mosse, (ed.), *Police Forces in History*, New York, 1982, is a useful comparative study of the historical development of police forces.

The Feme and the judiciary

Ingo Müller's *Hitler's Justice*, trans. Deborah Lucas Schneider, Cambridge, Mass, 1991, provides a good source to aid in understanding the courts and the justice system during the Weimar and Nazi years. Jane Caplan's *Government without Administration: State and Civil Service in Weimar and Nazi Germany*, Oxford, 1988, is a complex but interesting study which considers the judiciary in the context of the civil service. Richard Bendix, *From Berlin to Berkeley: German Jewish Identities*, New Brunswick, New Jersey, 1986, describes the struggles of an embattled Jewish labor judge who was a strong Weimar supporter.

The Golden Age

Harry Kessler's *In the Twenties: the Diaries of Harry Kessler*, trans. Charles Kessler, New York, 1971, is a record of the period by a cosmopolitan supporter who knew everyone and provides a sense of the vitality of the Weimar years. Henry Pachter's *Weimar Etudes*, New York, 1982, describes the great intellectual freedom of the period. Henry Turner's *Stresemann and the Politics of Weimar*, Princeton, New Jersey, 1963, is an insightful study of one of the principle reasonable men of the Weimar period.

Culture and the Bauhaus

Peter Gay's *Weimar Culture*, New York, 1968, is a provocative study of the cultural battleground that was Weimar Germany. Woodruff Smith's *Politics and the Sciences of Culture in Germany 1840–1920*, New York, 1991, is an interesting look at the "cultural sciences" that affected how the Germans viewed culture when the Weimar Republic was born. Anthony Phelan, *Weimar Dilemma: Intellectuals, in the Weimar Republic*, Manchester, 1985, is a helpful collection of essays on major cultural themes. Frank Whitford and Julia Engelhardt, (eds), *The Bauhaus – Masters and Students by Themselves*, London, 1992, is a comprehensive selection of original letters and documents by participants combined with insightful commentary on the major Bauhaus figures. Gillian Naylor, *The Bauhaus Reassessed: Sources and Design Theory*, New York, 1985, is a thorough presentation of the development of the Bauhaus. Eva Forgacs' *The Bauhaus Idea and Bauhaus Politics*, trans. John Batki, Budapest, 1995, is the most recent study relating the politics of the time to the life and work of the Bauhaus personalities.

The rise of the Nazis

Karl Dietrich Bracher's *The German Dictatorship: The Origins, Structure and Effect of National Socialism*, trans. Jean Steinberg, New York, 1972, is the classic study by a prominent German scholar of the failure of the Weimar Republic and the rise and nature of Nazism. Conan Fischer's *The Rise of the Nazis*, Manchester, 1995, is the most up-to-date overview of the subject, which takes stock of current debates and provides important reassessments. Martin Broszat's *The Hitler State: the Foundation and Development of the Internal Structure of the Third Reich*, London, 1981, is an important structural analysis of the Nazi movement and the Nazi state. Michael Kater's *The Nazi Party: a Social Profile of Members and Leaders 1919–1945*, Cambridge, Mass., 1983, indicates the types of people who supported the Nazis and made up their leadership. Thomas Childers and Jane Caplan (eds), *Reevaluating the Third Reich*, New York, 1993, provides useful essays on major disputes among historians concerning the nature of the Nazis, their successful seizure of power and their regime.

Index